SQL for IBM i:
A Database Modernization Guide

Rafael Victória-Pereira

MC PRESS

MC Press Online, LLC
Boise, ID 83703 USA

SQL for IBM i: A Database Modernization Guide

Rafael Victória-Pereira

First Edition
First Printing—January 2018

MC Press offers excellent discounts on this book when ordered in quantity for bulk purchases or special sales, which may include custom covers and content particular to your business, training goals, marketing focus, and branding interest.

MC Press Online, LLC
Corporate Offices: 3695 W. Quail Heights Court, Boise, ID 83703-3861 USA
Sales and Customer Service: (208) 629-7275 ext. 500;
service@mcpressonline.com
Permissions and Bulk/Special Orders: mcbooks@mcpressonline.com

www.mcpressonline.com • www.mc-store.com

ISBN: 978-1-58347-449-5

Acknowledgments

Ex nihilo omnia—From a blank page, a book

First of all, I'd like to thank you, dear reader, for investing your time in this book.

I'd like to thank Victoria Mack, longtime editor of my TechTips, for believing in my ability to write; Anne Grubb, editor of this work; and the rest of the dedicated staff of MC Press who made it happen.

A big, big thanks to Mike Jones for being a fantastic technical sounding board and for gracing me with his insightful suggestions and remarks. This book wouldn't be the same without his help.

My dear colleague Nuno Gama also helped to shape this book, by peppering me with questions and tough challenges about SQL for i, often pushing it to its limits.

I'd also like to thank David Ford, Hassan Farooqi, Dan Lovell, Robert Pietrzykowski, and Keith Hodges for sharing their "Christmas wish list for a proper SQL book." Much of what is discussed in this book came from their combined topic lists.

Finally, I'd like to thank the readers of the SQL 101 TechTip Series, who, with their questions and comments, inspired and helped to shape this book.

If I forgot someone, which is highly likely, and you are that someone, please find it in your heart to forgive my lapse!

Contents

Why You Need This Book

At the core of the IBM i, beneath the ever-growing landscape of hardware features, programming languages, and weird acronyms, lies its database: DB2 for i. This is the machine's most remarkable feature, a true differentiator that has kept the IBM i "modern" and a step ahead of the competition for decades. Everything goes through the database, from performance data to business data, in a uniquely integrated and seamless fashion. It's actually funny that the system's most remarkable feature is often neglected by system administrators, developers, and integrators. They simply ignore it or at least don't take full advantage of its power and versatility.

This book's objective is to provide people with beyond-the-basics SQL knowledge and the tools to get more out of the IBM i database. This means the book can be useful to IBM i veterans who have RPG and COBOL roots, system administrators who are looking to get more information out of the system, or even Java and .NET developers who need to "talk" to the IBM i database.

How Can You Get More Out of the Database?

This journey begins with the very foundations of SQL, by recapping the data definition and data manipulation SQL instructions, commonly referred to as DDL and DML. However, SQL is not a theoretical "thing": it's used to manipulate real data. The difference between this book and many SQL tomes is that every concept, example, and technique will be applied to a close-to-reality database. The UMADB database serves an application that is supposed to run a university. I say supposed to run because, as you'll see in a few pages, this database is poorly constructed and not very flexible. As the book progresses, this database will be improved, chapter by chapter. Applying the techniques explained in each chapter will result in a much better database that really takes advantage of what DB2 for i has to offer.

The early chapters will recap DML and DDL, explore the system catalog, and help you build a database that is friendlier to both users (for instance, through the use of longer and descriptive column names) and programmers (with views, stored procedures, user-defined functions, and triggers, to name just a few enhancements).

Since we've entered the database-design realm, there's no harm in taking another step and improving the database, by normalizing it. An entire chapter is devoted to the database normal forms concept; here, again, the UMADB will be used as an example to illustrate every concept and technique.

The next hot topic is making the database more business-aware, by moving as many business rules and validations into it as possible. Why? Well, doing so solves a common problem with IBM i installations: the database is dumb, simply a repository of data, and the applications (usually "legacy" RPG or COBOL applications) handle all the validations in often cryptic and huge blocks of monolithic code. The problem is that more and more businesses are looking to integrate their core systems' data (which sits comfortably on an IBM i) with the rest of the business applications. These applications are Web or mobile oriented and written using different, "modern" technologies that connect directly to the database, not the "legacy" applications. If the database doesn't "know" the business rules, then the validations will have to be rewritten in new technology—every single time. Naturally, moving business rules into a database requires solid knowledge of a few concepts from the database-design realm, such as column-level constraints, triggers, and referential integrity. Don't worry, these concepts will all be explained in depth and accompanied with plenty of examples, built over the UMADB.

After reading this book, I hope that you, dear reader, will also gain a more profound and useful knowledge of SQL, particularly the "flavor" offered by the DB2 for i—whether you're a developer, system administrator, or an all-round "IT person."

1

Meet the UMADB: Our Example Database

This chapter introduces UMADB, a database for a university management application. It's important to have a notion of how this database is built—its flaws and shortcomings—because I'll be using it in almost every example in the book. UMADB is in bad shape and will be improved throughout the book, by applying the concepts discussed in each chapter.

Behind (almost) every application worthy of that name is a database. Some databases are small, some are huge, some are simple, and some (I'd say most) are complex. In IBM i's world, they're usually old, big, and confusing. Although our example database, UMADB, is not very big (I downsized it for simplicity's sake), it is also poorly built and can be rather confusing to both programmers and users.

Let's start with what this database should do. It supports a university management application. This means it should manage student, teacher, class, course, classroom, grade, and timetable records. In its current state, it kind of does, but with some room for improvement. The UMA application, an "old-style" RPG application, should keep track of the students' academic lives: the classes they attended, the grades they received, and so on. It should also keep track of classroom usage and timetables, for both students and teachers. However, these last two tasks were deemed "too complex for the application" by the application's manager, and were left out of the database. In other words, these are manual tasks, performed by the university administrative staff. This is one of the many shortcomings of the application and its database.

There are plans to change the existing application, and we (you, dear reader, and I) are part of them. We are going to improve the current database, which is basically a set of DDS-defined physical files, by applying DB2 for i SQL techniques, tricks, and novel features!

But first, you need to get to know the database in some depth. Let's take a look at the current database structure, table by table, starting with the Students table.

The Students Table

The Students table started with a simple student name column and grew to include other pieces of data, as do many DB2 tables in real-life applications. However, the growth was not planned properly (again, as in many real-life DB2 tables), and there are some problems in this table, which might not be obvious at first. But we'll get back to that later; now let's have a look at the actual table (Table 1.1).

Table 1.1: The Students table structure					
Table Name	**Column Name**	**Data Type**	**Length**	**Dec. Pos.**	**Description**
PFSTM	STNM	Char	60		Name
PFSTM	STDB	Decimal	8	0	Date of birth
PFSTM	STAD	Char	60		Home address
PFSTM	STPN	Char	15		Home phone number
PFSTM	STMN	Char	15		Mobile number
PFSTM	STEM	Char	60		Email address
PFSTM	STDL	Char	20		Driver's license
PFSTM	STSN	Char	11		Social Security number
PFSTM	STSC	Char	1		Status

This looks just like most IBM i physical files I've seen: cryptically short file (or table) and field (or column) names, concentrating a lot of information in a single row. The columns are mostly unremarkable as well: the list includes student contacts (addresses and phone numbers) and IDs (driver's license and Social Security number).

There are a couple of eyebrow-raising features. First, the column that stores the date of birth is a decimal with a length of 8,0, meaning that it's a number, not a date. Note that the database isn't prepared to validate the content of the field—it's just a number that some convention says represents a date. Another noticeable "feature" is the absence of the student's record unique identifier. This identifier was deemed unimportant, because all searches are done using the student's name.

These flaws are just a couple of examples of textbook problems with IBM i tables: they are, in a word, dumb. Even though it's possible, for instance, to perform basic checks like the validity of a date at database level, this and many other similar tasks are almost always performed at application level, thus making the database a simple (and dumb) repository of data. The same could be said about the absence of a record ID. The problem occurs when there are other, non-native applications accessing and manipulating the data. Without checks at the database level, it's possible, and very likely, to insert rubbish into the tables. Introducing those checks is actually very easy to do. Later in this book, you'll learn how to create validations that mimic (and can even go a step further and actually replace) business rules that currently exist for RPG programs.

There's something else wrong with this table, but it's not obvious yet. We'll need to go over a couple more tables for you to see it. Let's move on to the Courses table.

The Courses Table

Let me take a moment to explain the structure of the information in this database. The students take classes, which are taught by teachers, and are part of courses. At the end of each semester, the teachers grade the students in each of the classes they attended. This may sound obvious and redundant, but it's important to keep the structure in mind from this point on. In a way, the Students and Courses tables are the center of the database, because all the other tables are somehow linked to one (or both) of these tables.

Now let's take a look at the Courses table structure, shown in Table 1.2.

Table 1.2: The Courses table structure					
Table Name	**Column Name**	**Data Type**	**Length**	**Dec. Pos.**	**Description**
PFCOM	CONM	Char	60		Course name
PFCOM	CODS	Char	100		Course description
PFCOM	CODN	Char	50		Department name
PFCOM	CODE	Char	60		Course director name
PFCOM	COTA	Char	60		Course teaching assistant name
PFCOM	COSC	Char	1		Status

Again, the table is pretty typical: the same cryptic names and the lack of a unique record identifier that characterized the Students table. By the way, I imagine that you're curious about the hidden flaw in the Students table, mentioned earlier. Don't worry, it's going to become obvious in the next section, where we'll look at the Teachers table.

Meanwhile, there's something common to all the tables in this database: a status column. As the name implies, it indicates the status of the record. The convention used here is the following:

- 0—Created but not active record
- 1—Active record
- 9—Inactive (deleted) record

This is something that has to be taken into account when querying the database, and it has been the source of many misunderstandings. Sometimes the users forget to include a condition in their queries and end up mixing active and inactive records, which leads to inconsistent or just plain wrong information.

The Teachers Table

The teachers are a very important part of any teaching system. They're also a very important part of the application our database supports, although the table that keeps their records is not very "polished." You'll see what I mean when we analyze the Teachers table, shown in Table 1.3.

Table 1.3: The Teachers table structure					
Table Name	Column Name	Data Type	Length	Dec. Pos.	Description
PFTEM	TENM	Char	60		Teacher name
PFTEM	TETR	Char	20		Teacher rank
PFTEM	TEDB	Decimal	8	0	Date of birth
PFTEM	TEAD	Char	60		Home address
PFTEM	TEPN	Char	15		Home phone number
PFTEM	TEMN	Char	15		Mobile number
PFTEM	TEEM	Char	60		Email address
PFTEM	TEDL	Char	20		Driver's license
PFTEM	TESN	Char	11		Social Security number
PFTEM	TEST	Char	200		Subjects taught
PFTEM	TESA	Decimal	11	2	Salary
PFTEM	TESC	Char	1		Status

This table is similar to the previous ones, but it includes a sensitive piece of information: the teacher's salary. As things stand, anyone with access to the table can see how much each teacher earns, which might not be a very good idea. I'll get back to this later, when I discuss how to hide a column's data from prying eyes.

Notice the similarities between this and the Students table: the personal information (addresses and IDs) is the same. Even though this makes sense—both teachers and students are people and share the same type of information, it begs the question: what if a student becomes a teacher, or vice versa? There will be duplicate and possibly inconsistent information in the database. I'll address this issue later, in the discussion about database normalization and how that translates to SQL.

Having said that, let me take a moment to explain the other columns in the table. Besides the obvious teacher name and the aforementioned personal information, this table also includes a "teacher rank" (which can be something like Assistant Professor, Professor, and so on) and a "subjects taught" column. The latter is supposed to link to the Classes table, presented in the next section, but the connection is kept by humans, not the database. Because the same person can teach multiple classes in the same school year, the application's manager thought it would be simpler to manually track the link between teachers and classes—yet another shortcoming we'll need to solve later.

It's now time to move on to the next section and review the Classes table.

The Classes Table

Here's where things start to get interesting: finally, a table with links to other tables. The Classes table contains information about the students who form a class of a given subject during a given year and the course to which the class belongs. As I said before, the teacher is not part of the setup, at least not at database level. Table 1.4 shows the complete Classes table structure.

Table 1.4: The Classes table structure					
Table Name	**Column Name**	**Data Type**	**Length**	**Dec. Pos.**	**Description**
PFCLM	CLNM	Char	60	0	Class name
PFCLM	CLCY	Decimal	4	0	Class year
PFCLM	CLCN	Char	60	0	Course name
PFCLM	CLSN	Char	60		Student name
PFCLM	CLSA	Char	60		Student home address
PFCLM	CLSE	Char	60		Student email address
PFCLM	CLSC	Char	1		Status

As you can see from this table, the links I mentioned before are based on the names of the student and the course, which might cause some problems. The ideal situation would be to have record identifiers in each of the tables and keep those IDs, instead of the respective names, in the Classes table records. The next issue is the duplicate student information. The application manager thinks this duplication makes sense, because the student information might change from school year to school year, and keeping the information here allows the teacher to contact the student using the most current addresses. We'll also have to deal with this situation later.

Finally, the last table of the downsized version of the UMADB database is the Grades table. Let's analyze it in the next section.

The Grades Table

After the end of the semester, the students are graded on their performance in each of the classes they attended. The results are stored in the Grades table, shown in detail in Table 1.5.

Table Name	Column Name	Data Type	Length	Dec. Pos.	Description
Table 1.5: The Grades table structure					
PFGRM	GRSN	Char	60		Student name
PFGRM	GRCN	Char	60	0	Class name
PFGRM	GRCY	Decimal	4	0	Class year
PFGRM	GRGR	Char	2		Grade

Just like the Classes table, this one also depends on another table's information to form its unique key. In this case, that key is formed by the student name, the class name, and class year. Of these three, two are names stored in character strings. This makes them prone to error (character fields usually make awful keys because of the possible mismatches caused by different character cases—"John" is not the same as "john", for example) and slower to work with (because it takes longer to process a string of characters than a numeric value). The other problem with this table is the Grade column: there's no validation in the database to prevent inconsistent values, such as invalid grades. It's assumed that the letters A, B, C, D, and F will be used, optionally followed by a plus/minus sign, but there's no actual check for a valid grade at the database level. Just like the student's date of birth validation, this one also exists at the application level, buried in some RPG program.

Just a Few Tables, and So Many Problems

From what you've read so far, you probably concluded this (exaggerated) scenario has some similarities with real-life issues in IBM i databases you've seen. Probably not all at the same time, but you know what I mean. It's true that some of the issues are very basic and easy to solve, while others require some database redesign and ingenuity. I'll address all these issues and a few more, which are related to the non-implemented functionalities that are currently handled outside the application's scope, over the next chapters of this book.

You can skip a chapter or two, but keep in mind that the database will evolve, and each chapter will build upon the foundations laid by its predecessor. If you're comfortable with the topics discussed in a chapter, you can simply have a quick look at the SQL code samples to keep track of the changes to the database. (You can download the code samples and other supplementary book materials on the book's page at *https://www.mc-store.com/products/sql-for-ibm-i-a-database-modernization-guide*.)

Before starting in earnest, I'll start by reviewing some SQL data manipulation language (DML) statements and sharing a few tricks I've learned over the years that can, hopefully, help you get more productive when it comes to manipulating data using SQL.

In This Chapter, You've Learned ...

The UMADB is a mess! Here's why:

- The existing tables don't have unique record identifiers, which makes the connections between its tables weak, to say the least.
- There's no data checking at database level, which can ... well, let me rephrase that ... probably *will* cause inconsistencies in the data, such as invalid dates and meaningless grades (yup, I'm talking receiving a G or a 24 as a final grade), just to name a couple.
- The table and column names are short and cryptic, following the age-old IBM i tradition, which makes querying the database rather user-unfriendly.

These issues will be addressed throughout the book, accompanied by the discussion of the relevant underlying concepts.

2

A Data Manipulation Language Basics Recap

This chapter recaps the basic data manipulation language (DML) statements and uses the sample UMADB database in all its examples. It will go over the SELECT, INSERT, UPDATE, and DELETE statements. However, this chapter won't discuss the syntax of these statements. Here we will explain how you can write shorter and clearer statements by resorting to a few keywords that you might not be aware of. If you want to play around with the examples, be sure to restore the UMADB_CHP2 library from the downloadable source code, at *https://www.mc-store.com/products/sql-for-ibm-i-a-database-modernization-guide*.

I'm going to assume that you're familiar with the most commonly used DML statements and will not explain their syntax in depth. Instead, I'll focus on some details that can simplify the statements—for instance, shorter "implementations" of concepts.

Using the BETWEEN and IN Predicates

Let's get started with a simple yet very powerful keyword. If you started querying the IBM i's database using Query/400 (as most of us did), one of the things you might miss is the RANGE keyword. This simple-to-use tool allows you specify the lower and upper limits of a range of values in a clear and concise way. What you might not know is that

SQL has a RANGE equivalent: BETWEEN. This keyword's equally easy to use, but it has a different syntax, which is closer to common English than the robot-speak of RANGE.

It's easier to explain with an example, so let's imagine that a user needs a list of all the university students who were born in the 1990s. The knee-jerk reaction would be to write something like this:

```
SELECT      STNM
            , STDB
   FROM     UMADB_CHP2.PFSTM
   WHERE    STDB >= 19900101
            AND STDB <= 20000101
;
```

Even though this statement is correct (assuming that the student's birth date, column STDB of the PFSTM table, is in YYYYMMDD format), it can be made clearer with BETWEEN:

```
SELECT      STNM
            , STDB
   FROM     UMADB_CHP2.PFSTM
   WHERE    STDB BETWEEN 19900101 AND 20000101
;
```

Notice how using the BETWEEN predicate made the statement easier to read. By the way, I'm a big fan of clear code, so you'll see a lot of indentation in my code examples. It makes the code easier to read and, more important, easier to maintain. For instance, if I want to add a new column to the query, I simple add a new line wherever I need to add it, and insert a comma followed by the column name. If all the columns are in the same line, this might not be so simple, especially in queries with a lot of columns. The only downside to this is that my queries tend to get a bit long. However, if you use IBM Access Client Solutions' Run SQL Scripts or any other non-native query tool (IBM Rational Developer for i's query tool, WinSQL, Toad, and so on), this is not a big issue.

All the examples shown here were written in Run SQL Scripts. You'll notice the SQL syntax with the period (.) separating the library (schema) and file (table) names, instead of the system's native syntax with the slash character (/) acting as a separator between the library (or schema) and the table, and the semicolon (;) terminating each statement.

Even if you knew BETWEEN, you might not know that you can invert the selection by adding a simple keyword: NOT. Here's an example to illustrate what I mean: the user actually wanted a list of all the students who weren't born in the 1990s. Well, let's not waste the statement we just wrote. Let's modify it instead:

```
SELECT      STNM
            , STDB
    FROM    UMADB_CHP2.PFSTM
    WHERE   STDB NOT BETWEEN 19900101 AND 20000101
;
```

See how with a very simple change you can get the exact opposite result of the original query? You can use NOT in all sorts of ways to easily negate a comparison. It's particularly useful when the opposite of a comparison is complex to write down. Instead, you can simply write NOT (original comparison), and you're done. I'll provide additional examples in a moment.

Another tedious and error-prone situation is when you want to find all the records that have one of several values in a given column. For instance, let's say that someone wants a list of all the teachers with the rank of Dark Master, Maximus Praeceptor, or Praeceptor. (Yes, the Teachers table is a bit quirky—actually, the entire database is! Take a moment to query the tables, and you'll see what I mean.) In Query/400 you'd use LIST, but I've noticed many people still write the comparison statement using something like this:

```
SELECT      TENM
, TETR
    FROM    UMADB_CHP2.PFTEM
    WHERE   TETR = 'Dark Master'
            OR TETR = 'Maximus Praeceptor'
            OR TETR = 'Praeceptor'
;
```

Instead of using LIST's SQL equivalent IN keyword:

```
SELECT      TENM
, TETR
    FROM        UMADB_CHP2.PFTEM
    WHERE       TETR IN ('Dark Master', 'Maximus Praeceptor', 'Praeceptor')
;
```

Naturally, you can also use NOT to quickly list all the teachers who don't hold one of these ranks:

```
SELECT      TENM, TETR
    FROM        UMADB_CHP2.PFTEM
    WHERE       TETR NOT IN ('Dark Master', 'Maximus Praeceptor',
'Praeceptor')
;
```

I've shown examples of BETWEEN using numeric values and IN using character values, mainly because this is their most common use. Keep in mind, though, that you can use these SQL predicates with any types of values and in any SQL clause that requires the use of a comparison, in addition to the WHERE clause.

Joining Tables

Listing the contents of a table, even with comparisons (or search conditions) that limit the output, as shown in the previous section, is a bit limited in a real-life situation. Typically, our queries are built using information from multiple tables. I'll go through almost all the ways you can join tables in SQL; I'll leave a special type of join, called EXCEPTION JOIN, for later. Let's start with the simplest of them all: the INNER JOIN.

The JOIN You've Been Using Without Realizing: INNER JOIN

The INNER JOIN is arguably the most-used type of join. Actually, you've probably been using it without realizing it, because it can be hidden in the WHERE clause, in what is commonly called an *implicit join*.

For instance, let's say you want to list all the students who have enrolled in at least one class. This is a complete intersection between the Students and Classes tables—a classic INNER JOIN (even though it could be simply a SELECT over the Classes table because it contains the student name—but let's ignore that for the moment, because it will be useful to illustrate another type of join). We know, from the previous chapter, that the link between the PFSTM (Students table) and the PFCLM (Classes table) is the student name. It's true that it's not a brilliant solution, but we'll have to live with it—for now. An SQL statement that lists all the students that have, at any given point, enrolled in a class is often written using an implicit join, like this:

```
SELECT      STNM
            , CLNM
            , CLCN
    FROM    UMADB_CHP2.PFSTM ST, UMADB_CHP2.PFCLM CL
  WHERE CL.CLSN = ST.STNM
  ;
```

However, if there are more than two tables in the SELECT statement, things might get a little hazy. That's why I think it's much clearer to write the same statement using an INNER JOIN:

```
SELECT      STNM
            , CLNM
            , CLCN
    FROM    UMADB_CHP2.PFSTM ST
    INNER JOIN UMADB_CHP2.PFCLM CL ON CL.CLSN = ST.STNM
  ;
```

If you're familiar with the INNER JOIN syntax, there's really nothing new for you here—perhaps the use of aliases for the tables (ST and CL), which make the statement slightly more readable. However, if you're used to the implicit join instead, there are a couple of things worth mentioning. First, notice how the line following the FROM clause starts with the join type: in this case it's an INNER JOIN, but there are others, as you'll see in a moment. The type of join identifier is then followed by the table name (and optionally, an alias), which in turn is followed by the ON keyword. This keyword is used to specify how the connection between the tables is supposed to work. In this case, the link between the Students and Classes tables is achieved via the student name, but it could be a more complex condition, resorting to multiple columns.

Let me close this section with a more complete example that uses multiple INNER JOINs to link all the tables of our sample database. The objective is to obtain a bit more information about a student's grades and the classes he or she attended. Here's the statement:

```
SELECT       STNM AS STUDENT_NAME
             , CONM AS COURSE_NAME
             , CODE AS COURSE_DIRECTOR
             , TETR AS TEACHER_RANK
             , CLNM AS CLASS_NAME
             , CLCY AS CLASS_YEAR
             , GRGR AS GRADE
    FROM     UMADB_CHP2.PFSTM ST
    INNER JOIN UMADB_CHP2.PFCLM CL ON     ST.STNM = CL.CLSN
    INNER JOIN UMADB_CHP2.PFGRM GR ON     GR.GRCN = CL.CLNM
                                          AND GR.GRCY= CL.CLCY
                                          AND GR.GRSN= ST.STNM
    INNER JOIN UMADB_CHP2.PFCOM CO ON     CO.CONM = CL.CLCN
    INNER JOIN UMADB_CHP2.PFTEM TE ON     TE.TENM = CO.CODE
    WHERE     GRSN = 'Anthony, Mark'
;
```

Even though the statement is a bit longer than the previous examples, it's a simple SELECT. The difference is that it uses many more tables, which can make it confusing really quickly. I'd like emphasize the importance of indentation to improve the statement's readability and the use of user-friendly column names. Also note that I've used aliases for all the tables. At this time, the aliases are not critically important, because the column names all identify the name of the table to which they belong. Later in the book, I'll show you how to "get the best of both worlds" by providing long, human-readable names and keeping the short "RPG-standard" cryptic names that currently exist. Then you'll see that making a habit of using aliases for the tables and using them when referring to columns in your statements is of paramount importance to the readability and maintainability of your code.

Start Joining Tables Left and Right

I bet you have already used INNER JOIN. Now imagine that the user asks you to modify the query, so that all registered students, regardless of whether or not they have taken a class, are listed. But the user still wants to know which classes the students took. Although it's very similar to the previous query, it is not simply an intersection between the tables. Nope, this time you'll have to include all the records from the first table (Students) and the records from the second table (Classes) that have matching student names. Instead of first and second tables, let's call them left and right tables, respectively. You now need all the records from the left table plus the ones that intersect with the right table, as depicted in Figure 2.1.

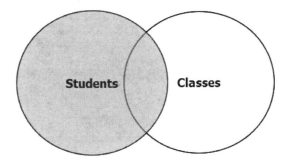

Figure 2.1: A LEFT JOIN between the Students and Classes tables

Let's see how this translates to SQL lingo:

```
SELECT      STNM
            , CLNM
            , CLCN
    FROM    UMADB_CHP2.PFSTM ST
LEFT JOIN   UMADB_CHP2.PFCLM CL ON CL.CLSN = ST.STNM
;
```

The only difference in the statement is the LEFT JOIN instead of INNER JOIN, but the result set tells a slightly different story: a student record was omitted from the previous result set because it doesn't have a match in the Classes table, which now appears, even though it has incomplete information. The class and course name columns (CLNM and CLCN, respectively) display a "no data available" sign (a dash, or -) instead of the expected contents. The - sign indicates NULL.

Similarly, if the request were to list all the records from the Classes table (the right table) plus the matches on the Students table (the left table), you'd use a RIGHT JOIN. Visually, a RIGHT JOIN looks very much like the previous figure, but with the table roles reversed, as depicted in Figure 2.2.

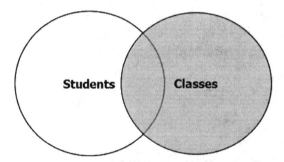

Figure 2.2: A RIGHT JOIN between the Students and Classes tables

As you'd expect, the SQL statement is also very similar to the previous one:

```
SELECT      STNM
            , CLNM
            , CLCN
    FROM    UMADB_CHP2.PFSTM ST
RIGHT JOIN  UMADB_CHP2.PFCLM CL ON CL.CLSN = ST.STNM
    ;
```

The result will be the same as the INNER JOIN, but only because there are no records in the classes table that don't have a match in the students table.

"Just Get Me Everything": FULL JOIN

So far, I've shown you how to select the matching records between two tables, then add to that all the records from the left table, and finally, add to that all the records from the right table. As you've probably guessed, there's also a type of join that includes everything from both left and right tables: it's the FULL OUTER JOIN, or FULL JOIN, for short:

```
SELECT       STNM
             , CLNM
             , CLCN
   FROM      UMADB_CHP2.PFSTM ST
   FULL JOIN UMADB_CHP2.PFCLM CL ON CL.CLSN = ST.STNM
;
```

In this case, you're selecting everything from both tables, which might not be a good idea. But who knows, maybe it can be useful in a particular situation? This example selects students with or without classes, plus classes with or without students.

A Join Summary

Even though this joining business is not complex with two tables, it's important to fully understand it. Database relations can get pretty complicated, and being able to join two or more tables correctly might save you some time. Figure 2.3 offers a summary of the join types discussed thus far:

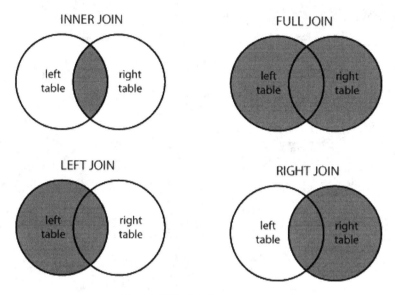

Figure 2.3: A join summary

Later I'll revisit this topic, to explain what happens when the value of columns used to link the tables (also known as key columns) is null. The next section will return to single-table queries to explore a few SQL functions. I'll stick to the most commonly used ones, but there are many more, with varying degrees of complexity.

My book, *Evolve Your RPG Coding: Move from OPM to ILE ... and Beyond* (*https://www .mc-store.com/products/evolve-your-rpg-coding-move-from-opm-to-ile-and-beyond*) has a very comprehensive chapter about most of the SQL functions (and a lot more basic SQL stuff).

A Handful of Column Functions

SQL's many functions are incredibly useful and can save you a lot of time. However, they can also be the cause of major headaches, so you need to understand and use them correctly. I'll go over a few of these functions now and explore a few more later in the book. Let's start with everybody's favorite: the COUNT function.

The COUNT Function

We've all used it, more times than we can count. It's the simplest way to determine how many records will be included in a query (unless you specify a FETCH FIRST clause). If you aren't familiar with FETCH FIRST, don't worry, because I'll cover it in several chapters. Here is a textbook example of the use of COUNT: to count the number of rows in the Students table:

```
SELECT      COUNT(*)
    FROM    UMADB_CHP2.PFSTM;
```

COUNT(*) includes rows even if they contain NULL values. COUNT(*expression*) excludes NULL values from the count.

The interesting thing about COUNT that you might not know is that you can use it in conjunction with other functions. Next I'll talk about finding the minimum and maximum values of a column and then show you an example that includes all three functions.

Finding the Minimum and Maximum Values of a Column

In a high-level programming language, finding the minimum or maximum value of a given column typically requires cycling through the whole table and storing the minimum/maximum value in a temporary variable that gets updated whenever the last record read contains a relevant column value. In SQL, it's a column function that you can use in a SELECT statement column list or, not as commonly done but also possible, in a HAVING clause. By the way, I'll also discuss the HAVING clause later, just in case you're not familiar with it. Here's how to determine the minimum and maximum salaries of the university's teachers:

```
SELECT      MIN(TESA) AS MIN_SALARY
            , MAX(TESA) AS MAX_SALARY
    FROM    UMADB_CHP2.PFTEM
;
```

This example has two very interesting elements: it shows that you can use different column functions together, and it also addresses a typical problem that derives from the use of any column function: the name of the column. If you run the same statement without the "AS *xxxx*" bits, you're still going to get correct results, but unless you remember which is which when you're analyzing the data (OK, in this case it should be obvious, but bear with me), they're going to be pretty useless because the columns will be named 00001 and 00002, respectively. What I'm getting at is that it's important to use aliases for your columns whenever you use a function or any other expression, such as a string concatenation or an arithmetic expression, so that its contents are obvious to whoever is looking at the output data. Speaking of arithmetic expressions, the functions I've presented so far can work with numbers and characters alike, but the last two of my examples only work on numbers.

Sums and Averages Made Easy

As in the minimum/maximum scenario, summing up a column of values or finding its average in a high-level programming language requires some work, but in SQL there's a column function that does that for you. Let's start with the one you've probably used before:

```
SELECT       SUM(TESA) AS TOTAL_SALARIES
    FROM     UMADB_CHP2.PFTEM
;
```

This statement returns the sum of the teachers' salaries and can be used in conjunction with other column functions without any problems. However, if you try to sum the teachers' ranks, a non-numeric column, the database engine will return the SQL0402 error message, which explains that you can "only" use INTEGER, SMALLINT, BIGINT, DECIMAL, ZONED, FLOAT, REAL, DOUBLE (or DOUBLE_PRECISION), and DECFLOAT data type values as an argument to the SUM function. If you have a numeric value stored in a character column, you can try to use the DIGITS function to convert it to a number and then calculate the sum. Something like SUM(DIGITS(YOUR_CHARACTER_FIELD)) should work, as long as the values of the character column are convertible to numeric format. Similarly, you can calculate the average of numeric values, and the same rules apply.

However, the AVG function can have an unpleasant side-effect that is also often misleading for the end user: its precision. Let's run a quick example to illustrate this problem. You can calculate the average salary of the teachers, with the following statement:

```
SELECT      AVG(TESA)   AS AVERAGE_SALARY
    FROM    UMADB_CHP2.PFTEM
;
```

If you run a full SELECT of the table and calculate the average yourself, you'll see that this output value is accurate and perhaps even too accurate (138333.3333333333333333333333) for the end user. After all, the user is expecting an amount, which usually means a number with two decimal places, not a huge train of 3s that can be confusing. I chose this example because it allows me to introduce another column function that is akin to the DIGITS function on steroids.

The Shape-shifting CAST Function

While DIGITS allows you to convert a character string into its numeric value, it doesn't allow you to be very specific about the number of decimal places of the number. It's true that there are other conversion functions that you can use, depending on your specific need, such as BIGINT, BINARY, BLOB, CHAR, CLOB, and DATE, to name just a few. But the beauty of the CAST function is that it can do the same as all the others and allow you to specify the number of decimal places.

Let's revisit the SQL statement that returns the average salary and modify it, in order to return a user-friendly amount instead of that awful number:

```
SELECT      CAST (AVG(TESA) AS DECIMAL (11, 2)) AS AVERAGE_SALARY
    FROM    UMADB_CHP2.PFTEM
;
```

What's going on here? Well, it's a function within another function: AVG(TESA) calculates the average of the salaries, just like before, but then the CAST function that encloses it converts the ugly numeric result returned by the AVG function into a DECIMAL(11, 2). I've used CAST in many different scenarios—from "data beautification," as in this case, to situations in which different tables that share a key don't have the key fields in the same format or even data type. CAST is indeed a powerful tool, and I prefer its readability when it comes to specifying the output data type over the aforementioned conversion functions.

Aggregating Data with GROUP BY

User requests often require little more than a regular SELECT statement, but standardized reports usually include aggregated information obtained with some of the column functions I've mentioned before. Let's say the university's board wants to know the average salary by teacher rank and how many teachers are in each of these ranks. So far, the column functions used included a single piece of data, like a count or an average, or at most, two functions combined. To answer this question, we'll need to list the teacher rank, which is a column of the teachers table, and two functions (a count of the teachers per rank and their average salary).

My guess is that you already figured out how to write this statement, based on what I've shown before. However, if you try to run this statement without a GROUP BY clause, it will end in error. Why? Well, because you'll be trying to aggregate data (by using the functions) and display all the records at once (the teachers' ranks). That's where the GROUP BY clause comes into play: it allows you to, well, group information by a given expression—typically a column of the select list. If you're having trouble following my train of thought, take a moment to analyze the following statement:

```
SELECT      TETR AS TEACHER_RANK
            , CAST (AVG(TESA) AS DECIMAL (11, 2))  AS AVERAGE_SALARY
            , COUNT(TETR) AS NUMBER_OF_TEACHERS
     FROM   UMADB_CHP2.PFTEM
     GROUP BY TETR
;
```

This is the magic of GROUP BY: you can use quite a few column functions and present sectioned results. Even though I'm only using one column in the GROUP BY clause, it's possible to use as many as you want or even more complex grouping expressions, which can resemble a Microsoft Excel pivot table (presenting both the grouped rows and the subtotals)—more about that later.

The Two Flavors of INSERT

Most programmers are familiar with the INSERT SQL statement, and some (including myself) prefer it to Data File Utility (DFU), because it's reproducible, controlled, and most important, easy to track. It's true that you can save all those spool files produced by DFU somewhere, but it's not easy to re-input or even reuse inputted data. With INSERT, a simple copy-paste-adjust operation is all it takes to add a second or third record that shares some similarities with the original statement.

Vanilla INSERT: Plain, Simple, and Kind of Boring

You're certainly familiar with the "insert one record with these values" INSERT statement. What you might not know is that there are some tweaks you can introduce into the most basic form of the INSERT statement. Let's say I want to add a course to the Courses table. There are two ways to do this: you can either specify which columns you'll be providing values for and what those values are, or simply specify a list of values. Here's an example of creating a new course with the two alternatives, starting with the longer of the two:

```
INSERT INTO UMADB_CHP2.PFCOM
(CONM, CODS, CODN, CODE    , COTA, COSC)
VALUES(
'Advanced Trickery'
        , 'This course will help you take your trick-or-treat Halloween
tricks to the next level!'
        , 'Manual Crafts'
        , 'The Joker'
        , 'Dennis the Menace'
        , '1'
)
;
```

Note that I'm providing values for all the columns. If I hadn't, then the default value for the column (zero for numeric columns and " for the character fields) would be used. I'll show you later how this can be customized via Data Definition Language (DDL). However, because I'm providing all the necessary information, I can omit the column names, like this:

```
INSERT INTO UMADB_CHP2.PFCOM
VALUES(
'Advanced Trickery'
        , 'This course will help you take your trick-or-treat Halloween
tricks to the next level!'
        , 'Manual Crafts'
        , 'The Joker'
        , 'Dennis the Menace'
        , '1'
)
;
```

Even though this second option is shorter (which makes it rather tempting to use), I favor the longer version, for two reasons:

- Clarity—the lists of column names and their matching values unambiguously state "what goes where" when the record is inserted. Also, you're not bound to the order by which the columns appear in the table record. The columns might be alphabetically ordered, but you want to start your statement with the columns that form the record's unique key and then fill in the rest of the data. With the shorter version, this is simply not possible, because you have to stick to the order of columns imposed by the table definition.

- Reusability—Even if new columns are added to the table, the longer INSERT statement will still work as expected, regardless of the position of the new columns in the table. With the shorter version, this might not be true, unless you always add the new columns after the last existing column of the record. Note, however, that if the values for the new columns are not specified, they'll be filled with the default value, which is not always a good option.

Strawberry (or Whatever Your Favorite Ice Cream Flavor Is) INSERT

My guess is that you're used to the "vanilla" INSERT and use it regularly. However, there are situations, such as copying a group of records from a table to another, in which you fall back to the CPYF (Copy File) CL command. This command is nice and simple, but it falls short when you don't want all the records from the original table to be copied to the destination table. Yes, you can use the FROMRCD/TORCD or FROMKEY/TOKEY keywords to limit the records being copied, but it's still a bit cumbersome.

This second flavor of INSERT (sorry about the lame section title; I'm a big fan of strawberry ice cream) allows you to selectively copy records. The best part is that you can list the records you'll be copying easily: using a SELECT statement. Interested? Let me explain how it works with an example.

The university managed to resurrect two reputed scholars—Max Planck and Albert Einstein—to teach a summer course on physics. They need to be added to the Teachers table, which would typically be a manual insertion operation performed by the administrative staff. However, someone secured a copy of the relevant data and uploaded it to a temporary table, named PFTEMP_TEM, which happens to have almost the exact same format as the Teachers table. It's missing only the status column. Let's see how you could copy its data to the Teachers table with an INSERT statement:

```
INSERT INTO UMADB_CHP2.PFTEM
SELECT      TMP.*, '1'
FROM    UMADB_CHP2.PFTEMP_TEM TMP
;
```

Notice the simplicity of the statement: with just a few lines, I copied all the data from one table to another and added the missing information. An INSERT with a nested SELECT statement is a powerful tool because the flexibility of the SELECT statement allows you to tailor the original data to the destination table, by changing its format; translating information (for instance, it's possible to translate a percentage to the respective letter grade, as you'll see later); and surgically selecting which records to copy. For instance, if PFTEMP_TEM had a different column arrangement (a different number of columns or simply a different order), you'd just change the SELECT clause to match the destination table's column order.

Data Adjustments with UPDATE

"Data adjustments" is a nice euphemism for those times when you have to get your hands dirty changing data at a very low level. A lot of programmers I know use DFU exclusively for these tasks, but I prefer to use SQL. The UPDATE instruction allows multiple, finely targeted, and reproducible changes to a group of records, while DFU can only act upon a record at a time. This flexibility is often the reason why some people don't like to use UPDATE: if you aren't careful, you might end up updating more than you wanted (or the whole table) with one incorrect UPDATE statement. That's why I always follow a methodology for my updates:

- Run a SELECT with the UPDATE record selection conditions in the WHERE clause.
- Double check the SET clause, either visually, if it's a simple change, or on the SELECT column list of a SELECT statement.
- Run the UPDATE statement.
- Extra step: if there's a risk of something going wrong with a large UPDATE, perform it under commitment control.

Let's see this in action with an example from our sample database. In the previous section, I inserted two new teachers into the Teachers table: Max Planck and Albert Einstein. However, the original data had a typo. The teacher rank was incorrect: the teacher rank of these two records currently reads "Profesor Emeritus" instead of "Professor Emeritus". Oops. Let's correct that mistake, following the steps mentioned before:

```
SELECT      TENM
            , TETR
    FROM    UMADB_CHP2.PFTEM
    WHERE   TENM in ('Planck, Max', 'Einstein, Albert')
    ;
```

In this case, the change is minimal, and a visual check suffices, so I'm ready to run the UPDATE:

```
UPDATE      UMADB_CHP2.PFTEM
SET         TETR = 'Professor Emeritus'
   WHERE    TENM in ('Planck, Max', 'Einstein, Albert')
;
```

You can also use UPDATE in slightly more complex scenarios, such as updating multiple columns at once or even using the current value of a column to calculate its new value. For instance, let's say the university wants to cut the teachers' salaries by 10 percent. With a single UPDATE statement, you can enforce this (probably unpopular) decision:

```
UPDATE      UMADB_CHP2.PFTEM
   SET      TESA = TESA * 0.9
   WHERE    TESC = '1'
;
```

Note that in this case, I'm only updating the active records (TESC = '1').

As I said before, it's possible to update multiple columns at once and even use the same column as the updater and the updated. For instance, you can update column A with the value of column B and, in the same statement, also update the value of column B with something else. You just need to carefully pick the order of the changes in the SET clause, as they'll be executed by the order in which you write them. Here's a generic example:

```
UPDATE      TABLE_XX
   SET      COL_A = COL_B, COL_B = 0
   WHERE    COL_X = '123'
;
```

I'll revisit the UPDATE instruction, to share a few tricks later in the book. Now it's time to discuss the last DML instruction of this chapter: DELETE.

DELETE: A Blessing and a Curse

I'm one of those programmers who doesn't like to (permanently) get rid of information. I'm not a hoarder, I just know that when someone asks me to delete something from a database, there's a good chance that, at some point in the future, they'll want that piece of data back. So, I'm a big fan of the soft delete: keeping the information exactly where it was, but with a different status to indicate that it's been "deleted" (or inactivated, if you will), thus indicating that it shouldn't be used by the application. However, there are times when you really have to get rid of stuff. For those situations, I still prefer a controlled way of deleting information. All of this to tell you a bit more about the DELETE instruction.

I assume you know the basic syntax of DELETE, and you've used it before to clear a table with the classic DELETE FROM *<table_name>*. However, I can't stress enough that you should be EXTREMELY careful when you use DELETE. There is no undo. And if you forget the WHERE clause or make a mistake in it, you run the risk of clearing the entire table, just like a CLRPFM (Clear Physical File Member) CL command would! That's why I consider the DELETE to be both a blessing and a curse: it can save you a lot of time—or cost you a lot of time, depending on how you use it. Just as with an UPDATE statement, I heartily recommend that you try a SELECT statement using the WHERE clause before you do a DELETE, just to make sure it works like you expect it to. In other words, the same methodology I mentioned before applies here:

1. Run a SELECT with the DELETE record selection conditions in the WHERE clause.

2. Double check everything before actually running the DELETE statement.

3. Run the DELETE statement (and pray you didn't botch it because there's no way back—except for restoring a backup, if you have one).

4. Extra step: if there's a risk of something going wrong with a large DELETE, perform it under commitment control.

Here's an example of a controlled DELETE, which will also use all the other SQL instructions discussed in this chapter. Let's say I want to reuse the temporary teacher table mentioned before, PFTEMP_TEM, for enrolling additional teachers, and one of them will also teach Advanced Quantum Mechanics and is from Germany, like Professor Max Planck. I could simply clear the table by using a CLRPFM CL command or a DELETE statement without a WHERE clause and then insert the new data. However, because there are no unique IDs in the table, I can reuse the good professor's record and type a little less. In other words, I can update an existing record and save some time. So, here's what I'm going to do:

1. I'll delete everything from the PFTEMP_TEM table except Professor Max Planck's record:

```
DELETE
    FROM       UMADB_CHP2.PFTEMP_TEM
WHERE TENM <> 'Planck, Max'
;
```

2. Insert the new teachers' records (I'll just insert one, for brevity's sake):

```
INSERT INTO UMADB_CHP2.PFTEMP_TEM
    (TENM, TETR, TEDB, TEAD , TEPN, TEMN,
TEEM, TEDL, TESN, TEST, TESA)
VALUES(
'Feynman, Richard'
        , 'Professor Emeritus'
        , 19180511
        , 'USA'
        , 'N/A'
        , 'N/A'
        , 'N/A'
        , 'N/A'
        , 'N/A'
        , 'Quantum Electrodynamics'
        , 100000.0
    )
;
```

3. Update Professor Max Planck's record with the necessary changes:

```
UPDATE        UMADB_CHP2.PFTEMP_TEM
SET           TENM = 'Schrodinger, Erwin'
              , TETR = 'Professor Emeritus'
              , TEDB = 18870812
    WHERE     TENM = 'Planck, Max'
;
```

4. Finally, insert the new data into the Teachers table:

```
INSERT INTO UMADB_CHP2.PFTEM
SELECT      TMP.*, '1'
FROM    UMADB_CHP2.PFTEMP_TEM TMP
;
```

In This Chapter, You've Learned ...

- A few tricks you can use in WHERE clauses, like the BETWEEN and IN predicates. These can help clarify and simplify future maintenance of complex SQL instructions. I also mentioned how to use the NOT operator and provided a couple of examples.

- How you can join tables and what the implications of those joins are in the output data. Particularly relevant to this topic is Figure 2.3, which provides an overview of the join types.

- There are a few handy functions to perform the most basic data aggregation operations: COUNT, SUM, calculate the AVeraGe, and find the MINimum and MAXimum values of a column (I've written the names of the functions in upper case, for brevity's sake).

- Some of these operations produce unexpected (let's called them "over-precise") results that don't sit well with the end user, and there's a nice function to change the data type of a piece of data into another type: the CAST function.

- It's possible to use the aggregation functions with non-aggregated data, as long as you use the GROUP BY clause.

- There are two "flavors" of UPDATE, and how to use the "strawberry-flavored UPDATE" to insert multiple records at once.

- How to update multiple columns with one statement and even use a column to update another, while changing the first column's contents on the same update.

- How to safely use the UPDATE statement, by using a simple methodology.

- Finally, how to apply that same methodology to the DELETE instruction and avoid wasting time cleaning up messes that could have been avoided.

The next chapter will be the last "warm-up" chapter and will recap the basics of DDL, while offering some insights, much as this chapter has done.

3

A Data Definition Language Basics Recap

Just as the previous chapter recapped Data Manipulation Language (DML) basics, this one does the same for Data Definition Language (DDL). The main DDL instructions (CREATE, ALTER, and DROP) and objects (TABLE, VIEW, and INDEX) will be discussed. However, the discussion won't focus on their syntax but will instead cover how to convert physical files to SQL tables and how to create self-managing unique keys.

Chapter 2 reviewed the main DML instructions and showed sample statements built over the UMADB database. Well, calling it a database at this stage is stretching the truth a bit: UMADB is just a set of physical files, not actually linked to each other at database level. Instead, they share some common string fields that work as keys at the application level.

Converting UMADB's Physical Files to SQL Tables

The first step in transforming UMADB from an amalgamation of files into a coherent, organized database is to convert the physical files into proper SQL tables, with all the bells and whistles. There are several ways to do this. For instance, you can type the complete CREATE TABLE statements by hand—not very efficient, but it gives you practice with the CREATE TABLE statement. But we're not going to do that! We're going to take a shortcut and use a nifty feature of IBM Access Client Solutions' (ACS) Run SQL Scripts: the Generate SQL option. (In the examples here, I use System i Navigator, but the instructions will also work with more recent versions of the product.)

In order to do that, let's fire up System i Navigator (ACS), expand the **My Connections** handle (it sits in the left sidebar of the window). Then we'll expand the **Databases** handle and its sub-handle with the system's name on it. Finally, let's click **Schemas**. Something similar to what's shown in Figure 3.1 should be displayed.

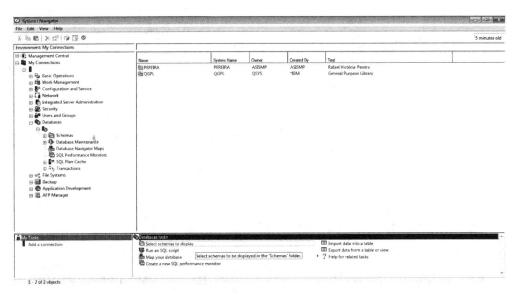

Figure 3.1: System i Navigator(ACS) database schemas

The list of schemas shown at the right side of the screen will vary, but there's a high probability that the one you want, UMADB_CHP2 (assuming you downloaded and restored to your IBM i the save file containing this library from Chapter 2's downloadable source code), is not displayed. Let's fix that. In the bottom right pane of the window, under **Database tasks**, there are several options. The first one from the top is **Select schemas to display**. If you click that option, you'll see something resembling Figure 3.2.

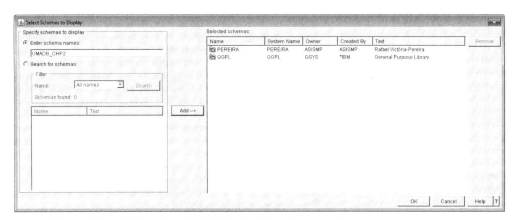

Figure 3.2: Adding the UMADB_CHP2 schema to the schemas to display

In order to add UMADB_CHP2 schema to the schemas to display panel, you have two options: you either type the library (or schema) name in the box in the top left corner of the window, or you click **Search for schemas:**. If you choose the latter, it's possible to refine your search by entering part of the schema's name followed by the percent (%) character and clicking the **Search** button. After any of these options, you simply click the **Add ->** button, followed by **OK**.

This closes the window, and you'll now see the UMADB_CHP2 schema in the schema's list in the left sidebar. Let's expand the UMADB_CHP2 database folder and click **Tables**. You'll see something similar to Figure 3.3, without the context menu—I'll get to that in a second.

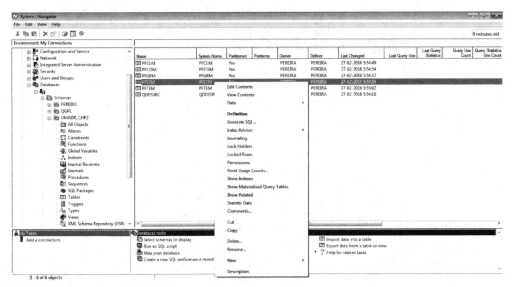

Figure 3.3: Expanded UMADB_CHP2 schema, showing the list of tables

To get exactly what's shown in Figure 3.3, you'll need to right-click a table. This opens a context menu; I'll explore a few of the options on this menu later. For the moment, let me just focus on the **Generate SQL…** option. What does it do? Well, IBM can come up with some very obscure names for things sometimes, but in this case, there's no doubt: this option generates the SQL code required to create the selected object.

Note that there are things that are possible in DDS that SQL can't do, and vice-versa. As you'll find out in a moment, the output of this option will list the things it can't convert to SQL. But first, let's generate the SQL statements for all the tables in the UMADB_CHP2 schema. Try selecting all the tables, pressing the right mouse button, and choosing the **Generate SQL…** option. You should see something resembling Figure 3.4.

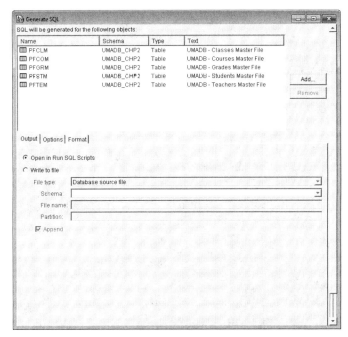

Figure 3.4: Generating SQL for multiple tables

Here you can save the generated SQL statements to a source file or open a new **Run SQL Scripts** window instead. I prefer this last option because it's easier to inspect and change the statements in a non-native SQL tool, so let's leave the selection as it is (the default should be **Open in Run SQL Scripts**) and click **OK**.

CREATE TABLE Fundamentals

If everything went according to plan, you should see a new **Run SQL Scripts** window with the generated SQL code for the tables' creation. Let's analyze the PFSTM's CREATE TABLE statement:

```
CREATE TABLE UMADB_CHP2.PFSTM (
--   SQL150B   10    REUSEDLT(*NO) in table PFSTM in UMADB_CHP2 ignored.
        STNM CHAR(60) CCSID 37 NOT NULL DEFAULT '' ,
        STDB DECIMAL(8, 0) NOT NULL DEFAULT 0 ,
        STAD CHAR(60) CCSID 37 NOT NULL DEFAULT '' ,
                                                      Continued
```

```
    STPN CHAR(15) CCSID 37 NOT NULL DEFAULT '' ,
    STMN CHAR(15) CCSID 37 NOT NULL DEFAULT '' ,
    STEM CHAR(60) CCSID 37 NOT NULL DEFAULT '' ,
    STDL CHAR(20) CCSID 37 NOT NULL DEFAULT '' ,
    STSN CHAR(11) CCSID 37 NOT NULL DEFAULT '' ,
    STSC CHAR(1) CCSID 37 NOT NULL DEFAULT '' )

    RCDFMT PFSTMR      ;
```

Notice the column definition for STNM, for instance: it uses the DDS field definition (60A) to create a CHAR(60) column, but it adds a few things. It takes the CCSID from the physical file definition and adds the NOT NULL and a default. All the columns include the NOT NULL indication and have data-type–related defaults, mimicking DDS's default behavior. This is exactly what can be expected, considering that corresponds to the "SQL version" of a DDS-defined file. If you look closely, you'll see that the same record format name of the DDS file was extracted—essential for keeping RPG programs that use this table functioning without modification.

Also notice the comment line just below the first line of the statement: this is the database engine's way of telling you, "Hey, I'm not DDS, there's stuff I can't do. Find a way to take care of this yourself." In this case, it's not a big deal, but there are situations in which you need to do some extra work to fully replicate a DDS-defined file. For instance, the EDTCDE keyword is not automatically converted, nor does it have an SQL equivalent. It's true that it doesn't directly impact the file itself, but if the field is referenced during a display or printer file creation, this keyword matters. There's no silver bullet for this. You just have to be careful and analyze the impact of the changes.

If you run the statement "as is," you'll get an error because PFSTM already exists in schema UMADB_CHP2. So, I'll create schema UMADB_CHP3 and change the schema name in the CREATE TABLE statement to UMADB_CHP3. Now let's run the statement. It should create the table in UMADB_CHP3, but you'll see there's something missing: all the descriptions are gone! If you scroll down a bit, you'll see a couple of LABEL ON statements. Let's change the schema name to UMADB_CHP3 in both statements, like this:

```
LABEL ON TABLE UMADB_CHP3.PFSTM
       IS 'UMADB - Students Master File' ;

LABEL ON COLUMN UMADB_CHP3.PFSTM
( STNM TEXT IS 'Student name' ,
       STDB TEXT IS 'Date of birth' ,
       STAD TEXT IS 'Home address' ,
       STPN TEXT IS 'Home phone number' ,
       STMN TEXT IS 'Mobile number' ,
       STEM TEXT IS 'Email address' ,
       STDL TEXT IS 'Driver''s license' ,
       STSN TEXT IS 'Social security number' ,
       STSC TEXT IS 'Status' ) ;
```

Now let's run these statements. Badabing, badaboom, the descriptions are back. Now seriously, this is just a reminder that the CREATE and ALTER instructions don't include descriptions like DDS definitions do. For that you need to use a LABEL ON statement. It's important to keep this in mind and make a habit of writing a LABEL ON statement right after every CREATE TABLE statement.

Moving a Step Closer to a Real SQL Table

Now that we have the PFSTM table created in UMADB_CHP3, let's start enhancing it. The objective is to make the data handling less application-dependent by "pulling down" to the database level some application features that impact the way data is stored and handled in the system. This allows other, non-native applications to handle the database as the native RPG application would. As you'll see, this is not a simple process, and I'll just scratch the surface in this chapter, with a few changes.

Adding a Unique, Self-Managed Key

The first step is to create a unique key, controlled by the database. Remember, the table already has a key, the student name column (STNM), but its uniqueness is enforced by the application. This quickly becomes a problem when other, non-native applications start using the database. In order to maintain the database, a consistent and coherent unique key, enforced at the table level, is required. In an ideal situation, you'd go a step further and implement a key that is transparent for the outside world: a key that automatically gets a new and unique value every time a record is inserted. DDS can enforce this with the UNIQUE keyword. However, it can't automatically generate a value that's unique. SQL can specify unique keys that are generated by the database engine.

Let's implement one on the Students table and make it the table's primary key. (Note: an Excel file containing the tables discussed in this chapter—Students, Courses, Teachers, Classes, and Grades—is included in the downloadable materials for this book, available at *https://www.mc-store.com/products/sql-for-ibm-i-a-database-modernization-guide*.)

Instead of using DROP to destroy the table, let's change the table structure with the ALTER TABLE instruction. But don't worry, I'll discuss DROP later. The ALTER TABLE instruction is to an SQL table what the CHGPF (Change Physical File) CL command is to a DDS-defined physical file: it allows you to change certain characteristics of the table without destroying and recreating it. In this case, I'll use it to add a primary key column, named STID. Keep in mind that I'm changing an empty table in UMADB_CHP3, but this could be performed over any SQL table. Here's the statement to add a primary key to PFSTM:

```
ALTER TABLE  UMADB_CHP3.PFSTM
    ADD COLUMN STID INTEGER
            PRIMARY KEY
            GENERATED ALWAYS
            AS IDENTITY(START WITH 1 INCREMENT BY 1)
  ;
```

As this might be new to you, let me go over it line by line. The ALTER TABLE statement is fairly straightforward up to the third line, where I'm defining STID as this table's primary key. The fun starts on the following line: GENERATED ALWAYS ensures that a value for this column is generated automatically by the database engine. Then AS IDENTITY indicates that this is an auto-incrementing column to which you do not have to assign values. In fact, you're not allowed to assign values to an auto-incrementing column, unless you override this restriction on an INSERT using the OVERRIDING SYSTEM VALUE keyword (which overrides GENERATED ALWAYS so it works like GENERATED BY DEFAULT instead for the duration of the INSERT).

The rest of the fifth line of the statement defines how the database engine will assign those values. Note that defining this column as INTEGER limits the maximum value of the unique key to 2,147,483,647. If you feel that this is not enough, you can use a BIGINT instead, which has a max value of 9,223,372,036,854,775,807, according to IBM's *DB2 for i SQL* reference manual. If this weren't a primary key column, you could specify the CYCLE keyword, which would cause the number generation to reset to the initial value (1 in this case) when the maximum possible value was reached.

Identity columns were added to DB2 for i in V5R2 and are immensely useful, but most people don't even know they exist. Because they simplify application development, all tables should be defined with a unique primary key, and identity columns are often an excellent choice for tables without a non-changing natural key. If you're not familiar with the concept, don't worry—I'll explain it in detail in a couple of chapters.

Providing Proper Default Values for Optional and Audit-Related Columns

Now that I have created a primary key for this table, let's see what other enhancements can be performed. A quick inspection of the application's student enrollment screen shows that the fields *Email address*, *Driver's license*, and *Social Sec. Number* have a default value of N/A. However, this is an application-only behavior: if a record is inserted via SQL and a value for these fields is not provided, they'll be left blank because that was the default value specified on the CREATE TABLE statement (go back a few pages and confirm, if you don't believe me). The screen also shows the current user, time, and date, even though those details are not stored with the student's record. This is a shortcoming of the application, because auditors really like to know this kind of stuff when they come snooping around.

Let's address all these issues. Again, I could destroy the table with a DROP statement, fix the CREATE TABLE statement, and recreate the table. However, this would also delete the data in the table, if there is any. Instead, I'll use another ALTER TABLE statement:

```
ALTER TABLE  UMADB_CHP3.PFSTM
ADD COLUMN STCU VARCHAR(18) DEFAULT USER
ADD COLUMN STCT TIMESTAMP DEFAULT CURRENT TIMESTAMP
   ALTER COLUMN STEM SET DEFAULT 'N/A'
   ALTER COLUMN STDL SET DEFAULT 'N/A'
   ALTER COLUMN STSN SET DEFAULT 'N/A'
   ALTER COLUMN STSC SET DEFAULT '1'
;
```

A couple of notes about this statement. First, it shows that you can change more than one thing at a time; I'm adding new columns and changing existing ones at the same time. Second, there are a few keywords, known as *special registers*, which you can use to refer to "system things," such as the current user's name or the current timestamp. There are others, such as CURRENT_DATE, CURRENT_TIME, CURRENT TIMEZONE, CURRENT SERVER, and CURRENT SCHEMA, to name just a few. These will allow you to mimic a typical native application's behavior. In fact, storing information about the record-creation user and timestamp is a good practice—and the auditors love stuff like that. I'll show you later how to do the same for the last update user and timestamp, another auditor-favorite feature of a proper table.

I don't want to sound repetitive, but remember: SQL is not DDS. If you add new columns to a table, always remember to execute the appropriate LABEL ON statement to provide clear and concise descriptions for your columns. Let's do that for the three new columns added to PFSTM:

```
LABEL ON COLUMN UMADB_CHP3.PFSTM
   (
        STID TEXT IS 'Record ID'
      , STCU TEXT IS 'Created by'
      , STCT TEXT IS 'Created on'
   )
;
```

If you back up a bit, to the last ALTER TABLE statement, you'll probably notice I also provided a new default for the STSC column. This is just another example of how you can simplify data insertion: specifying that new records are in active status ('1') by default saves me the trouble of including that information on future INSERT statements. Speaking of INSERT statements, let's see how the table changes I've performed impact those statements. Here's how I'd mimic the native application's student enrollment functionality before my ALTER TABLE statements:

```
INSERT INTO UMADB_CHP3.PFSTM
(STNM, STDB, STAD, STPN, STMN, STEM, STDL, STSN, STSC)
VALUES(
'Mailer, Norman'
     , 19750318
     , '2234 Blackstone Avenue, Joyville, South Carolina'
     , '555-001-123'
     , '999-010-469'
     , 'N/A'
     , 'N/A'
     , 'N/A'
     , '1'
)
;
```

Even though I don't have a value for the email, driver's license, and Social Security number, I still had to mention them on the INSERT, in order to force the appropriate "not available" value the application is expecting. I also had to include STSC with the value '1' to indicate that the record is active. Now let's see how the same INSERT looks like after the changes performed via ALTER TABLE:

```
INSERT INTO UMADB_CHP3.PFSTM
(STNM, STDB, STAD, STPN, STMN)
VALUES(
```

Continued

```
'Mailer, Norman'
        , 19750318
        , '2234 Blackstone Avenue, Joyville, South Carolina'
        , '555-001-123'
        , '999-010-469'
)
;
```

The statement is much shorter, but there's no loss of functionality because the defaults are used by the database engine to fill the columns for which I didn't specify a value. Additionally, the three new columns (the unique ID, record-creation user, and respective timestamp) are automatically filled in by the system.

Time for Some Practice

Before moving on to the section on views, it's time for you to practice what you've learned so far. Try to modify the CREATE TABLE and LABEL ON statements that were automatically generated for the rest of the tables in order to include the three new columns I added to PFSTM: the unique ID, the creation user, and the creation timestamp. Try following the same naming convention I'm using for the column names: a two-character prefix indicates the table (for instance, CO for courses), followed by two characters that define the type of value the column will hold (for instance, CU for creation user).

Let me get you started: here are the modified CREATE TABLE and LABEL ON statements for the Grades table:

```
CREATE TABLE UMADB_CHP3.PFGRM
    (
        GRID INTEGER
            PRIMARY KEY
            GENERATED ALWAYS
            AS IDENTITY(START WITH 1
                INCREMENT BY 1)
                                                    Continued
```

```
              , GRSN CHAR(60) CCSID 37 NOT NULL DEFAULT ''
              , GRCN CHAR(60) CCSID 37 NOT NULL DEFAULT ''
              , GRCY DECIMAL(4, 0) NOT NULL DEFAULT 0
              , GRGR CHAR(2) CCSID 37 NOT NULL DEFAULT ''
              , GRCU VARCHAR(18) DEFAULT USER
              , GRCT TIMESTAMP DEFAULT CURRENT TIMESTAMP
         )
      RCDFMT PFGRMR
   ;
LABEL ON TABLE UMADB_CHP3.PFGRM
         IS 'UMADB - Grades Master File' ;

LABEL ON COLUMN UMADB_CHP3.PFGRM
      (
         GRID TEXT IS 'Record ID'
         , GRSN TEXT IS 'Student name'
         , GRCN TEXT IS 'Class name'
         , GRCY TEXT IS 'Class year'
         , GRGR TEXT IS 'Grade'
         , GRCU TEXT IS 'Created by'
         , GRCT TEXT IS 'Created on'
      )
   ;
```

The next task is to copy the data from UMADB_CHP2's physical files to UMADB_CHP3's tables. You can either use the traditional CPYF or use what you've learned in the previous chapter and issue INSERT ... SELECT statements instead. If you need some help, the downloadable source code for this chapter, available at *https://www.mc-store.com/products/sql-for-ibm-i-a-database-modernization-guide*, contains a file with all the necessary statements.

A First Step Toward Easier Data Access: Creating a Few Simple Views

Now that I have (and I hope you have, too) created all the tables on the UMADB_CHP3 schema, with their primary keys, it's time to simplify data access. However, although

I've created primary keys based on unique IDs for all the tables, this doesn't accurately represent the links between the tables that are kept by the application. For instance, the Classes table's real key is composed of the student name, class name, and class year. For now, I'll keep the keys as they are and use those columns to establish the necessary links. I'll return to this issue later and replace these faux primary keys with the real ones. First, let's take a first small step toward easier data access by creating a few simple views.

Why Do You Need Views?

Typically, views are used to hide database complexity and/or protect sensitive data. Let's start with the database-complexity issue: even in our simple database, it's not very practical to include the same INNER JOIN lines on every single SELECT statement to establish the appropriate connections between tables. The pragmatic response is to create a view that joins the tables (much like a joined logical file) and use it in the SELECT statements, instead of the direct access to the tables.

This is very practical, but it doesn't offer much security-wise. But note that by using the view instead of the table(s), you're accessing a single, separate object. Because you can specify different authorities for different objects, you can actually hide a table behind a view, by changing the table object authorities in order to prevent access to it (with a PUBLIC *EXCLUDE, for instance) and granting limited access to the view itself. This way, you can ensure that only the columns mentioned explicitly in the view are accessible. For instance, I can create a view over the Teachers table that doesn't include the teacher salary column. If I combine that with a change in PFTEM's authorities, I can prevent whoever needs to use the teachers' other data from seeing the teachers' salaries.

How Do You Create Views?

Having said that, let's go through my usual process for creating a view:

1. Identify the tables and columns for the view.
2. Determine how the tables are linked.
3. Write a SELECT statement with the appropriate tables, columns, and JOINs.
4. Test, adjust, test, adjust ... until you get it right.
5. Finally, create the view using the SELECT statement, fine-tuned by the tests.

Let's start with a simple example that links the Students, Courses, and Classes tables. This view doesn't include every single column of these three tables, only a select few. Let's include the student, class, and course names plus the course description. Naturally, I only want students that are enrolled in classes—that way I can simplify the joins and use only INNER JOINs. So let's follow the steps I mentioned before and get started!

I've already identified the tables: I'll need the Students, Classes, and Courses tables. I already know how to link them (in case you missed it, it's described in Chapter 1). I'm now ready to write the appropriate SELECT statement:

```
SELECT      STNM AS "Student_Name"
            , CLNM AS "Class_Name"
            , CONM AS "Course_Name"
            , CODS AS "Course_Description"
    FROM    UMADB_CHP3.PFSTM ST
    INNER JOIN UMADB_CHP3.PFCLM CL ON ST.STNM = CL.CLSN
    INNER JOIN UMADB_CHP3.PFCOM CO ON CL.CLCN = CO.CONM
;
```

Note that I'm not using the newly defined primary keys. This is because the Classes and Courses tables are not fully modified to use the new primary keys. We'll discuss those modifications later.

If you run this statement, you should get the expected results and even nice column headers. Because this is a simple SELECT, there's no actual need for testing and adjusting the statement, so let's create the view by adding the SELECT statement to a CREATE VIEW statement:

```
CREATE VIEW  UMADB_CHP3.View_Students_Classes_1
AS
SELECT      STNM AS "Student_Name"
            , CLNM AS "Class_Name"
            , CONM AS "Course_Name"
            , CODS AS "Course_Description"
```

Continued

```
FROM        UMADB_CHP3.PFSTM ST
INNER JOIN UMADB_CHP3.PFCLM CL ON ST.STNM = CL.CLSN
INNER JOIN UMADB_CHP3.PFCOM CO ON CL.CLCN = CO.CONM
;
```

It's important to follow along, either by typing or copy-pasting from the downloadable source code, because of what I'll show next. To check whether the view is properly created, let's run a simple SELECT over it:

```
SELECT       *
FROM    UMADB_CHP3.View_Students_Classes_1
;
```

Again, the result is what's expected: an exact match of the previous SELECT's result. Now let's include a WHERE clause to list all the classes for a particular student:

```
SELECT       *
FROM    UMADB_CHP3.View_Students_Classes_1
WHERE STNM = 'Anthony, Mark'
;
```

Oops! The statement ends in error, complaining it doesn't know STNM. But it's right there on the SELECT statement ... or is it? What's happening is that my effort to embellish my view with nice headers did a bit more than I expected: in a regular SELECT statement, the column header (that bit following the *<column name>* AS part) is just that: a column header. However, when you use it in a CREATE VIEW statement such as the one I wrote here, it becomes more than that. It turns into the actual column name! So the correct SELECT statement over the view becomes this:

```
SELECT       *
FROM    UMADB_CHP3.View_Students_Classes_1
WHERE "Student_Name" = 'Anthony, Mark'
;
```

While not necessarily a bad thing, using this type of naming is dangerous because it's case-sensitive. Try replacing "Student_Name" with "Student_name", and run the statement again. It will fail with the same error as it did when I ran it with STNM: it complains that column doesn't exist on the specified tables (in this case, our newly created view). I'll discuss the topic of user-friendly names in greater depth in the next chapter, but let's fix this view, so that both ugly four-letter cryptic names and human-readable longer names work.

The CREATE VIEW statement used before was basically the SELECT statement plus a line that gave the view its name. However, just as you can specify the names of the columns on an INSERT statement, you can also do the same in this case. However, in order to keep both short and long names, I need to introduce an additional reserved expression: FOR COLUMN. This allows you to provide a system-friendly (and by that I mean a short 10-letters-tops) name to an SQL column. I know this may sound confusing, so let's examine the new and improved CREATE VIEW statement:

```
CREATE VIEW  UMADB_CHP3.View_Students_Classes_1
    (
                "Student_Name" FOR COLUMN STNM
              , "Class_Name" FOR COLUMN CLNM
              , "Course_Name" FOR COLUMN CONM
              , "Course_Description" FOR COLUMN CODS
    )
AS
SELECT        STNM
              , CLNM
              , CONM
              , CODS
    FROM       UMADB_CHP3.PFSTM ST
    INNER JOIN UMADB_CHP3.PFCLM CL ON ST.STNM = CL.CLSN
    INNER JOIN UMADB_CHP3.PFCOM CO ON CL.CLCN = CO.CONM
;
```

The SELECT part is exactly the same, but the CREATE VIEW part is now much longer, and it resembles the first part of an INSERT statement, with a list of columns. However, note that after each column name there's a FOR COLUMN followed by a shorter name, which you'll recognize as the names given to the columns on the original tables. Before running this statement, you need to destroy the existing view, using a DROP statement:

```
DROP VIEW    UMADB_CHP3.View_Students_Classes_1;
```

You're now ready to create the new version of the view. Let's run the statement and then try a couple of different SELECT statements. The first one is the original SELECT, which failed because of the column STNM's name:

```
SELECT       *
FROM    UMADB_CHP3.View_Students_Classes_1
WHERE STNM = 'Anthony, Mark'
;
```

This now works, because of the FOR COLUMN clause that identifies the "Student_Name" column as a system-friendly column named STNM. Now let's try to run the same statement with the longer column name:

```
SELECT       *
FROM    UMADB_CHP3.View_Students_Classes_1
WHERE "Student_Name" = 'Anthony, Mark'
;
```

As expected, this also works. The FOR COLUMN is a very nice tool to have in your arsenal, as I'll explain in greater depth later. Now let's focus on a different aspect of an SQL view.

Repeat After Me: A View Is Not a Logical File

This may shock a few readers, because there's a lot of literature that clearly states that a view and a logical file (LF) are the same thing. Well, they're not exactly the same.

The first difference is related to performance: while an LF has a maximum page size of 8Kb, a view is capable of handling up to 64Kb. That's eight times more! However, this may not always translate to an equivalent performance gain, as tests performed by Jon Paris and Susan Gantner for an *IBM Systems Magazine* special on DDS versus DDL (see *www.ibmsystemsmag.com/ibmi/developer/modernization/A-Debate--DDS-vs--DDL/*) showed. There are performance gains, to be sure, but views sometimes have quirky behavior, which IBM continues to work on eliminating.

Note that I'm not in any way implying that you should not use views—quite the contrary! I'm a big fan of modernization, not for the sake of modernization but because of the benefits it can bring. Performance improvements are an important part of that, and even if sometimes the final result is not exactly what was expected, modernizing your database is still worth the effort. Why else would I have written this book?

Anyway, the second and probably most important reason that a view is not an LF is almost counter-intuitive: while most LFs have a key, views cannot have one. Try creating a view using a SELECT statement ending with an ORDER BY clause, and you'll see what I mean. The database engine will complain, and you won't be able to create the view. Sure, you can say that a keyless LF and a view are the same thing. However, always keep in mind that most LFs have keys, and that's why you should repeat after me: a view is not a logical file.

The Missing Piece: SQL Indexes

If a view can't have a key, what is SQL's equivalent of a keyed LF? It's not one but two things: a view and an index. Let's create an index to complement the view created in the previous section.

The index is something most programmers are not entirely familiar with, so I'll make an exception and discuss the syntax of this SQL statement in a bit of detail. In its simplest form, a CREATE INDEX statement can be written like this:

```
CREATE INDEX UMADB_CHP3.Index_Students_By_Name
   ON       UMADB_CHP3.PFSTM (STNM)
;
```

This creates an index over PFSTM, using STNM (the student name) as key. You can specify a multipart key by including multiple column names, separated by commas, between the parentheses. The following statement creates an index similar to the previous one, but with an expanded key that includes the student's date of birth:

```
CREATE INDEX UMADB_CHP3.Index_Students_By_Name_And_Birth
   ON        UMADB_CHP3.PFSTM (STNM, STDB)
;
```

Running the SELECT statement over the View_Students_Classes_1 view should, theoretically, produce faster results. I say theoretically because there's not a lot of data in this sample database's tables, and the performance gain, if any, is negligible in this case. For the moment, just know that View_Students_Classes_1 and Index_Students_By_Name allowed me to create an SQL version of an LF over PFSTM that uses STNM as a key.

A Side Note: Why Is It So Important to Keep the Source Statements Safe?

Let's take a step back and analyze View_Students_Classes_1 and Index_Students_By_Name from a system's point of view. If you try to use PDM to find these objects, you'll have a bit of a surprise, because they're not there. Instead, you'll see LFs on UMADB_CHP3: VIEW_00001 and INDEX00001. This happens because I didn't specify a system name for the view or the index—I'll get to that in a moment. For now, let's see how the system describes these objects.

If you type DSPFD UMADB_CHP3/VIEW_00001, you'll see an LF without a key. By pressing **Page Down**, you'll note that output of the DSPFD command (which is the description of the view, from the system's point of view) also includes the SQL statement that was used to create the view, which is nice. However, don't think even for a moment that you don't have to keep the source code of a view stored safely somewhere, because what's displayed here may not correspond to the source statement of the view. If the statement is long, as useful views tend to be, it simply won't fit here.

Similarly, DSPFD UMADB_CHP3/INDEX00001 shows another LF, correctly identified by the system as "externally described." You can **Page Down** all you want, but there's no source statement here—one more reason to keep all DDL statements safe somewhere. Unlike the view, you'll note that this "LF" has a key, just as a regular LF would.

There's yet another good reason to keep the source code: if you want to change a view or an index, the logical choice would be using an ALTER statement to do so. The problem is that there are no ALTER VIEW or ALTER INDEX statements: you need to use DROP VIEW or DROP INDEX followed by the respective CREATE statement.

It's true that by using ACS or System i Navigator's Generate SQL option you can get the original source code, but if the SQL object is somehow damaged, this may not be possible. I can't stress this enough: always keep your source statements stored in a safe location.

Exploring a Few CREATE INDEX Options

Let's start by fixing the ugly, system-generated name of my Index_Students_By_Name index into something more agreeable. Well, not too agreeable, because it can only be a maximum of 10 characters long. In order to do that, I'll use the FOR SYSTEM NAME expression, inserted right after the index name, just as the FOR COLUMN followed the column name on the view syntax. Here's what my index looks like after this change:

```
CREATE INDEX UMADB_CHP3.Index_Students_By_Name FOR SYSTEM NAME IDX_STM_NM
    ON        UMADB_CHP3.PFSTM (STNM)
;
```

A programmer familiar with the naming convention quickly identifies this as an index over PFSTM, using STNM as a key. Of course this doesn't work at all with longer keys, so you might need to use the respective description (created using a LABEL ON statement, if you recall what was discussed earlier in this chapter) to explain to whomever looks at the index using native tools, such as PDM, exactly what the index is. It's important to mention that FOR SYSTEM NAME and KEEP IN MEMORY, presented later in this section, only work on V7.1 or higher.

Now let's say I wanted an index by name, but in reverse alphabetical order. Just like in a regular ORDER BY clause, I can use ASC and DESC after each column name to specify the order. This means that my index, modified to sort the student name in reverse alphabetical order, looks like this:

```
CREATE INDEX UMADB_CHP3.Index_Students_By_Name FOR SYSTEM NAME IDX_STM_NM
   ON          UMADB_CHP3.PFSTM (STNM DESC)
;
```

I've also mentioned that a typical index has a larger page size than an LF. However, the default value for PAGESIZE, the keyword used to specify that value, is determined by the length of the key and has a minimum value of 64Kb. What I didn't say at the time is that you can choose the page size, by specifying the intended value on the CREATE INDEX statement! It's as simple as writing this:

```
CREATE INDEX UMADB_CHP3.Index_Students_By_Name FOR SYSTEM NAME IDX_STM_NM
   ON          UMADB_CHP3.PFSTM (STNM DESC)
   PAGESIZE  128
;
```

This creates an index with a 128Kb page size. Naturally, this affects performance, but it's not the only way to "juice up" your indexes. You can also use a couple of keywords to use a faster disk unit (a solid state disk, or SSD, to be more precise), if available, and to bring the index data into the main storage pool. Let's change the sample index to include these options:

```
CREATE INDEX UMADB_CHP3.Index_Students_By_Name FOR SYSTEM NAME IDX_STM_NM
   ON          UMADB_CHP3.PFSTM (STNM DESC)
   PAGESIZE  128
   UNIT      SSD
   KEEP IN MEMORY    YES
;
```

Finally, let me add one more thing, which is so obvious that you're probably wondering what it looks like in SQL: the DDL equivalent of an LF with the UNIQUE keyword. It's obvious because it's the same keyword, inserted in the middle of the CREATE INDEX statement. Here's an example that creates an index over PFSTM while ensuring that the student name is unique across the table:

```
CREATE UNIQUE INDEX UMADB_CHP3.Index_Students_By_Name
    FOR SYSTEM NAME IDX_STM_NM
    ON          UMADB_CHP3.PFSTM (STNM DESC)
    PAGESIZE  128
    UNIT        SSD
    KEEP IN MEMORY    YES
;
```

There are other interesting keywords to explore, and I'll discuss some of them later, properly contextualized with an example.

In This Chapter, You've Learned ...

I hope this has been an interesting chapter, filled with novelties for some readers, while providing a solid review of DDL for others. Here's a summary of what I've tried to explain here:

- How to convert a physical file to an SQL table, using the Generate SQL System i Navigator (ACS) option
- How to use LABEL ON statements to add descriptions to tables and columns
- How to use the ALTER TABLE statement to add columns, change default values, and add primary keys
- Why and how to create views
- Why a view is not (necessarily) the same as a logical file
- Why and how to create indexes
- How to add a few extras to your CREATE INDEX statements

This doesn't cover all the DDL you need to know—it only just scratches the surface. This chapter provided the basics of DDL. There's much more DDL to cover in the next chapters!

4

Making the Database User-Friendly

Following up on the previous chapter's refresher on Data Definition Language (DDL), this chapter will focus on making the database more user-friendly, by using longer and more descriptive names for the tables and the respective columns and explaining how to create views to hide the database complexity from the users, among other things.

Chapter 3 led us on the first step toward a true database, but it kept most of the hallmarks that make a DB2/400 database very "user-unfriendly": the table and column names are short, in the typical and old-fashioned way of the AS/400. However, end users' demands in regard to data queries have evolved significantly in recent years. The users of our UMADB are particularly data-hungry and are overtaxing the university's IT staff labor resources. This added burden on the IT staff is something that often occurs when you "open up" the database to the end users. The problem is that the database is not always ready to be used by someone not used to short, cryptic names, and this ends up causing additional stress on the IT staff, because it requires additional time and effort to "explain the database" to users and help them navigate the nearly indecipherable table and column names.

Using Longer Table and Column Names

The next step is fixing that, by providing longer names that users can relate to. As you've probably guessed, this will require changes to the tables' definition. Just as was explained in the previous chapter, this operation can be performed with a DROP TABLE/CREATE TABLE combination.

Let's help the university's IT staff and enhance the Grades table, but first, make sure you duplicate the UMADB_CHP3 library to a new UMADB_CHP4 library. This way you can always "go back" and repeat any of the statements mentioned in this chapter. Back in Chapter 3, all tables were changed to include a primary key and some auditing information. After these changes, PFGRM looks like Table 4.1.

Table 4.1: The Grades table structure					
Table Name	**Column Name**	**Data Type**	**Length**	**Dec. Pos.**	**Description**
PFGRM	GRID	Integer			Record ID (primary key)
PFGRM	GRSN	Char	60		Student name
PFGRM	GRCN	Char	60	0	Class name
PFGRM	GRCY	Decimal	4	0	Class year
PFGRM	GRGR	Char	2		Grade
PFGRM	GRCU	Varchar	18		Created by
PFGRM	GRCT	Timestamp			Created on

Now we're going to make it a bit more usable for non-IT people. Time for some hands-on reading! When you're ready, type the following statement:

```
DROP TABLE UMADB_CHP4.PFGRM;
```

And issue the new CREATE TABLE statement, with longer names for the table and its columns:

```
CREATE TABLE UMADB_CHP4.TBL_GRADES
    (
        GRADE_ID FOR COLUMN GRID INTEGER
            PRIMARY KEY
            GENERATED ALWAYS
            AS IDENTITY(START WITH 1
                INCREMENT BY 1)
                                                    Continued
```

```
        , STUDENT_NAME FOR COLUMN GRSN CHAR(60) CCSID 37 NOT NULL DEFAULT ''
        , CLASS_NAME FOR COLUMN GRCN CHAR(60) CCSID 37 NOT NULL DEFAULT ''
        , CLASS_YEAR FOR COLUMN GRCY DECIMAL(4, 0) NOT NULL DEFAULT 0
        , GRADE FOR COLUMN GRGR CHAR(2) CCSID 37 NOT NULL DEFAULT ''
        , CREATED_BY FOR COLUMN GRCU VARCHAR(18) DEFAULT USER
        , CREATED_ON FOR COLUMN GRCT TIMESTAMP DEFAULT CURRENT TIMESTAMP
    )
    RCDFMT PFGRMR
;
```

Now let's test it:

```
SELECT * FROM UMADB_CHP4.TBL_GRADES;
```

You should get no results, because we've just created the table, but the statement shouldn't end in error. Notice, however, that the column names have changed: you now see longer, human-readable column names instead of the cryptic four-letter acronyms. The "magic" is being provided by the FOR COLUMN instruction on each column specification. The syntax is quite simple: instead of simply specifying the column name, as we did before, we're now saying something like "this SQL column has a system name of *yyy*," where the *yyy* is the cryptic four-letter name, and the SQL column name is the longer version.

Let's review an example to make this clearer. Look at the student name line:

```
, STUDENT_NAME FOR COLUMN GRSN CHAR(60) CCSID 37 NOT NULL DEFAULT ''
```

Here you have the SQL name, STUDENT_NAME, followed by the FOR COLUMN instruction, which in turn is followed by what was already there on the table creation statement from Chapter 3: the "old" column name, GRSN, and the rest of the column definition.

As explained in the previous chapter, in the section that discussed creation of the view, it is possible to access the column using both the "old" and "new" names, which is great because programs can keep using the short names and people can now use the longer ones. Unfortunately, this doesn't apply (not yet, anyway) to the table name: the following statement will produce an error, complaining that the table doesn't exist:

```
SELECT * FROM UMADB_CHP4.PFGRM;
```

Why is that? Well, it's because we created an SQL table with the columns of PFGRM, but it has a different name. For all intents and purposes, PFGRM doesn't exist in UMADB_CHP4—yet. In order to keep all the programs that use PFGRM working and recognizing TBL_GRADES as the PFGRM that they "know," we'll need to create an alias, like this:

```
CREATE ALIAS UMADB_CHP4.PFGRM FOR UMADB_CHP4.TBL_GRADES;
```

If the new table name was not a valid system name, this extra step wouldn't be necessary. In this particular case it is, because TBL_GRADES is 10 characters long and doesn't start with a "forbidden" character. After issuing this CREATE ALIAS statement, you should be able to run the SELECT statement using the "old" name of the grades table.

Let's repeat the process for PFSTM, the Students table, so that I can show you how to do the renaming, or more accurately, double naming, process in one step. The current Students table looks like Table 4.2.

Table 4.2: The Students table structure					
Table Name	Column Name	Data Type	Length	Dec. Pos.	Description
PFSTM	STID	Integer			Record ID (primary key)
PFSTM	STNM	Char	60		Student name
PFSTM	STDB	Decimal	8	0	Date of birth
PFSTM	STAD	Char	60		Home address
PFSTM	STPN	Char	15		Home phone number
PFSTM	STMN	Char	15		Mobile number
PFSTM	STEM	Char	60		Email address
PFSTM	STDL	Char	20		Driver's license
PFSTM	STSN	Char	11		Social Security number
PFSTM	STSC	Char	1		Status
PFSTM	STCU	Varchar	18		Created by
PFSTM	STCT	Timestamp			Created on

Again, we're going to use DROP TABLE to get rid of the existing PFSTM:

```
DROP TABLE UMADB_CHP4.PFSTM;
```

And then we'll issue a modified CREATE TABLE statement to create a table recognizable by its SQL and system names:

```
CREATE TABLE UMADB_CHP4.TBL_STUDENTS
    FOR SYSTEM NAME PFSTM
    (
        STUDENT_ID FOR COLUMN STID INTEGER
            PRIMARY KEY
            GENERATED ALWAYS
            AS IDENTITY(START WITH 1
                INCREMENT BY 1)
        , NAME FOR COLUMN STNM CHAR(60) CCSID 37 NOT NULL DEFAULT ''
        , DATE_OF_BIRTH FOR COLUMN STDB DECIMAL(8, 0) NOT NULL DEFAULT 0
        , HOME_ADDRESS FOR COLUMN STAD CHAR(60) CCSID 37 NOT NULL DEFAULT ''
        , HOME_PHONE_NBR FOR COLUMN STPN CHAR(15) CCSID 37 NOT NULL
DEFAULT ''
        , MOBILE_NBR FOR COLUMN STMN CHAR(15) CCSID 37 NOT NULL DEFAULT ''
        , EMAIL_ADDRESS FOR COLUMN STEM CHAR(60) CCSID 37 NOT NULL DEFAULT
'N/A'
        , DRIVERS_LICENSE FOR COLUMN STDL CHAR(20) CCSID 37 NOT NULL
DEFAULT 'N/A'
        , SOCIAL_SEC_NBR FOR COLUMN STSN CHAR(11) CCSID 37 NOT NULL
DEFAULT 'N/A'
        , STUDENT_STATUS FOR COLUMN STSC CHAR(1) CCSID 37 NOT NULL DEFAULT
'1'
        , CREATED_BY FOR COLUMN STCU VARCHAR(18) DEFAULT USER
        , CREATED_ON FOR COLUMN STCT TIMESTAMP DEFAULT CURRENT TIMESTAMP
    )
    RCDFMT PFSTMR
;
```

Here the long names are truly descriptive: SOCIAL_SEC_NBR is a bit abbreviated, but it's far more obvious than STSN. Note that I've added a FOR SYSTEM NAME PFSTM instruction (see the second line of the statement), which removes the need for a separate CREATE ALIAS statement. This is very practical, but not always possible: you can only do this if you use an SQL name that's not a valid system name, as I mentioned before.

This table is particularly interesting because it has some moderately long names that users might or might not want to use. I'm bringing this up to show you that you can refer to short and long names in the same statement; the database engine will figure out which column you're referring to and show the appropriate data. Here's an example:

```
SELECT STUDENT_ID
     , NAME
     , STDB
     , HOME_ADDRESS
     , STPN
FROM   UMADB_CHP4.TBL_STUDENTS
;
```

As you can see here, I'm using a mix of short and long names in this statement. This can be especially useful when the long names are too long or you're in a hurry to get things done. The RPG programs will still work as before, because they "see" the column system names, which are the same as the "old" DDS field names. You (and your end users) get the best of both worlds with this simple technique, but keep in mind that you need to back up the table's data before performing the DROP operation and restore it again (using an INSERT statement with a nested SELECT, for instance) once you've created the table with the appropriate table and column names.

Time for Some Practice

By now, you've realized the power of longer and more descriptive names. Before changing the tables in your own application, why don't you practice with the rest of UMADB's tables? I've included a spreadsheet in this chapter's downloadable source code with the new layout of the tables, sporting the short and long names for both tables and columns. Go and have a look at it. You'll also find all the SQL statements mentioned in this chapter and the "solutions" to this exercise. Don't cheat, just peek if you get stuck!

There's something I've neglected to mention, and it's a bit important: naming conventions. I followed a simple naming convention for the table names, prefixing them with TBL_. I'll do the same later with the views, using the VIEW prefix, and the indexes, resorting to the Index prefix. I followed a looser naming convention for the column names, but adhered to the so-called underscore convention: I used an underscore character (_) to separate the words in the column name. It's a bit longer, but it's far more clear than camel case, especially because SQL tends to return column names in all caps when you query it.

I followed a few other, more subtle conventions regarding the column names: for example, all the ID and status columns were prefixed with the name of the table; whenever a table contains data from another table, I indicated where the data is coming from—for instance, there's a "student name" column in the Grades table, so its long name is Student_Name. With this information, you should be able to create all the tables in the UMADB database.

Hiding Database Complexity

Now the users love their new explicitly named tables and are starting to build their own queries. But they're still coming back to the IT staff with questions like "how do I link this table to that one?" or "Where can I find this information? I can find the header record, but where are the details?" and so on. This leaves you with a couple of options: you can either build a database "map" (which I'll discuss later), or you can hide the database complexity.

For the moment, let's explore the second option. How are we going to do that? Well, the previous chapter introduced views and actually showed a big view that links all the tables in the UMADB database. It's a cumbersome construct that probably won't have any real-world use. Instead, let's build a couple of smaller, more focused views. I'll use the opportunity to introduce some Data Manipulation Language (DML) details you might not know about.

Using the Same Table Twice in a Query

Let's start with a more or less simple view: Course Information. This view provides extended information about each course, listing the course and its staff (course director and teaching assistant). The problem resides in the fact that the Courses table has two links to the Teachers table: both the Course Director and the Teaching Assistant are teachers. To display their information, I could devise a complicated solution, filtering data and displaying two lines for each course, or I could use the same table twice in the same query.

This simple and elegant solution relies on the use of correlation names. Whenever you use a table in a SELECT statement, you can specify a correlation name (also known as an alias) in order to make the statement more readable. The same technique can be used to solve our little problem. Let's follow the methodology I usually use to create views, which is described in Chapter 3:

1. Identify the tables and columns for the view.
2. Determine how the tables are linked.
3. Write a SELECT statement with the appropriate tables, columns, and JOINs.
4. Test, adjust, test, adjust ... until you get it right.
5. Finally, create the view using the SELECT statement, fine-tuned by the tests.

I already know that I'll be using the Courses and Teachers tables, and I know I'll link the Courses table twice to the Teachers table (one for the Director's data and the other for the Teaching Assistant's), so let's skip directly to step 3. Here's the SELECT statement:

```
SELECT COURSES.COURSE_ID
     , COURSES.NAME
     , COURSES.DESCRIPTION
     , COURSES.DEP_NAME
     , DIRECTOR.NAME as "DIRECTOR_NAME"
     , DIRECTOR."RANK" as "DIRECTOR_RANK"
     , TA.NAME as "TA_NAME"
     , TA."RANK" as "TA_RANK"
                                        Continued
```

```
FROM    UMADB_CHP4.TBL_COURSES COURSES
        INNER JOIN   UMADB_CHP4.TBL_TEACHERS DIRECTOR
ON COURSES.CODE = DIRECTOR.NAME
        INNER JOIN   UMADB_CHP4.TBL_TEACHERS TA
ON COURSES.COTA = TA.NAME
;
```

Note that I'm using two aliases for my copies of the Teachers table in this statement. SQL will allow you to treat them as two different tables. By choosing appropriate aliases for these copies, I manage to keep some degree of readability on an otherwise messy and complicated query. If you run this query, you should get the expected output: details about the courses, coming directly from the Courses table, plus the ranks of both the course director and teaching assistant. This means that we're ready to create the view, which is basically the statement above plus a pair of lines:

```
CREATE VIEW  UMADB_CHP4.VIEW_COURSE_INFORMATION
    FOR SYSTEM NAME V_COURSE_1
    AS
SELECT COURSES.COURSE_ID
            , COURSES.NAME
            , COURSES.DESCRIPTION
            , COURSES.DEP_NAME
            , DIRECTOR.NAME AS "DIRECTOR_NAME"
            , DIRECTOR."RANK" AS "DIRECTOR_RANK"
            , TA.NAME AS "TA_NAME"
            , TA."RANK" AS "TA_RANK"
FROM    UMADB_CHP4.TBL_COURSES COURSES
            INNER JOIN   UMADB_CHP4.TBL_TEACHERS DIRECTOR
ON COURSES.CODE = DIRECTOR.NAME
            INNER JOIN   UMADB_CHP4.TBL_TEACHERS TA
ON COURSES.COTA = TA.NAME
;
```

Using Sub-queries

Now let's say I want to extend the information provided by this view to include the number of classes for each course. I need to link the Courses and Classes table by the course name, right? Let's ignore the fact that the Classes table also includes a "class year" column that is part of its unique key (at the application level, because as far as the database is concerned, Classes' primary key is its unique ID: column Class_Id). I can extend the SELECT statement I've been working with to include the Classes table, using another INNER JOIN, and add a COUNT to the SELECT clause, like this:

```
SELECT COURSES.COURSE_ID
        , COURSES.NAME
        , COURSES.DESCRIPTION
        , COURSES.DEP_NAME
        , DIRECTOR.NAME AS "DIRECTOR_NAME"
        , DIRECTOR."RANK" AS "DIRECTOR_RANK"
        , TA.NAME AS "TA_NAME"
        , TA."RANK" AS "TA_RANK"
        , COUNT(CLASSES.COURSE_NAME)
FROM    UMADB_CHP4.TBL_COURSES COURSES
        INNER JOIN UMADB_CHP4.TBL_TEACHERS DIRECTOR
            ON COURSES.CODE = DIRECTOR.NAME
        INNER JOIN UMADB_CHP4.TBL_TEACHERS TA
            ON COURSES.COTA = TA.NAME
        INNER JOIN UMADB_CHP4.TBL_CLASSES CLASSES
            ON COURSES.NAME = CLASSES.COURSE_NAME
GROUP BY    COURSE_ID
, COURSES.NAME
, DESCRIPTION
, DEP_NAME
, DIRECTOR.NAME
, DIRECTOR."RANK"
, TA.NAME
, TA."RANK"
;
```

This works, no doubt. But it can get really confusing, really fast: just try adding a few more tables, and you'll see what I mean. Instead, you can use a sub-query, which is nothing more than a query within a query. It can be used almost anywhere in an SQL statement and provides more flexibility and readability than the solution above. Let's rewrite the statement above using a sub-query to replace that COUNT(CLASSES.COURSE_ NAME) line and all the associated "baggage":

```
SELECT COURSES.COURSE_ID
        , COURSES.NAME
        , COURSES.DESCRIPTION
        , COURSES.DEP_NAME
        , DIRECTOR.NAME AS "DIRECTOR_NAME"
        , DIRECTOR."RANK" AS "DIRECTOR_RANK"
        , TA.NAME AS "TA_NAME"
        , TA."RANK" AS "TA_RANK"
        , (
            SELECT    COUNT(COURSE_NAME)
            FROM      UMADB_CHP4.TBL_CLASSES CLASSES
            WHERE     CLASSES.COURSE_NAME = COURSES.NAME
            GROUP BY COURSE_NAME
        )
FROM    UMADB_CHP4.TBL_COURSES COURSES
        INNER JOIN UMADB_CHP4.TBL_TEACHERS DIRECTOR
            ON COURSES.CODE = DIRECTOR.NAME
        INNER JOIN UMADB_CHP4.TBL_TEACHERS TA
            ON COURSES.COTA = TA.NAME
;
```

This is a "cleaner" solution, but it comes with a cost: the database engine can't always properly optimize a query with sub-queries. In other words, sub-queries tend to run slowly. Lateral join (left/right inner/outer joins) are almost always faster than a sub-query. You need to experiment with the data and figure out whether performance is (or can be, in the future) a problem. Later I'll discuss how you can "see" what the database engine is doing, but for now it's important to keep this in mind: using sub-queries in the SELECT clause is sometimes useful but it should be the exception, not the rule. If you really need this type of functionality and the all-in-one query is not working for you, consider using a temporary table instead. It's a two-step process, but it's often a better solution.

There are other interesting uses for sub-queries, such as inline views, for instance. I'll also use a sub-query in a different setting later in this chapter to achieve something totally different.

Using EXISTS to Omit Records on a SELECT Statement

Another typical request from users is to show only records from a table that meet some condition, which doesn't depend directly on that table. In other words, something that you can't easily put in the WHERE clause. Here's an example: imagine that I want to refine the Course Information view to hide the courses that don't offer classes at the moment (or some other convoluted restriction).

You can do this with OUTER JOINs or really complex statements, but there's a (probably) simpler solution: just use the EXISTS predicate. Let me show you an example: let's take the SELECT statement from the Course Information view and "hide" courses without classes. In other words, only the course names that have at least one match in the Classes table will be shown. Seems complex? It's actually quite simple:

```
SELECT COURSES.COURSE_ID
        , COURSES.NAME
        , COURSES.DESCRIPTION
        , COURSES.DEP_NAME
        , DIRECTOR.NAME as "DIRECTOR_NAME"
        , DIRECTOR."RANK" as "DIRECTOR_RANK"
        , TA.NAME as "TA_NAME"
        , TA."RANK" as "TA_RANK"
FROM    UMADB_CHP4.TBL_COURSES COURSES
        INNER JOIN   UMADB_CHP4.TBL_TEACHERS DIRECTOR
ON COURSES.CODE = DIRECTOR.NAME
        INNER JOIN   UMADB_CHP4.TBL_TEACHERS TA
                                                    Continued
```

```
ON COURSES.COTA = TA.NAME
WHERE   EXISTS (
SELECT 1
FROM UMADB_CHP4.TBL_CLASSES CLASSES
WHERE CLASSES.COURSE_NAME = COURSES.NAME
)
;
```

I added a WHERE clause, with an EXISTS predicate and a query inside it. Note that this is not a sub-query, in the traditional sense: I'm not interested in how many rows or columns are returned by this inner query. I just need to know if the number of rows returned is zero or not, for the specified condition (in this case, CLASSES.COURSE_NAME = COURSES .NAME). If at least one record is returned by the inner query, then the condition with the EXISTS predicate will evaluate to TRUE, meaning that the Courses table record with that course name will be returned. Otherwise, if there aren't any classes with that course name (i.e., the inner query doesn't return a single record), the condition evaluates to FALSE and the Courses record is ignored. This is a simple way to restrict which records are returned by a query based on complex conditions. You can also use NOT EXISTS to make the conditions more readable and maintainable.

Let's create the conditions necessary to see this in action. As things stand, all courses have classes associated with them. In the downloadable source code, you'll find data about three courses, each with four classes. You can confirm this by running the SELECT statement with the EXISTS predicate I've just shown. Now let's add an additional course record and run the SELECT again to see what happens. If you're following along, type the following statement:

```
INSERT INTO UMADB_CHP4.PFCOM
(CONM, CODS, CODN, CODE, COTA, COSC)
VALUES(
'Philosophy Studies and Shakespeare'
        , 'To be or not to be? Checking my EXISTance'
        , 'Philosophy'
```
Continued

```
               , 'Dr. Doom'
               , 'Vader, Darth'
               , '1'
    )
    ;
```

If you run the SELECT statement again, you'll still see the same three courses, even though you've just added a fourth to the Courses table. This is because there's no match for "Philosophy Studies and Shakespeare" in the Classes table. Now let's create a class for this course:

```
INSERT INTO UMADB_CHP4.PFCLM
    (CLNM, CLCY, CLCN, CLSN, CLSA, CLSE, CLSC)
VALUES('Hamlet and Mao Tse Tung'
        , 2016
        , 'Philosophy Studies and Shakespeare'
        , 'Dalton, Joe'
        , '52 SloMo Boulevard, San Fernando, California'
        , 'joe.dalton@aol.com'
        , '1'
    )
;
```

Finally, run the SELECT statement once again. Now there are four courses, as many as exist in the Courses table, because we just added a Class record to match the "Philosophy and Shakespeare" course.

Checking Database Consistency with the Exception Join

A couple of chapters ago, I mentioned the exception join as something I'd discuss later, because it was a bit unusual. Now that you know how the EXISTS predicate works and have a good grip on the whole INNER/OUTER JOIN thing, explaining the exception join will be a breeze.

Like many IBM i databases in the real world, this database has no true structure. It's just a set of tables, informally joined by fields with the same name, or similar names, in different tables. The actual table relationships are kept by the RPG programs that use the database. Naturally, this can potentially lead to database inconsistencies and loss of database integrity. A typical example in our little fictional database would be a class with the wrong course name. Let's create that scenario by inserting a record in the Classes table with a course name that doesn't exist in the Courses table:

```
INSERT INTO UMADB_CHP4.PFCLM
   (CLNM, CLCY, CLCN, CLSN, CLSA, CLSE, CLSC)
VALUES('Macbeth meets Friedrich Nietzsche'
      , 2016
      , 'Philosophy Studies'
      , 'Dalton, Joe'
      , '52 SloMo Boulevard, San Fernando, California'
      , 'joe.dalton@aol.com'
      , '1'
   )
;
```

To confirm that an inconsistency exists, let's run a SELECT using your newly acquired knowledge of EXISTS:

```
SELECT CLASSES.NAME
FROM    UMADB_CHP4.TBL_CLASSES CLASSES
WHERE   NOT EXISTS   (
                     SELECT 1
                     FROM    UMADB_CHP4.TBL_COURSES COURSES
                     WHERE   COURSES.NAME = CLASSES.COURSE_NAME
                     )
;
```

This will return a single row, matching the "Macbeth meets Friedrich Nietzsche" class that was created moments ago. Now let's rewrite this query using EXCEPTION JOIN instead of EXISTS:

```
SELECT              CLASSES.NAME
FROM                UMADB_CHP4.TBL_CLASSES CLASSES
EXCEPTION JOIN      UMADB_CHP4.TBL_COURSES COURSES
ON      CLASSES.COURSE_NAME = COURSES.NAME
;
```

It looks like a regular JOIN, similar to the ones discussed in Chapter 2, but the functionality is totally different. In fact, it's similar to the Query/400 "unmatched records with primary file" option. It offers a simple way to check for data problems that's unique to the IBM i. It's true that you can use EXISTS/NOT EXISTS to implement similar functionality, at least most of the time, but the EXCEPTION JOIN's compact and "natural" syntax is faster to write and easier to maintain. There's a catch: writing an EXCEPTION JOIN with three or four tables might not produce the results you're looking for. There will be times when an EXISTS predicate will yield better results, even if it's not as readable as an EXCEPTION JOIN. Anyway, this is a new tool to add to your kit, and, as most things, there will be appropriate times to use it and other times you will want to look elsewhere for the solution for a specific problem.

To keep our fictional database as "clean" as possible, let's delete this anomalous record:

```
DELETE
FROM    UMADB_CHP4.TBL_CLASSES
WHERE   NAME = 'Macbeth meets Friedrich Nietzsche'
;
```

Time for Some (More) Practice

Now that I've shown you an example of the EXCEPTION JOIN, how about rolling up your sleeves and writing the necessary SELECT statements to check the consistency of the entire database? Or, even better, create a few views that you can use from time to time, just to check whether the database is still fully consistent. This will be a temporary measure, because I'll show you later how you can (and should) maintain your database consistency using referential integrity and other constraints. For the moment, let me give you a hand and explain how the tables are linked to one another.

- The Courses table links with the Teachers table twice, via the Course_Director_ Name and the Course_TA_Name columns. Note that these links to the Teachers' Name column are independent from one another, which means you'll have to write two very similar SELECT statements.

- The Classes table links with the Courses table, as shown before, but also with the Students table. The Classes Student_Name column must match the Students' Name column.

- Finally, the Grades table links separately to the Students table, via Student_Name, and the Classes table, via the Class_Name/Class_Year combination, which match the Name and Year columns of the Classes table, respectively.

In case you get stuck, I've included the solutions in this chapter's downloadable source code.

Using CASE to Return "Friendlier" Column Values

A common complaint from the users is that the data they see in queries doesn't match what they have in the program's output. For instance, a program may read a 1 from the database and show "Active" on the screen, or translate "*RDY" to "Ready for delivery". Typically, programs do this sort of data translating using If-Else or Case (Select-Case in RPG) decision structures. In order to get similar results when querying the database, a similar functionality is required.

SQL provides a CASE structure, similar to many other languages. SQL's version acts at the column level, which means you can use it nearly anywhere in an SQL statement. Let's start with a very simple example and build upon it to create a nice informational view over the Grades table.

If you're American, or familiar with the American academic grading system (*https:// en.wikipedia.org/wiki/Academic_grading_in_the_United_States*), you know what a final grade of F means: bad news. This translation is automatic, imbued in your brain after many years of academic life. That's basically the reason I chose it for this example. Let's take the Grades table and build a query over it, providing all the relevant data (student, class, and grade data) in a user-friendly way that hides the database complexity from the user. To begin with, let's just show the student's name, class name, and class year, along with the grade achieved:

```
SELECT      STUDENT_NAME
            , CLASS_NAME
            , CLASS_YEAR
            , GRADE
FROM        UMADB_CHP4.TBL_GRADES;
```

The grade is recognizable, but a simpler classification, such as "PASSED" or "FAILED," would be better. We'll do that translation with the CASE expression, but before showing the modified SELECT statement, let me refresh the CASE syntax:

```
CASE <expression>
WHEN <value to match> THEN <value to return>
...
ELSE <value to return when a match is not found>
END
```

Here *<expression>* is a column name or some expression based on it, such as a SUBSTR or another scalar function's result. After this first line, one or more WHEN conditions may follow. If a condition is met, a matching value is found, when the *<value to return>* is output instead of the initial expression. If the optional clause ELSE is specified and none of the WHEN statements match the value produced by the expression in the first line of the CASE, then the *<value to return when a match is not found>* value is output. This will become clearer in a moment, with an example. Before that, let me just show you an alternative syntax:

```
CASE
WHEN <condition> THEN <value to return>
                                            Continued
```

```
...
ELSE <value to return when a match is not found>
END
```

In this syntax, the WHEN lines hold both the expression and the value to match, forming a condition. The nice thing about this syntax is that it provides additional flexibility. However, note that after the first condition is met, the corresponding value is returned and the check stops. We're finally ready to add the CASE to the SELECT statement I showed a while ago:

```
SELECT      STUDENT_NAME
            , CLASS_NAME
            , CLASS_YEAR
            , CASE GRADE
                    WHEN 'F' THEN 'FAILED'
                    ELSE 'PASSED'
            END AS FINAL_GRADE
FROM        UMADB_CHP4.TBL_GRADES;
```

This is comparable to an IF statement in most programming languages. To demonstrate the alternative syntax of CASE, let's rewrite this query to look even more like an IF statement:

```
SELECT      STUDENT_NAME
            , CLASS_NAME
            , CLASS_YEAR
            , CASE
                    WHEN GRADE = 'F' THEN 'FAILED'
                    ELSE 'PASSED'
            END AS FINAL_GRADE
FROM        UMADB_CHP4.TBL_GRADES;
```

Notice how I omitted the expression after the CASE keyword and used a condition in the WHEN line instead. This provides additional flexibility and can be useful when you're transferring business rules from a high-level programming language to SQL. This is one of the neat tricks I'll use later on the book to "beef up" the database. For now, let's return to our Grades example and upgrade it to unleash the full power of CASE with a more detailed classification of the final grade:

```
SELECT      STUDENT_NAME
          , CLASS_NAME
          , CLASS_YEAR
          , CASE GRADE
                  WHEN 'F' THEN 'FAILED'
                  WHEN 'D' THEN 'BARELY MADE IT'
                  WHEN 'C' THEN 'AVERAGE RESULT'
                  WHEN 'A' THEN 'EXCELENT SCORE'
                  WHEN 'A+' THEN 'MASTER!'
                  ELSE 'PASSED'
            END AS FINAL_GRADE
FROM    UMADB_CHP4.TBL_GRADES;
```

In this example, I'm using multiple WHEN lines to produce fine-grained results and a "catch-all" clause, with the final ELSE line. As you can conclude from these statements, CASE is a very nice tool to translate data, thus making that data more user-friendly, but it can do a lot more.

Using CASE in the ORDER BY Clause

As I said before, CASE can be used nearly anywhere in an SQL statement. A neat trick I use a lot is strategically placing a CASE in the ORDER BY clause of a SELECT statement to produce customized sorting sequences of data.

Let's say you were asked to display all the teachers, showing the Dark Masters at the top of the list and the Assistant Professors at the bottom. Sounds like a very convoluted request, but you might get something equally strange in real life. How can CASE help us with this? Well, you can use CASE to attribute a "weight" to each record, thus making it show higher or lower on the output list: "lighter" records float to the top, "heavier" records drop to the bottom. Based on this piece of information, let's write the statement that lists the teachers, showing Dark Masters at the top of the list and Assistant Professors at the bottom:

```
SELECT       NAME
             , RANK
FROM         UMADB_CHP4.TBL_TEACHERS
ORDER BY     CASE RANK
                  WHEN 'Dark Master' THEN 0
                  WHEN 'Assistant Professor' THEN 99
                  ELSE 1
             END
;
```

Here I'm assigning a weight of 0 to the records where the Rank is equal to "Dark Master" and a weight of 99 (any value greater than 1 would do, but 99 is "heavy" enough) to those records that have "Assistant Professor" in the Rank column. Everything ELSE gets a weight of 1. It's another interesting and often ignored way of using CASE, but it's not the only way to produce customized sorting sequences.

Using a Secondary Table to Produce Customizable Sorting Sequences

Often sorting sequences are natural to humans, but are totally undecipherable for machines. For instance, the American academic grading scale seems simple enough, and SQL can handle it—that is, until you try to use the plus and minus following the grade. This happens because strings or, in other words, everything that is not a number, are sorted character by character, with the code-page-defined sorting sequence. This sorting sequence doesn't "know" that a grade of C is smaller than a grade of C+ and greater than a C-.

With just a handful of values, you can use a CASE expression to customize the sorting sequence, but this presents a huge disadvantage: you're hard-coding the sort sequence, and any change to the data or an unforeseen value will disrupt the sorting and produce unexpected results. The solution seems simple: instead of hard-coding the sort sequence, let's soft-code it.

For this I'll use a secondary table, containing the possible values and respective weights, and use that to do the sorting. Let's start by creating a generic table that can be easily reused:

```
CREATE TABLE           UMADB_CHP4.TBL_SORT_SEQ
    FOR SYSTEM NAME    PFSRTSEQ
    (
        TABLE_NAME FOR COLUMN SSTN CHAR(50)
        , COLUMN_NAME FOR COLUMN SSCN CHAR(50)
        , VALUE_NAME FOR COLUMN SSVN CHAR(100)
        , VALUE_WEIGHT FOR COLUMN SSVW INTEGER
        , CONSTRAINT UMADB_CHP4.PK_SORT_SEQ
            PRIMARY KEY(TABLE_NAME
                , COLUMN_NAME
                , VALUE_NAME
            )
    )
    RCDFMT PFSRTSEQR
;
```

A couple of notes about this table: I'm using a composite primary key, which guarantees the uniqueness of each TABLE_NAME, COLUMN_NAME, and VALUE_NAME combination. In other words, I'm making sure the sort sequence is unambiguous. Then notice that I'm providing short and long names, even though I don't intend to use this table in RPG or another high-level programming language—at least, not now. It's a good practice to think ahead, because in real life it is usually not easy to replace a table definition. You can always use ALTER TABLE, but there are things it can't do. Always keep in mind that ALTER TABLE is not CHGPF, and SQL's DDL is not the system native's DDS!

Now that I've created the table, let's populate it with the numeric weights for the letter-based grade system. You can find those INSERT statements in the downloadable source code for this chapter. Take a moment to figure it out yourself (or just copy-paste the statements from the downloadable source code for this chapter), and then run the following statement:

```
SELECT       CLASS_NAME
             , CLASS_YEAR
             , STUDENT_NAME
             , GRADE
    FROM     UMADB_CHP4.TBL_GRADES
             INNER JOIN UMADB_CHP4.TBL_SORT_SEQ
                  ON TABLE_NAME = 'TBL_GRADES'
                             AND COLUMN_NAME = 'GRADE'
                             AND GRADE = VALUE_NAME
    WHERE    CLASS_NAME = 'Treachery'
ORDER BY     CLASS_NAME
             , CLASS_YEAR
             , VALUE_WEIGHT
;
```

I'm selecting a single class in order to show clear results. What you'll see is that the A+ is displayed before the C grade, which is something that wouldn't naturally happen, because of the code-page character sequence. If you omit the WHERE clause, you'll see a list sorted by class name, then by class year, and finally by letter-based-grade! This is possible because each grade that has a match in the sort sequence table will return its weight, and the database engine will take this factor into account when performing the final sort of the output data.

If you want a bit of practice, create the necessary records in TBL_SORT_SEQ for the teacher rank sequence, as shown in Table 4.3, and then write a SELECT statement, similar to the one just shown, to list the teachers, sorted by their rank.

Table 4.3: The Teachers' ranks, sorted by importance	
Rank	**Weight**
Dark Master	0
Maximus Praeceptor	1
Praeceptor	2
Assistant Professor	3

As usual, if you need help, you'll find the "solutions" in the downloadable source code.

That's all for now. Later in the book, you'll find other ways to help your users navigate the database—and free IT staff's time for other tasks!

In This Chapter, You've Learned ...

This chapter covered several different ways to make a database more user-friendly, sometimes in a slightly twisted way. Here's a summary of what I've tried to explain here:

- How to recreate a table to include both short (program-friendly) and long (user-friendly) names
- How to implement complex record selection with the EXISTS predicate
- How to check database consistency with the EXCEPTION JOIN
- How to translate column values into something more "human-readable" with the CASE decision structure
- How to use a secondary table to create customized sorting sequences

I'll explain more ways to make the database more accessible to the users in later chapters, so keep reading!

5

Tidying Up the Database

This chapter explains how to "tidy up" the database—for example, by correcting the database's structural issues, and preventing potential data anomalies. It starts by giving the reader a quick refresher on relational databases and all the concepts they encompass (keys and their types, relationship types, modality, and cardinality) and crow's foot notation, commonly used in entity relationship diagrams. The next step is addressing the database problems through database normalization up to third normal form. The corresponding data modeling will be performed in a very hands-on manner using Visual Paradigm, a data-modeling tool popular among Java developers. This will be the longest part of this chapter, but will be worth it.

After this step, the new database structure that resulted from the database normalization process will be created via a series of CREATE TABLE statements. The data migration from the old structure to the new one will follow, via a series of INSERT statements, along with some tips and tricks. Finally, a few views will be created, both to hide the increased database complexity and to provide a user-friendly way to access data.

The UMADB users are now happy with the recently acquired access to the database and the fact that they can, finally, make sense of the tables and columns. Or at least, they were happy until their queries started returning unexpected results. For instance, the student data seems to be out of sync: there are students with different postal addresses in the Students and Classes tables. Oops.

After a more thorough analysis (and a chat with the RPG programmers), I realized that the so-called "perfect data-synchronization mechanism," implemented at the application level, is flawed, and there are many inconsistencies throughout the database. The Students data is repeated in several tables, sometimes with conflicting values for the same student. The Teachers data is also in bad shape, because there are problems with the values of the Subject Taught column: since this is a char field with no check at database level, the contents are not reliable and contain repeated values, misspelled subjects, and other problems. The list goes on, with structural anomalies in the Classes table, which has duplicate information regarding the class name, as many times as there are students in that class/year combination. In summary, the database is one big mess.

Just a side note: you know that UMADB is a fictional database, but this scenario is very real. I dealt with something similar, although on a smaller scale, some years ago. Data anomalies, structural issues, and other (even weirder) problems are, unfortunately, common in aging, application-controlled databases, such as this one.

A Quick Refresher on Relational Databases

Before we actually dive into the database normalization task, let's quickly review a handful of relational database concepts, just to make sure the whole database transformation process is well understood. I'll try not to bore you with loads and loads of theory, but the concepts presented in this section are of paramount importance for the task ahead. Let's begin with a subject you're probably familiar with: keys.

Relational Databases and Their Use of Keys

A relational database gets its name from the fact that relations are established between the different information repositories—the tables—that comprise the database. These relationships are based on *keys*: special columns on the tables used to uniquely identify a record and simultaneously link it to one or more records (depending on the type of relationship—more about this later) in other tables. There are three types of keys: a primary key, a unique key, and a foreign key. Let's look at each one in greater detail.

Primary Keys

A *primary key* is used to uniquely identify a record in a table. Unique identification for each record is necessary because applications require unique row identifiers to accurately and efficiently process transactions. Our little fictional database already has primary keys in nearly all the tables: the *_ID columns I added when I converted the tables from DDS to DDL. However, you can have a unique key that is not the table's primary key.

Unique Keys

Like a primary key, a *unique key* is created on a column containing only unique values throughout an entire table. For instance, all the name fields in the database (such as the student, teacher, course, and class names) should be unique to ensure that no ambiguity exists when a report is generated or a grade is attributed. Those are unique keys that we'll add later, but they aren't the respective table's primary keys. This may seem strange and contrary to what you've done for years: creating a DDS-defined file and defining a unique key based on the field that defines each record, either directly on the physical file or on a separate logical file. More often than not, a name or another descriptive identifier is used as the unique key.

Why use an integer (you've probably already noticed that all the *_ID columns I added are integers) instead of the actual meaningful key? Well, first for performance reasons: it's much faster to sort and find an integer than a char or varchar field. Note that primary keys are also used to define relationships between tables. If you define a name as the primary key and then use it to link to another table (as UMADB is doing now, in most cases), you can't change the name because you'll lose track of the relationship, unless you change the name everywhere it exists.

Imagine this scenario: someone misspells a student name, and this student is enrolled in a class. Later, the student (or someone else, it really doesn't matter) realizes the mistake and corrects it in the Students table. The links to all the tables where the student name exists—Classes and Grades—are immediately lost. By using an ID as primary key, you ensure that database consistency is maintained, even when a student's name is changed, because the record ID will remain the same.

Foreign Keys

You've probably realized that one of the changes we'll perform is to replace the student name in the Classes and Grades tables with the respective student ID, because you need these IDs to match in order to keep the relationship between the Students and these two tables intact. The columns used in the dependent or *child* tables—Classes and Grades, in this case—to maintain the links to its parent table are called *foreign keys*.

In other words, foreign keys are the copies of primary keys created into child tables to form the opposite side of the link in an inter-table relationship: establishing a relational database relationship. A foreign key defines the reference for each record in the child table, referencing back to the primary key in the parent table, thus maintaining the respective link.

Table Relationship Types

If you didn't know already, you've realized by now that the whole primary-foreign key thing links two tables together. However, by itself this is not enough to define the relationship. It's also important to know the type of relationship. Relationships between tables can be zero, one, or many. *Zero* means that the record does not have to exist in the target table; *one with zero* implies that it can exist; *one without zero* implies that it must exist; and *many* simply implies many.

Looking at our database, you'll find that all the current relationships are one to many: each child table can have one or more records with foreign keys (in most cases, a name column) linking back to a single record of the parent table. It's important that you can define these relationships in a sentence. For instance, *each record in the Students table can have one or more records in the Classes table.* I'll be using this type of reasoning to review existing (and create new) relationships between the tables of our database.

Understanding Identifying and Non-Identifying Relationships

There's another perspective to the inter-table relationships. If the parent table primary key is included in the primary key of the child table, then their relationship is an *identifying* relationship and the child table is said to be *dependent* on the parent table. An example of this would be an intermediate table, typically used to implement a many-to-many relationship at database level. This table would sit between the two other tables (the ones that actually have the many-to-many relationship) and have one-to-many relationships with both. To keep the link between the two original tables consistent, the intermediate table needs to include both tables' primary keys in its own primary key. Intermediate tables are also known as *association tables*.

As you might have gathered, a *non-identifying* relationship is the exact opposite of what I just described: a relationship in which the child table holds the primary key of the parent table as a foreign key, and that key is not part of the child table's primary key.

Referential Integrity

Referential integrity functions just as its name states: it ensures the integrity of referential relationships between tables as defined by primary and foreign keys. In a relation between two tables, one table has a primary key and the other a foreign key. The primary key uniquely identifies each record in the first table. In other words, there can be only one record in the first table with the same primary key value. The foreign key is placed into the second table in the relationship such that the foreign key contains a copy of the primary key value from the record in the related table.

Entity Relationship Diagram Notation

Using sentences is a good way to evaluate one relationship, but we'll need to describe all the relationships between tables in our database. Using text to do that will get really confusing, really fast. So we'll use a picture instead. Because humans can handle visual information much faster and more efficiently than textual information, we'll use an *entity relationship diagram* (ERD) to describe the tables' relationships. An ERD describes the tables and their relations in a visual and very informative way, once you get used to its notation. I've already hinted at one of the two most-used notations: using zero, one, and many (or N, as it's more commonly known) to describe a relationship is part of *Chen's notation*, and it is commonly found in ERDs.

The other one is *crow's foot notation*. It's based on the same idea but uses symbols instead of numbers to depict the relationship's modality and cardinality, which are the indicators of the business rules around a relationship. *Cardinality* refers to the maximum number of times an instance in one entity can be associated with instances in the related entity. *Modality* refers to the minimum number of times an instance in one entity can be associated with an instance in the related entity.

Cardinality can be *1* or *many*, and the symbol is placed on the outside ends of the relationship line, closest to the entity. Modality can be *1* or *0*, and the symbol is placed on the inside, next to the cardinality symbol. For a cardinality of 1, a straight line is drawn. For a cardinality of many, a foot with three toes is drawn. For a modality of 1, a straight line is drawn. For a modality of 0, a circle is drawn. Figure 5.1 shows the possible combinations of modality and cardinality.

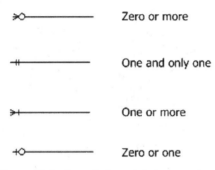

Figure 5.1: Crow's foot basic notation

Identifying and non-identifying relationships are also part of this notation: a dashed line indicates a *non-identifying relationship*, and a continuous line, as shown in Figure 5.1, indicates an *identifying relationship*. Naturally, this shows only one side of the relationship.

Let's look at some examples of actual relationships defined using this notation. Figure 5.2 depicts a couple of relationships between tables. First you'll see the relationship between Student and Seat. In this relationship, one and only one student fills one and only one seat: it's a one-to-one relationship. In the second example, you'll find the most common type of relationship: one Teacher teaches one or more Classes: it's a one-to-many relationship. Even though you can, theoretically, define many-to-many relationships, these are not easy to manage efficiently in actual databases. It's always best to use an intermediate table and have two one-to-many relationships between the three tables (the original two plus the intermediate table).

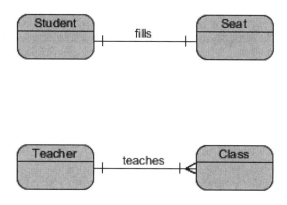

Figure 5.2: Crow's foot relationship examples

Solving UMADB's Database Problems Through Normalization

Most people take a quick look at the normal forms definitions—the "steps" to achieve normalization Nirvana—and dismiss the whole thing as being an academic and convoluted waste of time. Actually, normalization is, for the most part, easy and mostly common sense with some business knowledge thrown in. Once you understand the fundamental concepts, you'll see that it's actually useful and a great way to tackle aging and "broken" databases, such as UMADB. Let me start by introducing a few key concepts that will be used later to define each normal form. Don't worry, it won't be all long-winded, boring theory. I'll use examples taken from the current UMADB as often as possible to illustrate each concept.

Data Anomalies

UMADB is already suffering from data anomalies: I've told you about the different "versions" of the student data found in several tables. This is being caused by structural problems in the database, which I'll try to fix in this normalization process. But before we go any further, it's important to define what we're trying to fix. So let's take a moment to consider the different types of data anomalies, starting with the *insert anomaly*.

This type of anomaly occurs when a child record is inserted without a link to the parent record. For instance, creating a Grades record for a student that doesn't exist; this can be a simple misspelling error, but it will cause an insert anomaly and put the database into an inconsistent state. However, the same thing can happen when you're updating data: unless you have the proper safeguards in place, you can accidentally break the link between two tables, thus leaving the child table record "orphaned." This is called an *update anomaly*.

Imagine that you're updating the student information in the Classes table and inadvertently change the course name. Doing so causes the record to become orphaned, because the link to the Courses table will be compromised.

Finally, a *delete anomaly* occurs when you delete a parent table's record and don't do the same with the child's. Because UMADB tables' relationships are flimsy and defined at the application level, it's very easy to mess up the database with a couple of DML statements.

These are the anomalies that we'd like to prevent. We'll do that by applying the normal forms, as I mentioned earlier. But before that, there are some mathematical terms you need to know.

Some Boring, Yet Important, Math Jargon

Let's start with the simplest of them all: *dependency*. Dependency can come in many forms, but the easiest to understand is *functional dependency*: Y is functionally dependent on X if the value of Y is determined by X. In other words, if Y = X +1, the value of X will determine the resultant value of Y. Thus, Y is dependent on X as a function of the value of X.

Imagine that the university keeps a currency rates table because of its student exchange program. A sample of this table's content, at a given time (so disregard the fact that the rates are not current), is shown in Table 5.1.

Table 5.1: Currency rates table			
Currency_Code	Name	Rate	Country Name
JPY	Yen	101.689	Japan
CAD	Dollar	1.31075	Canada
AUD	Dollar	1.3217	Australia
INR	Rupee	66.725	India
NZD	Dollar	1.38535	New Zealand
GBP	Pound	0.7558	Great Britain

This table demonstrates functional dependency between the Name and Currency_Code columns: the currency name being Yen depends on the currency code being JPY.

The next notion is *determinant*. The determinant in the description of functional dependency in the previous paragraph is X, because X determines the value Y (at least partially because 1 is added to X as well). In Table 5.1, the determinant of the currency name being Rupee is the value of the currency code being INR. This means that the determinant is the currency code column. In other words, *a determinant is the inversion or opposite of functional dependency*.

So far, so good. Now it gets more interesting ... I hope. A *transitive dependence* describes the indirect dependency of a column on another: for instance, Z is transitively dependent on X when X determines Y and Y determines Z. Transitive dependence thus describes that Z is indirectly dependent on X through its relationship with Y. In Table 5.1, the foreign exchange rates in the Rate column (against the U.S. dollar) are dependent on the currency name (Name column). The currency name, in turn, is dependent on the country name (Country Name column). Thus, the rate is dependent on the currency, which is in turn dependent on the country name; *therefore, the Rate column is transitively dependent on the Country Name column*.

The next concept is something that you're probably already familiar with: a *candidate key*, also known as *potential* or *permissible key*, is a field or combination of fields that can act as a primary key field for a table—thus uniquely identifying each record in the table. Most of the tables that resulted from the adjustments performed in the previous chapter have an ID column, which fits all the requirements for being a candidate key: each ID is unique within the table and is, by itself, enough to identify a record.

These ID columns actually eliminated all *full functional dependencies* on UMADB's tables, because all the columns of each table depend on the primary key and this primary key is not a composite key—it's formed by the ID column alone. For instance, if the Classes table didn't have an ID field and its primary key was formed by the class name and class year, we could say that the course name was not fully functionally dependent on the table's primary key, because the course name would depend only on the class name and not the class year.

However, the adjustments performed in the previous chapter didn't solve all the database's problems, as you already know. One of the most common (and annoying, if you ask me) problems is the *multi-valued dependency* that exists on the Subjects_Taught column of the Teachers table. This column contains multiple values, separated by commas. These values depend on the table's primary key as a whole. If you want to do anything with one of these values, you'll have to isolate it from the rest of the values on the column; even so, the whole process is prone to error.

The last type of dependency doesn't happen very often, but when it does, it's a nightmare to untangle: *cyclic dependency* means that X is dependent on Y, which in turn is also dependent on X, directly or indirectly. Cyclic dependence, therefore, indicates a logically circular pattern of interdependence. Cyclic dependence typically occurs with tables containing a composite primary key of three or more fields (for example, where three fields are related in pairs to each other). In other words, X relates to Y, Y relates to Z, and X relates to Z. Ultimately Z relates back to X. This is not very common, but I've seen it happen in tables with complex keys and multiple identifying relationships to other equally complex tables.

These notions may seem farfetched and pointless now, but you'll see how the normal forms relate to them and how this can be of use when "tidying up" a database.

Introducing the Normal Forms, Academic Version

The steps to achieving Nirvana are long and hard ... wait, wrong book. No, they're actually simple and a very acceptable. A normalization pseudo-Nirvana state can be achieved with only three steps, explained next. Unlike the steps in other paths to enlightenment, these have logical, cold, and simple names (they were defined by the academic community, so what else could we expect?).

- *First normal form* (1NF)—Eliminate repeating groups so that all records in all tables can be identified uniquely by a primary key in each table. In other words, all fields other than the primary key must depend on the primary key.

- *Second normal form* (2NF)—All non-key values must be fully functionally dependent on the primary key. No partial dependencies are allowed. A partial dependency exists when a field is fully dependent on a part of a composite primary key.

- *Third normal form* (3NF)—Eliminate transitive dependencies, meaning that a field is indirectly determined by the primary key. This is because the field is functionally dependent on another field, whereas the other field is dependent on the primary key.

We'll be implementing these three steps in UMADB during this chapter, but the normalization path doesn't end here. It goes further with (even more) convoluted requirements:

- *Boyce-Codd normal form* (BCNF)—Every determinant in a table is a candidate key. If there is only one candidate key, BCNF and 3NF are one and the same.

- *Fourth normal form* (4NF)—Eliminate multiple sets of multi-valued dependencies.

- *Fifth normal form* (5NF)—Eliminate cyclic dependencies. 5NF is also known as projection normal form (PJNF).

- *Domain key normal form* (DKNF)—DKNF is the ultimate application of normalization and is more a measurement of conceptual state, as opposed to a transformation process in itself. It's normalization Nirvana.

You might be wondering why we'll stop at 3NF when the rest of the normal forms seem accessible. Well, the problem is that the higher the normalization state is, the harder it gets to query the database. This happens because higher normalization states cause more data fragmentation (read: more tables), and this affects performance. And we all know that a database with poor performance is not really useful. That's enough theory; let's apply the normal forms to UMADB!

Normalizing UMADB to 3NF

1NF is easy to understand, but sometimes it's not so easy to apply. In UMADB's case, a quick review of the tables shows that only the Classes table contains repeating groups of columns: the class name and class year columns have repeating values, one per each student who attended a certain class in a certain year. The first step is fixing this issue, by "exploding" this table into three tables and adding information: one of the class definitions, which will contain the class name; a link to the course table and a description; table two with the class for a given year, containing the teacher name; and finally a third table for student enrollment in that class/year combination.

2NF is somewhat similar to 1NF, but at value level, as opposed to 1NF's column level. There's only one example of columns holding multiple values: the Subjects_Taught column in the Teachers table. The logical thing to do would be to create a many-to-many relationship, because a teacher can teach many subjects and a subject can be taught by many teachers, but in practice many-to-many relationships should be avoided at all costs. They are conceptually sane, but hard to understand and maintain in a real database. A many-to-many relationship would imply creating a Subjects table and linking it to the existing Teachers table. Instead, we'll include an intermediate table, named Subjects_ Taught, and create one-to-many relationships with both the existing Teachers table and the new Subjects table.

3NF is not so easy to explain. Even if you understand what a transitive dependency is, it can be hard to identify it in a database. Let me give you a hand: I started this chapter by referring to some duplicate data across the database and went on to explain how and why this can cause data anomalies. The student data exists in multiple tables, but, in most cases, it shouldn't because it doesn't depend directly on the table's primary key. For instance, a student's home address shouldn't depend on the class he/she is taking. Instead, it should depend on the student information stored in the Students table. However, a closer look at the Students and Teachers tables reveals that they have a lot of information in common—after all, both students and teachers are people. This means that it might be a good idea to strip these tables of the information about a person that they contain and centralize that data in a new Persons table. Naturally, the partial information contained in the Classes table should also be eliminated and replaced with a link to the respective student record.

We'll also create new tables for the Department (only its name exists in the Courses table, which can lead to confusing situations) and Teacher Rank, to avoid inconsistencies. Finally, we'll introduce referential integrity to this database (at the moment, all the connections between tables are kept at the application level, and, from what we've seen, it's not working properly) by replacing the weak links (name references, mostly, such as the student name in the Classes table) with proper foreign keys.

In summary, here's what we'll have to do:

1. Create new tables for Class Definitions, Classes per Year, Class Enrollment, Subjects, Subjects Taught, Persons, Departments, and Teacher Ranks.

2. Remove duplicate columns, related with student data, in the Students, Teachers, and Classes tables.

3. Create proper foreign keys to link all the "informally linked" existing tables and link the new tables as well.

We could continue to change the tables the same way we've been doing so far—using DROP and CREATE TABLE statements. However, there are a lot of changes and it's going to be hard to keep track of everything. Instead, we'll "do it like the pros" and use a data-modeling tool.

Data Modeling with Visual Paradigm

This section introduces Visual Paradigm, a system and data design tool that is commonly used in the Java world to describe and implement complete and complex applications. Visual Paradigm provides a full complement of Unified Modeling Language (UML) diagrams and ERD tools used in system and database design, among them the Resource Catalog, Model Transitor, and Nicknamer features. Doc. Composer lets you easily produce detailed design specifications. Out of the many tools Visual Paradigm offers, we're interested only in its ERD tools. That and the fact there's a free version of the software!

Introducing Visual Paradigm Community Edition

We'll be using the Visual Paradigm Community Edition (VPCE) for the remainder of this chapter, but be advised that this version is not free for commercial use. I'll be using it as a teaching tool, to show you how to do data modeling and how it can help solve database problems such as the ones described earlier in this chapter. VPCE is a very powerful and complete tool. If you intend to use it professionally, outside of the scope of this book, please consider acquiring a license or subscription that legally entitles you to use the product.

Having said that, let's install VPCE. Go to *https://www.visual-paradigm.com/download/community.jsp* and press the big red button to download the software. Be sure to read the license terms carefully, and, once the installation process completes, launch VPCE. You'll be greeted by the tool's Welcome screen, shown in Figure 5.3.

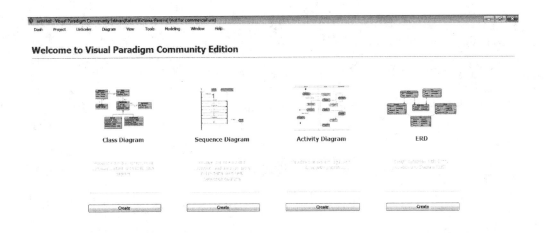

Figure 5.3: VPCE Welcome screen

Here you can choose to create different types of diagrams that help describe an application. The people who introduced me to the tool usually use all of these diagrams in several stages of an application's life to visually describe and document the different perspectives of the software being designed and developed. It's particularly useful for communicating with functional analysts and power users who are familiar with UML. But we're not going to create UML diagrams. We're interested in the rightmost option; click the **Create** button below the ERD box. This takes you to the program's main window, shown in Figure 5.4.

Figure 5.4: VPCE ERD design screen

On the vertical menu at the left you'll find all the tools we'll be using to design our new and improved UMADB database. Let's start by recreating one of the existing tables, to help you get the lay of the land.

Here's a step-by-step guide to creating a table:

1. Click the **Entity** button, the first button of the vertical menu, and then click somewhere on the right side of the screen. A new entity (i.e., a table) will be created, and its name, currently set to **Entity**, will be selected.

2. Let's name this table *TBL_Grades*. Once you've typed the name, press **Enter**.

3. Now right-click the table and choose **New Column**, or press Alt+Shift+C.

4. A new column definition will be created, under the table name. Update its name to *Grade_ID* and press **Enter**.

5. Automatically, another new column will be created. Use the spreadsheet from the Chapter 4's downloadable source code containing the tables' definition and add all seven columns of this table. Once you're done, press **Esc** to end the column creation. Your table should resemble Figure 5.5.

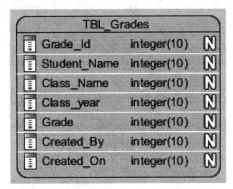

Figure 5.5: TBL_Grades initial form

6. We're not quite there yet: all the fields are 10-position integers, which don't match out current specifications. Let's change each column's definition to match our table's current specifications.

    Left-click the table and press **Enter**, or if you prefer, right-click the table and choose **Open Specification**. Either way, an **Entity Specification** window will result. Click the **Columns** tab, located at the top of the window. This new window should now look like Figure 5.6.

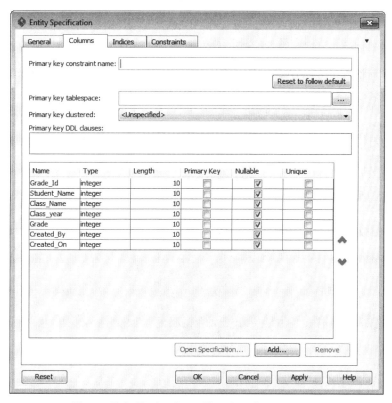

Figure 5.6: Entity Specification Columns tab

7. Let's change each column's details to match our requirements. Start by clicking the **Grade_Id** row's **Primary Key** box. This will automatically deselect the **Nullable** box for this column. However, in order to keep compatibility with RPG programs, we need to make all columns not null, so deselect away until the whole **Nullable** column is blank.

8. Now let's start adjusting the column specs. Double-click the **Student_Name** row. You'll be presented with a new window, named **Column Specification**.

9. Click the **Type** drop-down list and select **char**. Adjust the **Length**, just below the **Type**, to **60**, as depicted in Figure 5.7.

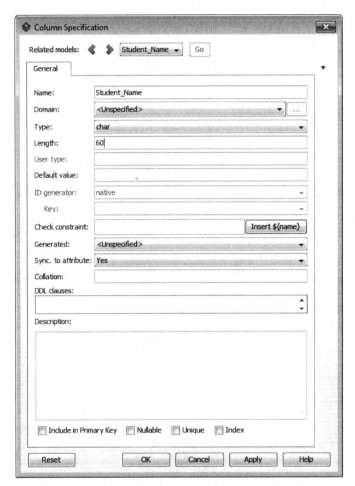

Figure 5.7: Student_Name column specification

10. Repeat the process with the remaining fields.

11. You have now successfully created your first table! Check whether what you've built so far resembles Figure 5.8.

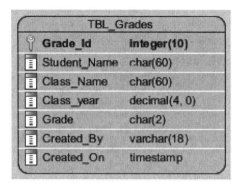

Figure 5.8: TBL_Grades final form

Time for Some Practice

Before moving on to the new and improved UMADB schema, why don't you take a moment to create the remaining tables, as they are described in Chapter 4's spreadsheet? It's only a handful of tables (literally—there are five of them left).

You can, for instance, fully define a column when you add it, by specifying its name, type, and length using the following notation: *<column name>:<blank space><column type>(<column length>)*. For types that allow decimal places, the notation is slightly different: *<column name>:<blank space><column type>(<column length>,<blank space><number of decimal places)*.

For instance, you can define the **Student_Name** column by typing **Student_Name: char(60)** when adding a new column to the Students table. For the Date of Birth column from the same table, you can type **Date_of_Birth: decimal(8, 0)**. Alternatively, you can select a group of fields from a table, such as the repeating person information that exists in both Students and Teachers table, and duplicate it, either by right-clicking the selected column(s) and choosing **duplicate** or by pressing Ctrl+E and moving the duplicate columns, suffixed with a 2, to the destination table. Then it's simply a question of removing the 2 suffix.

Once you're done, your ERD should resemble Figure 5.9. As usual, the "solutions," in this case in the form of a VPP (Visual Paradigm Project) file, are available in the downloadable source code for this chapter.

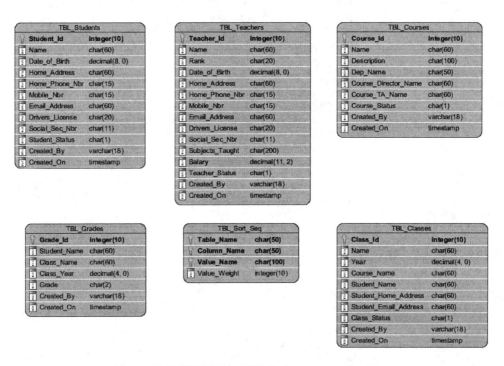

Figure 5.9: UMADB's ERD before normalization

Creating the New and Improved UMADB

Now that we've created an ERD that matches the current state of the UMADB database, let's use that diagram to build the new and improved UMADB ERD. Let's start by creating a copy of the "old" ERD and connecting to the DB2 for i database. Here are the steps for performing this task:

1. Open the UMADB ERD, either your own or the VPP file in the downloadable source code for this chapter.

2. Go to the Project menu, near the top of VPCE's window, and select **Save** and then **Save As**.

3. Name your new project *UMADB ERD After Normalization* and click the **Save** button.

4. Go to the Project menu again, select **Properties**, change the project name to *UMADB ERD After Normalization*, and click **OK**.

5. Before going any further, let's set up the connection to the IBM i database—you'll see why later. Right-click some blank space on the right side of the window (not on a table, just some blank space) and choose **Open Specification...**.

6. Type *UMADB_CHP5* in the Default Schema box and click **OK**.

7. Go to the Tools menu, near the top of VPCE's window, and select **DB** and then **Database Configuration...**.

8. A new window, similar to Figure 5.10, will be displayed.

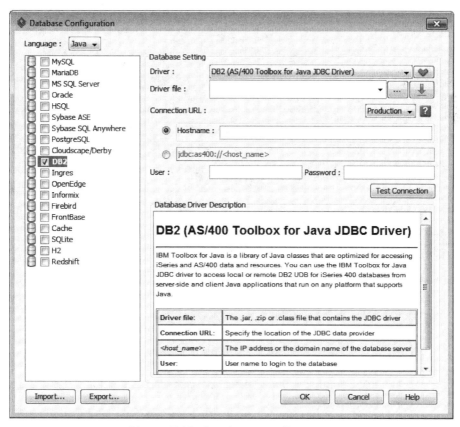

Figure 5.10: Database configuration

9. Select **DB2** from the left-side list and then choose **DB2 (AS/400 Toolbox for Java JDBC Driver)** from the **Driver** drop-down list.

10. Indicate the location of your copy of the JT400.Jar file; it should reside somewhere inside the IBM i Access (or whatever your version is called) folder. If you don't use IBM i Access, you can easily find this file online (just Google "jtopen driver download").

11. Fill in the system name, user, and password, and click **Test Connection**.

12. If everything went according to plan, you should receive a *Connection Successful* message.

You'll see later why establishing a connection to your IBM i database is important. Let's continue and create the Persons table and its links to the Students and Teachers tables.

13. Select the **TBL_Teachers**, **TBL_Courses**, **TBL_Sort_Seq**, and **Classes** tables and drag them to the right, to clear some space for a new table.

14. Go to the left-side vertical menu and click the **Entity** button.

15. Click between the **TBL_Students** and **TBL_Teachers** table to create a new table.

16. Name this new table *TBL_Persons*.

17. Add a *Person_Id* column, type integer, length 10.

18. Now comes the tricky part: the Persons table will replace the common columns of the Students and Teachers tables, centralizing that information in one place. In other words, we'll no longer need the Name, Date of Birth, and other columns in either the Students or Teachers tables.

    Let's select the **Name** column from **TBL_Students** and, keeping the **Shift** key pressed, click on the **Social_Sec_Nbr** column of the same table. The result should be the selection of all the columns between the two aforementioned columns.

19. Now drag that selection to the newly created Persons table.

20. Adjust the size of the Students table (there's a lot of empty space now, because of the column removal).

21. Add the *Created_By* and *Created_On* columns to **TBL_Persons**, with the same specs that were used for all the other tables.

22. Define *Person_ID* as **TBL_Persons**' primary key.

23. Next we'll add a link between the Students and Persons tables, but before doing that, check whether your ERD resembles the one shown in Figure 5.11.

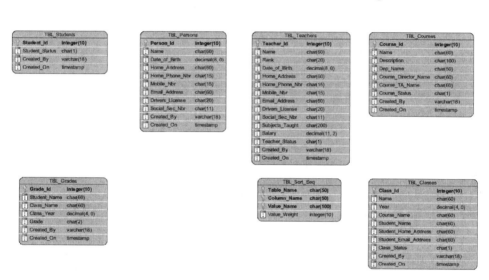

Figure 5.11: UMADB's ERD after adding the Persons table

24. Click the **One-to-Many Relationship** button in the left-side vertical menu, then left-click the **Persons** table. Without releasing the button, drag the cursor to the Students table. A new window, similar to Figure 5.12, should pop up.

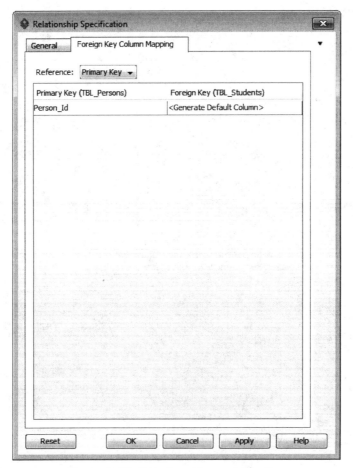

Figure 5.12: Relationship specification

25. This window allows you to review the columns used to define the relationship between the two tables and specify the name of the foreign key fields on the child table. We're going to use the default values, so simply click **OK**.

26. A new column appeared at the bottom of the column list of **TBL_Students**, with a little green arrow just above the column symbol; this indicates that this column is a foreign key.

27. Note that crow's foot notation, mentioned earlier in this chapter, is used by VPCE to define a one-to-many, non-identifying relationship between the two tables.

Now let's do the same for the Teachers table. But before that, let's remove the columns that we no longer need on **TBL_Teachers**.

28. Select the **Name**, **Date_of_Birth**, **Home_Address**, **Home_Phone_Nbr**, **Mobile_Nbr**, **Email_Address**, **Drivers_License**, and **Social_Sec_Nbr** columns, by clicking the first one, holding the **Ctrl** key down, and selecting the others.

29. When all the columns are selected, press the **Del** key to remove the columns from the table.

30. Adjust the size of the table to match its current number of columns.

31. Now add a link between **TBL_Persons** and **TBL_Teachers**, as you did before for the **TBL_Persons** - **TBL_Students** relationship. After you've completed that task, your ERD should look like Figure 5.13.

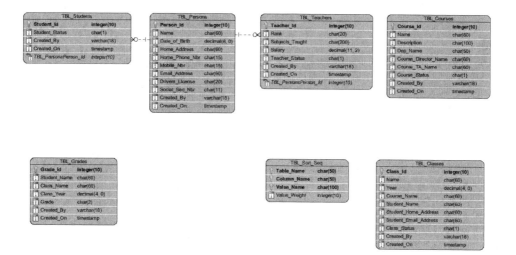

Figure 5.13: UMADB's ERD after connecting the Persons table

Now let's add the Subjects table and its many-to-many relationship with the Teachers table:

32. Remove the **Subjects_Taught** column from the Teachers table.

33. Move the **TBL_Sort_Seq** table to the space below **TBL_Classes**. Don't worry, the working area will "stretch" to accommodate this change.

34. Add a new table, by clicking the **Entity** button located on the left-side vertical menu and then clicking where the **TBL_Sort_Seq** used to be.

35. Name this table *TBL_Subjects*. Note that it will automatically be prefixed with the schema name.

36. Add the columns *Subject_Id (integer(10))*, *Name (char(60))*, and *Description (char(100))* to the newly created table. Don't forget to make these columns not nullable and to define Subject_Id as the table's primary key.

Now let's add the many-to-many relationship between this table and the Teachers table:

37. Select the **Many-to-Many Relationship** button from the left-side vertical menu, click the **Subjects** table and, without releasing the button, drag the mouse to the Teachers table.

38. A new intermediate table will be automatically created for you, with one-to-many relationships to both tables, as shown in Figure 5.14.

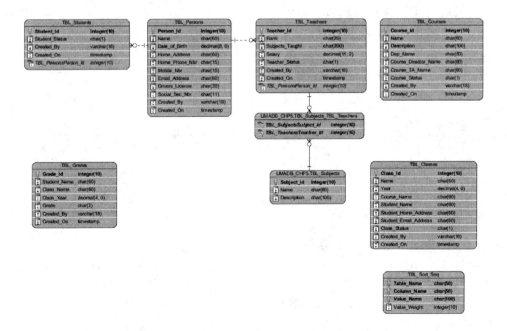

Figure 5.14: UMADB's ERD after adding a many-to-many relationship

Note that the one-to-many relationships between the intermediate table and both Teachers and Subjects tables are identifying relationships. This is a direct consequence of the fact that they define a many-to-many relationship. Feel free to rename the intermediate table to *Subjects_Taught*, or leave it as is.

Now let's split the Classes table into three tables: the Class Definition, Classes per Year, and Class Enrollment. Actually, this last one will be automatically created, because it spawns from the many-to-many relationship between the Students and Classes per Year tables. Let's get started.

39. Move the Grades table below the Persons table.

40. Move the Classes table to where the Grades table used to be.

41. Rename **TBL_Classes** to **TBL_Class_Definition** and add a *Description (char(100))* column to it. Remember to make the new column non-nullable.

42. Add a new table above **TBL_Class_Definition** and name it *TBL_Classes_per_Year*.

43. Add a primary key to the newly created table, with the name *Class_per_Year_Id*, and make it an integer (10).

44. Create a one-to-many relationship between the Class Definition and the Classes per Year tables. Keep in mind that one Class Definition can have many Classes per Year.

45. Create a many-to-many relationship between the Classes per Year and Students tables, just like we did for the Subjects/Teachers relationship.

46. Clean up the Class Definition table, by removing the **Year**, **Course_Name**, **Student_Name**, **Student_Home_Address**, and **Student_Email_Address** columns.

47. Resize the table to match its current number of columns.

One of the deleted columns was Course_Name, which was used to establish an informal relationship between the old Classes table and the Courses table. Now that the Classes table became Class Definition, the link should be kept and "formalized." Add a one-to-many relationship, in which one Course can have many Class Definitions. Additionally, you can replace the entire Grades table with just a new column in TBL_Classes_per_Year. I'll ask you to add this column and delete the Grades tables later this chapter.

I mentioned earlier that having a Classes per Year table would allow us to store additional information, such as who will be teaching a certain class in a certain year. Because many teachers can teach many classes, we'll have to add a many-to-many relationship between the Classes per Year and Teachers tables. This will force you to rearrange the diagram a bit. Feel free to rename the tables that result from the many-to-many relationships to more appealing names, such as Class Enrollment, as I suggested earlier. You might want to change the connectors' style to make it more appealing. Here's how it's done:

48. Right-click somewhere on the work area.

49. Select **Connectors** and then **Rectilinear**.

50. Because you'll have to cross connector lines sooner or later, right-click again on the work area, select **Connectors**, and then choose **Arc** from the **Line Jumps** list.

After these changes, your ERD should look like Figure 5.15.

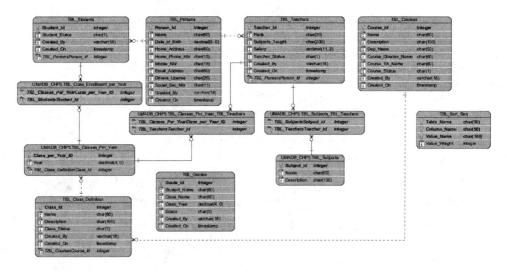

Figure 5.15: UMADB's ERD after splitting the Classes table

Note that you could merge the Subjects and Class Definition tables, thus removing a few database links. These changes would require analyzing the data in the tables carefully before making a decision. This is one of the many advantages of an ERD: it forces you to look at the database's structure and question the way it's built.

Time for Some (More) Practice

Now that you have a grasp of how to add tables and create relations, go ahead and complete the ERD using the spreadsheet you'll find in the downloadable source code for this chapter. Remember to delete the columns that were used to establish the informal links between the tables and replace them with proper one-to-many relationships.

If you analyze the spreadsheet carefully, you'll realize that I chose to remove the Subjects table, because all the subjects match classes and are linked to courses. I also changed the teachers' names columns in the Courses tables to teacher IDs, but I didn't add a link to the Teachers table. This will be handled later in the book. Finally, note that I applied the default schema defined earlier in this chapter to all the tables and changed the presentation option that controls the position of the connectors terminators by right-clicking the workspace and choosing **Presentation options** > **Foreign Key Display Options** > **Point Foreign Key End to Associated Column**. You'll find the "solutions" in the form of a VPP file in this chapter's downloadable source code.

Data Modeling Is Fun, but Where's the Code?

So far, you've been drawing boxes and setting properties. You might be wondering if it was really worth it. Sure, data modeling gives an interesting perspective on the database, but it doesn't create the database ... or does it?

Let's go back to VPCE and open the ERD we've been working on (at least that one I've been working on; I don't know about you). I'll guide you with another step-by-step set of instructions to generate the SQL code to create the database we've just drawn.

1. Make sure you're connected to the database: go to the Tools menu, select **DB** and then **Database Configuration...**.

2. Fill in the necessary information, as I explained earlier in this chapter.

3. Click the **Test connection** button, adjust the user/password if necessary, and when everything is working, click **OK**.

4. Now right-click the work area, go to **Utilities**, and choose **Generate SQL**.

5. A new window, similar to Figure 5.16, will pop up.

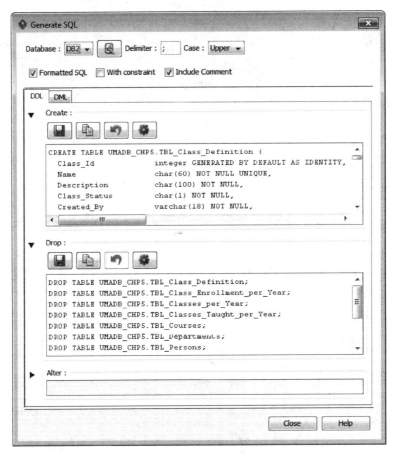

Figure 5.16: Generate SQL window

Yes, you're seeing it right: VPCE generated all the necessary SQL code to create the tables and their relations!

You can choose to save the code to a file, copy it (to use/modify on your favorite SQL editor), or even execute the code immediately. The green arrow is just to revert your changes, in case you modify the code manually.

6.   Choose to save to file—the CREATE TABLE statements are not 100 percent complete. Unfortunately, VPCE doesn't "know" DB2 for i SQL that well and doesn't offer a way to specify the system names for tables and columns.

7. You can do it yourself; it's good practice. As usual, if you get stuck, you'll find a modified version of the file in the downloadable source code for this chapter with the solutions.

8. Finally, execute the code to create the new and improved UMADB in the UMADB_CHP5 schema. You'll be using it in the next section of the chapter.

You're probably thinking that it isn't typical to have an actual production database as messed up as UMADB was. You're probably right. I intentionally created unusual structural problems to demonstrate the most common issues with databases that I have found, in my experience:

- The Teachers and Courses tables illustrate a mild data-consistency problem that can cause a lot of damage, even if the application handles the data properly. The fact that there's an unchecked department name column is a risk, but the multi-value column (Subjects_Taught) is an even bigger problem, because it can influence the user choices and create additional "trash" in the database.

- The absurd redundancy of student data throughout the database, even if properly managed at application level. (OK, that's a myth; it's never 100 percent secure, so manage it at database level, with checks and constraints.) Actually, this is a very common problem, especially in big databases, and it's important to look at the "big picture" before assuming something is "right" or "wrong." In this case, the problem was bigger than the student data: the teachers are also people, and their data is very similar to the students' data. In an ERP there's usually an "entity" or a "third-party" table that holds common data for suppliers and clients. Here the situation is similar, but in a different context.

- The Classes table depicts an "all-in-one table," an unfortunately very common problem that is a huge nightmare to manage. It stores different types and levels of information in the same record, leading to data duplication (not redundancy) and wasted resources. You need to analyze the data carefully and decide how to divide it. In this case, the Classes table was segmented into four tables, but sometimes it makes sense to use five or more.

Before moving on to the data migration section, let me share two more things with you. First: the good people of Visual Paradigm not only make great software, they make nice instructional videos, too! Go to *https://www.visual-paradigm.com/training/database-design-and-management/* and check out their Database Design and Management training course.

The second one is what my completed ERD looks like; see Figure 5.17. I wanted to put it here (not in the section in which it's referenced) so it wouldn't influence your data modeling.

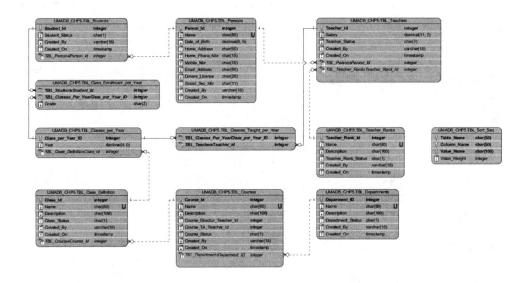

Figure 5.17: UMADB ERD's final version

Migrating the Data to the New, Improved UMADB

Now that we created the new and improved version of UMADB, the next step is migrating data to the new structure. We'll be using data from the UMADB_CHP4 schema, so if you don't have it on your IBM i's disk, you can restore it from Chapter 4's downloadable source code. I've included a save file with the UMADB_CHP4 library for your convenience. Let's start with an easy one: the Teacher Ranks table.

Populating the Teacher Ranks Table

The Teacher Ranks table depicts a simple way to enforce consistency in a database, by turning an unchecked character value into a multi-choice field. In this particular case, the data migration is quite simple: I'll take the unique (or non-repeated) values of the Rank column of the Teachers table and use that data to populate the Teacher Ranks table. In fact, this is so simple that the illustration in Figure 5.18 is not strictly necessary.

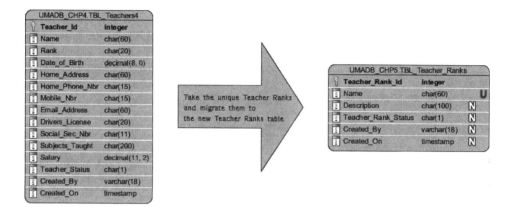

Figure 5.18: Teacher Ranks creation

I'm including it so that you get familiar with the methodology I'll use to explain the more complex INSERT statements used later in this section. Here's the INSERT statement for the Teacher Ranks table:

```
INSERT INTO UMADB_CHP5.TBL_TEACHER_RANKS
(NAME)
  (SELECT     DISTINCT RANK
   FROM       UMADB_CHP4.TBL_TEACHERS
  )
;
```

Note that this INSERT statement is a combination of the INSERT/SELECT statement I used to copy the data from UMADB_CHP3 to UMADB_CHP4 and a "regular" INSERT, with the column names and the VALUES clause. The reason I made most of the columns of this table and most of the tables nullable with a default value was to facilitate the data migration. This way I'm not forced to insert made-up values—I just let the database take care of things like the current time and logged-in user.

Populating the Departments Table

The Departments table is conceptually similar to the Teacher Ranks table: I'll take the unique department names and insert them in a new table. Figure 5.19 depicts the process, and the SQL statement below makes it happen:

```
INSERT INTO UMADB_CHP5.TBL_DEPARTMENTS
  (NAME)
  (SELECT    DISTINCT DEP_NAME
   FROM      UMADB_CHP4.TBL_COURSES
  )
;
```

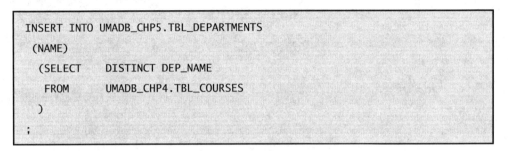

Figure 5.19: Departments creation

Creating the Persons Data

After this gentle start, let's move on to more complex data migrations. As you recall, the Persons table was created to store in a single place all the person-related data that was spread all over the database. Because there were inconsistencies with the student data, I decided to take the data from the Students table first and disregard the data in other related tables, namely the wrong addresses in the Classes table. I also "moved" the teachers' personal data to this new table. However, a student can later become a teacher, which means I need to check for data duplications before concentrating both student and teacher personal data in this new table.

There are different ways to do this: I could use an EXISTS statement or an EXCEPTION JOIN to figure out if there's data duplication, but you've already seen those in action, so I'll use something else. As you probably know, you can use a UNION statement to join the resulting data sets of two or more SELECT statements and present the result as a single table. In this case, we need the opposite: I want to figure out if there's data duplication between the Students and Teachers tables, so instead of a UNION I'll use an INTERSECT. Here's the statement that takes all the personal data from both Student and Teacher data and returns the matching records:

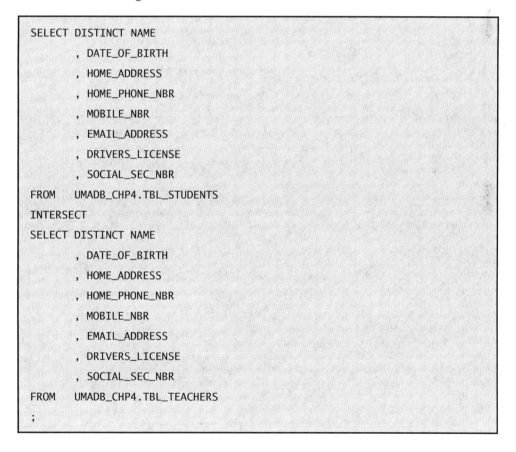

```
SELECT DISTINCT NAME
       , DATE_OF_BIRTH
       , HOME_ADDRESS
       , HOME_PHONE_NBR
       , MOBILE_NBR
       , EMAIL_ADDRESS
       , DRIVERS_LICENSE
       , SOCIAL_SEC_NBR
FROM   UMADB_CHP4.TBL_STUDENTS
INTERSECT
SELECT DISTINCT NAME
       , DATE_OF_BIRTH
       , HOME_ADDRESS
       , HOME_PHONE_NBR
       , MOBILE_NBR
       , EMAIL_ADDRESS
       , DRIVERS_LICENSE
       , SOCIAL_SEC_NBR
FROM   UMADB_CHP4.TBL_TEACHERS
;
```

In this case, there's no matching data, so we can populate the Persons table as depicted in Figure 5.20.

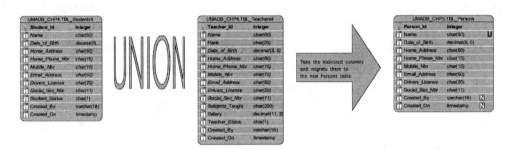

Figure 5.20: Persons creation

Because there's no duplication, I can use a UNION to join both Students' and Teachers' relevant data, shown in italics in Figure 5.20, and insert the result into the new Persons table. Here's the SQL statement that performs this operation:

```
SELECT DISTINCT NAME
        , DATE_OF_BIRTH
        , HOME_ADDRESS
        , HOME_PHONE_NBR
        , MOBILE_NBR
        , EMAIL_ADDRESS
        , DRIVERS_LICENSE
        , SOCIAL_SEC_NBR
FROM    UMADB_CHP4.TBL_STUDENTS
UNION
SELECT DISTINCT NAME
        , DATE_OF_BIRTH
        , HOME_ADDRESS
        , HOME_PHONE_NBR
        , MOBILE_NBR
        , EMAIL_ADDRESS
        , DRIVERS_LICENSE
        , SOCIAL_SEC_NBR
FROM    UMADB_CHP4.TBL_TEACHERS
;
```

Populating the Teachers Table

Here's where things start to get a bit more complex. The teachers' data is now spread across several tables. I took the teacher rank and moved it to the new Teacher Ranks table. I also migrated the personal data to the new Persons table. Now I need to figure out the record IDs for the rank and personal data of each teacher and insert it, along with the data that remains in the old Teachers table (just the salary, in this case) into the new Teachers table. Figure 5.21 depicts the process.

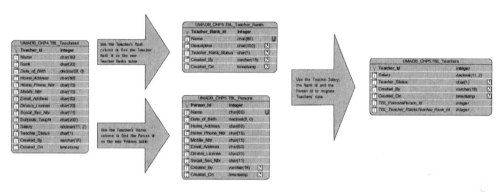

Figure 5.21: Teachers data migration

It's important that you take a moment to understand this picture before reviewing the SQL statement below, because I'll be using similar statements for the remainder of the data migration in this chapter. I'm saying this because the INSERT statement necessary to migrate the data might not be clear, as it "does everything at once" using INNER JOINs, instead of the step-by-step approach shown in Figure 5.21. Anyway, here's the statement:

```
INSERT INTO UMADB_CHP5.TBL_TEACHERS
  (SALARY, TBL_PERSONSPERSON_ID, TBL_TEACHER_RANKSTEACHER_RANK_ID)
  (SELECT    SALARY
            , PERSON_ID
            , TEACHER_RANK_ID
  FROM       UMADB_CHP4.TBL_TEACHERS TEACHERS
      INNER JOIN    UMADB_CHP5.TBL_PERSONS PERSONS
        ON TEACHERS.NAME = PERSONS.NAME

                                              Continued
```

```
       INNER JOIN    UMADB_CHP5.TBL_TEACHER_RANKS RANKS
            ON TEACHERS."RANK" = RANKS.NAME

   )

   ;
```

This is not very complex, as it uses only two INNER JOINs, but it will get more complex later, taking as many as five JOINs to gather all the necessary data to populate a table. You're probably wondering why the rank needs to be written between double quotes. That's because RANK is a reserved word, used for data aggregation and categorization—but that's a subject for another chapter.

Populating the Students Table

The Students table is conceptually similar to the Teachers table, in terms of data migration. I decided to provide an additional example of the same concept, just to reinforce the methodology and prepare you for more complex situations. Figure 5.22 illustrates the process.

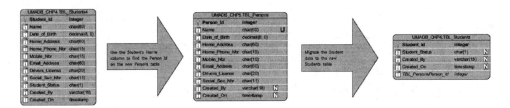

Figure 5.22: Students data migration

Take a moment to analyze the diagram, and compare it with the previous one and the respective SQL statement. This diagram is actually simpler, because it has only one INNER JOIN. Can you figure out what the statement necessary to migrate the Students data looks like? Here, check whether you got it right:

```
INSERT INTO UMADB_CHP5.TBL_STUDENTS
   (TBL_PERSONSPERSON_ID)
     (SELECT    PERSON_ID
```

Continued

```
    FROM        UMADB_CHP4.TBL_STUDENTS STUDENTS
        INNER JOIN    UMADB_CHP5.TBL_PERSONS PERSONS
            ON STUDENTS.NAME = PERSONS.NAME
    )
;
```

Populating the Courses Table

The Courses table would seem, at first glance, an easy one to migrate. After all, we only took the department name and stored it in the new Departments table. However, there were other, not-so-obvious changes: the teacher names used to indicate the course's Director and Teaching Assistant are now teacher IDs. This is part of the relationship enforcement I did to build proper referential integrity in the database, as opposed to the "application-maintained" weak relationships that existed before. Figure 5.23 depicts the necessary steps to get the data needed for the new course records.

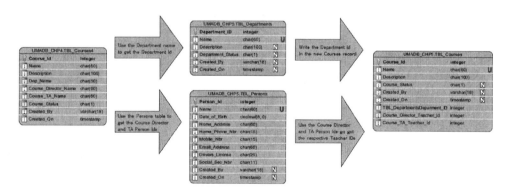

Figure 5.23: Course data migration

Note that, even though it appears only once, the Persons table is being used twice: once for the course Director and the other for the Teaching Assistant. This makes the SQL statement a tad more complex:

```
INSERT INTO UMADB_CHP5.TBL_COURSES

  (NAME, DESCRIPTION, COURSE_DIRECTOR_TEACHER_ID, COURSE_TA_TEACHER_ID,
TBL_DEPARTMENTSDEPARTMENT_ID)
```
Continued

```
(SELECT    COURSES.NAME
           , COURSES.DESCRIPTION
           , DIRECTOR_PERSON.PERSON_ID
           , TA_PERSON.PERSON_ID
           , DEPARTMENT_ID
 FROM       UMADB_CHP4.TBL_COURSES COURSES
           INNER JOIN   UMADB_CHP5.TBL_PERSONS DIRECTOR_PERSON
              ON COURSES.COURSE_DIRECTOR_NAME = DIRECTOR_PERSON.NAME
           INNER JOIN   UMADB_CHP5.TBL_TEACHERS DIRECTOR_TEACHER
              ON DIRECTOR_TEACHER.TBL_PERSONSPERSON_ID = DIRECTOR_
PERSON.PERSON_ID
           INNER JOIN   UMADB_CHP5.TBL_PERSONS TA_PERSON
              ON COURSES.COURSE_TA_NAME = TA_PERSON.NAME
           INNER JOIN UMADB_CHP5.TBL_TEACHERS TA_TEACHER
              ON TA_TEACHER.TBL_PERSONSPERSON_ID = TA_PERSON.PERSON_ID
           INNER JOIN UMADB_CHP5.TBL_DEPARTMENTS DEPARTMENT
              ON COURSES.DEP_NAME = DEPARTMENT.NAME
 )
;
```

Here everything happens at once, but conceptually, I'm using, in the first step, two copies of the Persons table to get the Person_Id of the teachers, and with that I'm retrieving the respective Teacher_Ids. Note that this is only possible because I know that the data is available—and I checked, by running the SELECT statement beforehand and comparing it with its UMADB_CHP4 equivalent—more about that in the next chapter.

Creating the Class Definitions Data

If you recall, I "exploded" the Classes table into four new tables:

- Class Definitions, which holds all the generic definition for a class
- Classes per Year, which lists which classes are available for each school year
- Class Enrollment per Year, a table that links the students to the yearly classes they attend and also holds their grades, replacing in this regard the old Grades table

- And finally, the Classes Taught per Year, which replaces the Subjects table that briefly existed in the beginning of this chapter to illustrate a many-to-many relationship and serves the purpose of indicating which teacher will be responsible for which class during each school year

The process of extracting and storing the data into these new tables follows the same methodology presented before, but takes it up a notch. Let's start with the simplest of the operations: the Class Definition migration.

The Class Definition table is, as its name implies, a definitions table, created to hold the class-related information that remains more or less static throughout time: the class name and description. Populating this table is somewhat similar to what was done with the Teacher Ranks name: I just take the unique class names and, because I've made the Description column optional and provided a default, insert those names into the new table, as shown in Figure 5.24.

Figure 5.24: Class Definition creation

However, because the same class can be taught in more than one course, I also need to supply the Course ID. In order to get it, a little detour through the Courses table is required: by passing the course name, I retrieve the course ID. Note that I could (and should, if I were to take the 3NF to the extreme) define a many-to-many relationship between the Class Definition and Courses tables with an additional table to act as intermediate table to avoid having repeated class names in the Class Definitions table. This is an example of knowing when to stop "fragmenting" tables. Just use your common sense and don't take the rules (in this case, the normal forms) literally, because what seems simple on the drawing can quickly become a nightmare to implement and maintain.

Let's see what the INSERT statement looks like:

```
INSERT INTO UMADB_CHP5.TBL_CLASS_DEFINITION
 (NAME, TBL_COURSESCOURSE_ID)
  (SELECT    DISTINCT CLASSES.NAME
             , COURSES.COURSE_ID
    FROM      UMADB_CHP4.TBL_CLASSES CLASSES
             INNER JOIN   UMADB_CHP5.TBL_COURSES COURSES
                 ON CLASSES.COURSE_NAME = COURSES.NAME
  )
;
```

Creating the Classes per Year Data

The next fragment of the "old" Classes table is a table that helps keep track of the class-related information that changes every year: the class' students and teachers. Because the same class can (and should) have more than one student and can have more than one teacher, this table doesn't store the data directly. Instead, it provides an identifier of a class/year combination, which will be used by the tables I'll discuss next. To populate this table, I'll start with the data from the Classes table and use the new Courses and Class Definition tables to get the correct Course and Class IDs, respectively. Then I'll combine that information with the unique Class/Year combinations and write the records into the new Classes per Year Table, as illustrated in Figure 5.25.

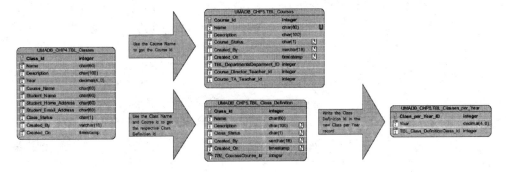

Figure 5.25: Classes per Year creation

Note that, even though I'm presenting these "things" as separate and consecutive steps, they happen more or less at the same time: the join operations of the statement shown next are executed in parallel whenever possible. I'll talk a bit about query optimization later, but this is something to keep in mind: the illustrations I'm providing show the thought process, not the SQL engine execution. Here's the INSERT statement that performs the operations depicted in Figure 5.25:

```
INSERT INTO UMADB_CHP5.TBL_CLASSES_PER_YEAR
  (YEAR, TBL_CLASS_DEFINITIONCLASS_ID)
   (SELECT    CLASSES.YEAR
              , CLASS_DEFINITION.CLASS_ID
    FROM      UMADB_CHP4.TBL_CLASSES CLASSES
              INNER JOIN   UMADB_CHP5.TBL_COURSES COURSES
                    ON CLASSES.COURSE_NAME = COURSES.NAME
              LEFT OUTER JOIN UMADB_CHP5.TBL_CLASS_DEFINITION CLASS_
DEFINITION
                    ON CLASSES.NAME = CLASS_DEFINITION.NAME AND CLASS_
DEFINITION.TBL_COURSESCOURSE_ID = COURSES.COURSE_ID
   )
;
```

If you look closely, you'll see something a little different: I'm using a LEFT OUTER JOIN instead of the usual INNER JOINs. This is because the Classes table has more than one match for each record of the Class Definitions table; remember, I took the unique Class Name/Course Name combinations from the Classes table and stored them in the Class Definitions table. This means there's more than one possible match, so I need to ensure I'm including all the records from the Classes table and match them with the Class Definitions table to get the proper Class IDs, hence the LEFT OUTER JOIN.

Creating the Class Enrollment per Year Data

Remember what I said I was just a warm-up for the real thing? Well, this is the real thing! The Class Enrollment per Year table is the smallest fragment of information of the Classes table. To populate it, I need to follow the breadcrumbs I left behind, with the creation of all the other class-related tables to get the necessary IDs to build the key for this table. Remember, the Classes table is always the starting point. Figure 5.26 illustrates the entire process.

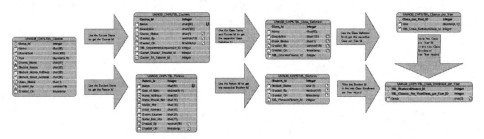

Figure 5.26: Class Enrollment per Year creation

As you can see, it's big and seems complex. Let analyze it in steps, starting with the most basic information: student and course IDs. To get the course ID, I'll use the course name. More or less the same happens with the student ID, but with a detour through the Persons table, just like in previous statements. Figure 5.27 shows these first two steps.

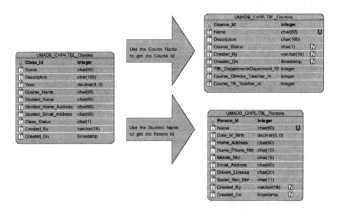

Figure 5.27: Class Enrollment per Year creation, step 1

The next step is using the course ID along with the class name (from the Classes table) to find the Class ID in the Class Definition table. Simultaneously, I'll use the Person ID to get the Student ID. Just as with the Teacher ID earlier, I can do this only because I know that the data is available and I'll find only one match. Figure 5.28 depicts this step.

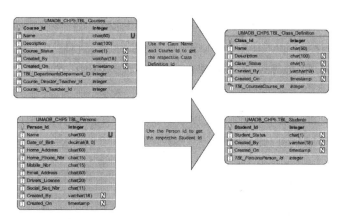

Figure 5.28: Class Enrollment per Year creation, step 2

Finally, I have to use the Class ID from the Class Definition table plus the Year from the Classes table to find the appropriate Class per Year ID from the Classes per Year table. After following all the class-related breadcrumbs to get to the class per year unique identifier and having found the appropriate student ID, I can finally write the records to the new Class Enrollment per Year table, as shown in Figure 5.29.

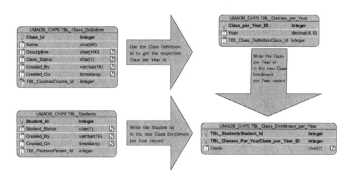

Figure 5.29: Class Enrollment per Year creation, step 3

As you might have gathered, the SQL statement is not simple. You should be able to understand it by matching each JOIN presented earlier (the arrows in figures 5.26, 5.27, and 5.29):

```
INSERT INTO UMADB_CHP5.TBL_CLASS_ENROLLMENT_PER_YEAR
  (TBL_STUDENTSSTUDENT_ID, TBL_CLASSES_PER_YEARCLASS_PER_YEAR_ID)
   (SELECT    STUDENTS.STUDENT_ID
             , CLASSES_PER_YEAR.CLASS_PER_YEAR_ID
    FROM      UMADB_CHP4.TBL_CLASSES CLASSES
             INNER JOIN   UMADB_CHP5.TBL_PERSONS PERSONS
                   ON PERSONS.NAME = CLASSES.STUDENT_NAME
             INNER JOIN   UMADB_CHP5.TBL_STUDENTS STUDENTS
                   ON PERSONS.PERSON_ID = STUDENTS.TBL_PERSONSPERSON_ID
             INNER JOIN   UMADB_CHP5.TBL_COURSES COURSES
                   ON CLASSES.COURSE_NAME = COURSES.NAME
             LEFT OUTER JOIN UMADB_CHP5.TBL_CLASS_DEFINITION CLASS_
DEFINITION
                   ON CLASSES.NAME = CLASS_DEFINITION.NAME AND CLASS_
DEFINITION.TBL_COURSESCOURSE_ID = COURSES.COURSE_ID
             INNER JOIN UMADB_CHP5.TBL_CLASSES_PER_YFAR CLASSES_PER_YEAR
                   ON CLASSES_PER_YEAR.TBL_CLASS_DEFINITIONCLASS_ID =
CLASS_DEFINITION.CLASS_ID
   )
;
```

You'll recognize some of the JOIN lines from previous statements. It's the "following of the breadcrumbs" I mentioned earlier. The only "new" part is the final INNER JOIN to get the Classes per Year ID.

Populating the Sort Sequence Table

The Sort Sequence table structure remains the same. However, this table's records use table and column names to provide sorting sequences (for the teacher ranks and grades, if you recall), which means I need to adjust the values in order to keep data consistency—a different kind of consistency, but consistency nonetheless.

I could do a two-step operation, with a simple INSERT/SELECT statement followed by an UPDATE statement. However, I can "copy" and transform the data at the same time, using

CASE structures to tweak the data as needed. Here's the SQL statement to populate the Sort Sequence table:

```
INSERT INTO UMADB_CHP5.TBL_SORT_SEQ
   (SELECT    CASE    TABLE_NAME
                    WHEN    'TBL_GRADES' THEN 'TBL_CLASS_ENROLLMENT_PER_
YEAR'
                    WHEN    'TBL_TEACHERS'     THEN 'TBL_TEACHER_RANKS'
                    ELSE    TABLE_NAME
               END
             , CASE        COLUMN_NAME
                    WHEN    'RANK'             THEN 'NAME'
                    ELSE    COLUMN_NAME
               END
             , VALUE_NAME
             , VALUE_WEIGHT
    FROM       UMADB_CHP4.TBL_SORT_SEQ
   )
;
```

The first CASE structure converts the occurrences of 'TBL_GRADES' into 'TBL_CLASS_ENROLLMENT_PER_YEAR' because the Grades column, which previously existed in the Grades table, was moved to the Class Enrollment per Year table. The same happens with the Rank, which was part of the Teachers table and now has its own table ('TBL_TEACHER_RANKS'). If there are any other values in the TABLE_NAME column, the ELSE part of the CASE structure ensures that they are migrated verbatim to the new table's record.

The second CASE structure does the same type of thing, but it only needs to transform the Rank into Name, because the Grades column kept its original name but the Rank column didn't.

Time for a Bit More Practice

The only missing piece of information belongs in the Classes Taught per Year table. This table serves as a link between the Teachers and the Classes per Year tables, thus indicating which teacher taught each class in a given school year. Since there's no data to migrate (the information in the "old" Subjects_Taught column was incomplete and unreliable), I leave it to you to populate this table. It's simple: just figure out which teacher you want to assign to a certain class and then write "regular" INSERT statements with the VALUES clause and fixed data.

Here's an example that makes Darth Vader (which has the Teacher_Id equal to 2) the teacher of the 2014 "Supervillainy 101" class (which has the Class_per_Year_Id equal to 6):

```
INSERT INTO UMADB_CHP5.TBL_CLASSES_TAUGHT_PER_YEAR
  (TBL_CLASSES_PER_YEARCLASS_PER_YEAR_ID, TBL_TEACHERSTEACHER_ID)
VALUES(6, 2)
;
```

Hiding the Database Complexity (Again) by Recreating the Views

If the database structure was already getting a bit complex by the end of the previous chapter, now it can be a real challenge to create a query with more than a couple of tables. Let's create some views to help the users create their own queries and simultaneously hide the database complexity. I'll start with something simple, and you'll take it from there.

Before the database redesign, listing the students' information was simple: a SELECT over the Students table yielded all the necessary data. With the creation of the Persons table and the respective data migration, listing the students' information got a little bit more complicated, so I'll create a view to facilitate the access to the Students data:

```
CREATE OR REPLACE VIEW UMADB_CHP5.VIEW_STUDENT_INFO
  FOR SYSTEM NAME V_STUDENT1
  AS
  SELECT      STUDENTS.STUDENT_ID
                                                    Continued
```

```
            , PERSONS.NAME
            , PERSONS.DATE_OF_BIRTH
            , PERSONS.HOME_ADDRESS
            , PERSONS.HOME_PHONE_NBR
            , PERSONS.MOBILE_NBR
            , PERSONS.EMAIL_ADDRESS
            , PERSONS.DRIVERS_LICENSE
            , PERSONS.SOCIAL_SEC_NBR
            , STUDENTS.STUDENT_STATUS
    FROM    UMADB_CHP5.TBL_STUDENTS STUDENTS
            INNER JOIN UMADB_CHP5.TBL_PERSONS PERSONS
                ON PERSONS.PERSON_ID = STUDENTS.TBL_PERSONSPERSON_ID
    ;
```

Note that I'm now using CREATE OR REPLACE VIEW, which will save you the additional
step of deleting (via a DROP statement) the view before recreating it. Other than that,
the code should be easy to understand, because it follows the same principles that were
presented back in Chapter 3 and revisited in Chapter 4, regarding SELECT and CREATE
VIEW statements. If you're not familiar with the database relations, have another look at
Figure 5.17, which contains the final database structure, complete with the relationships
between the tables.

It's important to properly document your code, especially because the views might be
used by users and programmers alike, so let's add a fitting description to it, using a LABEL
ON statement:

```
LABEL ON TABLE UMADB_CHP5.VIEW_STUDENT_INFO IS 'Student Information
View';
```

If you issue a WRKOBJ (Work with Objects) command or list the contents of the UMADB_
CHP5 library via PDM, Navigator, or another tool, you'll see 'Student Information View' as
the object's description.

The next stop is the Teachers information. The process is similar, but it includes an additional table: the Teacher Ranks. Let's include the teacher's rank, name, and personal information. Take a break from reading now, and try to do it yourself. But don't peek; the solution is just below!

```
CREATE OR REPLACE VIEW UMADB_CHP5.VIEW_TEACHER_INFO
 FOR SYSTEM NAME V_TEACHER1
 AS
 SELECT        TEACHERS.TEACHER_ID
              , TEACHER_RANKS.NAME AS TEACHER_RANK
              , PERSONS.NAME AS TEACHER_NAME
              , PERSONS.DATE_OF_BIRTH
              , PERSONS.HOME_ADDRESS
              , PERSONS.HOME_PHONE_NBR
              , PERSONS.MOBILE_NBR
              , PERSONS.EMAIL_ADDRESS
              , PERSONS.DRIVERS_LICENSE
              , PERSONS.SOCIAL_SEC_NBR
              , TEACHERS.TEACHER_STATUS
 FROM          UMADB_CHP5.TBL_TEACHERS TEACHERS
               INNER JOIN UMADB_CHP5.TBL_PERSONS PERSONS
                      ON PERSONS.PERSON_ID = TEACHERS.TBL_PERSONSPERSON_ID
               INNER JOIN UMADB_CHP5.TBL_TEACHER_RANKS TEACHER_RANKS
                      ON TEACHERS.TBL_TEACHER_RANKSTEACHER_RANK_ID =
                      TEACHER_RANKS.TEACHER_RANK_ID
 ;

 LABEL ON TABLE UMADB_CHP5.VIEW_TEACHER_INFO IS 'Teacher Information
 View';
```

Now let's improve upon this. The Courses table has two implicit relationships with the Teachers table, because it contains the Teacher IDs of the course's Director and Teaching Assistant. They are implicit relationships, and at this moment the data consistency is not being checked—that's something for a later chapter, but for now, I need to get the teachers' names and ranks to display the complete course information. This makes the next view's code slightly longer than the teachers' code I just presented:

```
/* Course Information View */
CREATE OR REPLACE VIEW UMADB_CHP5.VIEW_COURSE_INFO
 FOR SYSTEM NAME V_COURSE1
 AS
 SELECT       COURSES.COURSE_ID
              , COURSES.NAME AS COURSE_NAME
              , COURSES.DESCRIPTION
              , DEPARTMENTS.NAME AS DEPARTMENT_NAME
              , DIRECTOR_PERSON.NAME AS COURSE_DIRECTOR_NAME
              , TA_PERSON.NAME AS COURSE_TA_NAME
              , COURSES.COURSE_STATUS
  FROM        UMADB_CHP5.TBL_COURSES COURSES
              INNER JOIN UMADB_CHP5.TBL_TEACHERS DIRECTOR
                     ON DIRECTOR.TEACHER_ID = COURSES.COURSE_DIRECTOR_
TEACHER_ID
              INNER JOIN UMADB_CHP5.TBL_PERSONS DIRECTOR_PERSON
                     ON DIRECTOR_PERSON.PERSON_ID =
                     DIRECTOR.TBL_PERSONSPERSON_ID
              INNER JOIN UMADB_CHP5.TBL_TEACHERS TA
                     ON TA.TEACHER_ID = COURSES.COURSE_TA_TEACHER_ID
              INNER JOIN UMADB_CHP5.TBL_PERSONS TA_PERSON
                     ON TA_PERSON.PERSON_ID = TA.TBL_PERSONSPERSON_ID
              INNER JOIN UMADB_CHP5.TBL_DEPARTMENTS DEPARTMENTS
                     ON COURSES.TBL_DEPARTMENTSDEPARTMENT_ID =
                     DEPARTMENTS.DEPARTMENT_ID
 ;

LABEL ON TABLE UMADB_CHP5.VIEW_COURSE_INFO IS 'Course Information View';
```

This code is a bit more "twisted," but it follows the same principle as the previous SQL code examples. This happens because the data modeling that took place earlier in this chapter didn't fragment the Students, Teachers, or Courses tables. It simply rearranged the data and added a couple of new tables.

However, the "old" Classes table suffered a much greater (and much needed) redesign, which means that creating a view that, for instance, lists the classes each teacher taught in a given school year, requires careful consideration, as it involves the teacher-related tables (used in the teachers' view shown before) but also the new fragmented class-related tables.

A quick look at Figure 5.17 will tell you that the Classes Taught per Year table sits between the Teachers and the Classes per Year tables. The problem is that the Classes per Year table is just an intermediate table which contains very little data: it simply shows which class existed in each school year. It doesn't contain information that the users might find important, such as the class name and description. That requires bringing in the Class Definition table and linking all these tables together via INNER JOINs.

The complete code for this view is shown below. Analyze it carefully and use the final UMADB ERD (Figure 5.17) to fully understand all the relationships involved.

```
/* Classes Taught per Year by Teacher View */
CREATE OR REPLACE VIEW UMADB_CHP5.VIEW_CLASSES_TAUGHT_PER_YEAR
 FOR SYSTEM NAME V_TEACHER2
 AS
SELECT      CLASS_DEFINITION.NAME AS CLASS_NAME
            , CLASS_DEFINITION.DESCRIPTION AS CLASS_DESCRIPTION
            , CLASSES_PER_YEAR.YEAR AS CLASS_YEAR
            , TEACHER_RANKS.NAME AS TEACHER_RANK
            , PERSONS.NAME AS TEACHER_NAME
FROM       UMADB_CHP5.TBL_CLASSES_TAUGHT_PER_YEAR CLASSES_TAUGHT_PER_YEAR
            INNER JOIN UMADB_CHP5.TBL_TEACHERS TEACHERS
                ON CLASSES_TAUGHT_PER_YEAR.TBL_TEACHERSTEACHER_ID =
        TEACHERS.TEACHER_ID
            INNER JOIN UMADB_CHP5.TBL_TEACHER_RANKS TEACHER_RANKS
                                                    Continued
```

```
ON TEACHERS.TBL_TEACHER_RANKSTEACHER_RANK_ID =
   TEACHER_RANKS.TEACHER_RANK_ID
              INNER JOIN UMADB_CHP5.TBL_PERSONS PERSONS
                     ON TEACHERS.TBL_PERSONSPERSON_ID = PERSONS.PERSON_ID
              INNER JOIN UMADB_CHP5.TBL_CLASSES_PER_YEAR CLASSES_PER_YEAR
                     ON CLASSES_TAUGHT_PER_YEAR.TBL_CLASSES_PER_
YEARCLASS_PER_YEAR_ID

= CLASSES_PER_YEAR.CLASS_PER_YEAR_ID
              INNER JOIN UMADB_CHP5.TBL_CLASS_DEFINITION CLASS_DEFINITION
                     ON CLASSES_PER_YEAR.TBL_CLASS_DEFINITIONCLASS_ID
=
 CLASS_DEFINITION.CLASS_ID
;

LABEL ON TABLE UMADB_CHP5.VIEW_CLASSES_TAUGHT_PER_YEAR IS 'Classes
Taught per Year by Teacher View';
```

Finally, let's create a view to make the access to the students' class enrollment and grades information easier, as the table that contains that information sits in the middle of complex many-to-many relationships. In order to get the student's name, the class in which he/she is enrolled, the name of the course that class is part of, and the grade obtained, a handful of tables are required.

To get the student's personal information, I'll start with the Class Enrollment per Year table, which maps the many-to-many relationship between the Students and the Classes per Year tables. However, the Students table no longer contains the student's name; that piece of information is now stored in the Persons table, to which I'll link via the student's person ID. Finally, I'll add the Persons table to retrieve the student's name. That takes care of the student-related data.

Getting the class and course data requires a slightly longer route: from the Class Enrollment per Year to the Classes per Year table and from there to the Class Definition table. The Class Definition table contains the Course ID, which will allow me to add the link to the Courses table and get the course name.

You'll find the complete code below. Again, analyze it carefully and refer to Figure 5.17 to see how all the relationships are mapped in the INNER JOINs.

```
CREATE OR REPLACE VIEW UMADB_CHP5.VIEW_STUDENT_GRADES_INFO
 FOR SYSTEM NAME V_STUDENT2
 AS
 SELECT       STUDENTS.STUDENT_ID
              , PERSONS.NAME AS STUDENT_NAME
              , COURSES.NAME AS COURSE_NAME
              , CLASS_DEFINITION.NAME AS CLASS_NAME
              , CLASSES_PER_YEAR.YEAR AS CLASS_YEAR
              , ENROLLMENT.GRADE

 FROM         UMADB_CHP5.TBL_CLASS_ENROLLMENT_PER_YEAR ENROLLMENT
              INNER JOIN UMADB_CHP5.TBL_STUDENTS STUDENTS
                   ON STUDENTS.STUDENT_ID = ENROLLMENT.TBL_
STUDENTSSTUDENT_ID
              INNER JOIN UMADB_CHP5.TBL_CLASSES_PER_YEAR CLASSES_PER_YEAR
                   ON CLASSES_PER_YEAR.CLASS_PER_YEAR_ID =
ENROLLMENT.TBL_CLASSES_PER_YEARCLASS_PER_YEAR_ID
              INNER JOIN UMADB_CHP5.TBL_CLASS_DEFINITION CLASS_DEFINITION
                   ON CLASS_DEFINITION.CLASS_ID =
CLASSES_PER_YEAR.TBL_CLASS_DEFINITIONCLASS_ID
              INNER JOIN UMADB_CHP5.TBL_PERSONS PERSONS
                   ON PERSONS.PERSON_ID = STUDENTS.TBL_PERSONSPERSON_ID
              INNER JOIN UMADB_CHP5.TBL_COURSES COURSES
                   ON CLASS_DEFINITION.TBL_COURSESCOURSE_ID =
COURSES.COURSE_ID
 ;

 LABEL ON TABLE UMADB_CHP5.VIEW_STUDENT_GRADES_INFO IS 'Student Classes
 and Grades per Year View';
```

These examples should provide you with enough information to create your own views over the tables of this database and, hopefully, to apply what you've learned here, about normalization, database redesign, and relationships, to your own database. This is a very important chapter because a good database design and implementation are of paramount importance to what lies ahead.

In This Chapter, You've Learned ...

This was a very hands-on chapter, but it also contained a fair amount of theory. Here's a summary of what I've tried to explain:

- The fundamental notions of relational databases, namely the concepts of relationship, keys, and everything relevant to them

- The concept of data modeling and its representation in an ERD

- How to install and use Visual Paradigm Community Edition

- How to build the new and improved version of UMADB, with proper primary and foreign keys, and generate the corresponding SQL statements

- How to migrate data to a different structure using ERD-like schematics to facilitate the thought process and complex INSERT/SELECT statements to map the relations between the tables

- How to handle data transformation requirements using CASE structures

- How to create complex views using an ERD to map the relations between tables via JOIN clauses

6

Introducing Data-Centric Programming and SQL/PSM

> This chapter introduces the concept of data-centric programming, a different approach to programming that provides additional flexibility and in effect "opens" the database to the outside world. This is achieved via the SQL/Persistent Stored Modules (SQL/PSM) SQL extension, which is explored and explained with examples throughout the chapter.

A Call from the Dean's Office

Fast-forward a few months. Both users and IT staff are happy with their shiny new database, which is now more flexible, organized, and faster than ever. Everything seems perfect until I get a call from the Dean's office, scheduling a meeting ASAP. Naturally, I agree to the meeting and show up at the appointed time, not having a clue what the big boss might want from me.

Over tea and biscuits, the Dean congratulates us (yes, you're tagging along) on a job well done: everyone is finally getting proper reports, the IT department's productivity is up, and the user complaints are down—all thanks to the database redesign. However, the Dean wants more. He wants to provide additional decentralized services, by creating Web and mobile apps. "That's the new trend! I don't have a clue how it's done, but it would do wonders for the university's reputation!" he says. Even though the Dean doesn't know the details, he's been told that the database and the green-screen application it serves are closely knit together: every business rule, check, and procedure resides at application level, which is very difficult (read: very costly) to replicate on other applications. The Dean wants us to provide a (cheaper) solution for this problem, and he wants it fast!

Introducing Data-Centric Programming

We leave the Dean's office scratching our heads, wondering how to approach the problem. How are we going to open the database to the outside world, without rewriting code every time a new application is created? After some research, we determine that *data-centric programming* (DCP) offers a good solution. But what exactly is DCP?

DCP is both a methodology and a concept. In simple terms, it advocates that if you "pull" business logic and processes into the database or near it, the cost of developing applications that use the database goes down. The application will use the logic and processes provided by the database instead of "reinventing the wheel," which makes for faster and more consistent data processing/validation. It requires reviewing the entire application, if one already exists (as in our particular situation), and listing all the business rules/validations that are not already enforced by the database design, in the form of table relationships.

Bringing business rules into the database will require automating sequences of operations at the database level that are currently handled by the application using high-level languages, like RPG. How are we going to do that? Well, we'll be using stored procedures and user-defined functions, which I'll discuss later in more detail. Enforcing business validations can mean, among other things, adding constraints to columns. A common example is restricting the acceptable range of values for a certain piece of information—for instance, a teacher's salary must be a positive number.

We'll achieve all this by writing code—not your run-of-the-mill SELECT statement, but a mix of DDL, DML, and something new, called *SQL/PSM*. We'll place our code into stored procedures, user-defined functions, and triggers, depending on a few factors that I'll discuss later. But first, let's learn a bit more about SQL/PSM.

An SQL/PSM Crash Course

DB2 for i's SQL/PSM implementation is based on industry standards. As you'll see in a little while, it uses constructs common to many programming languages, including RPG, with which you're probably already familiar. This crash course will cover variable declaration and assignment, flow control, loop control, compound statements, calling procedures, dynamic SQL, cursors, and error handling. It looks like a lot, but it's actually quite simple. Let's start with the basics: declaring and assigning values to variables.

Variable Declaration

You can assign values to different variable types, namely input or output parameters (I'll explain these later) or your own variables. In order to declare your own variables, you need to use another SQL/PSM construct: DECLARE. SQL's DECLARE is similar to CL's DCL: you state the name and type of the variable, and you're done. Here's how I'd declare a variable named min_passing_grade:

```
DECLARE min_passing_grade INT;
```

Note that you must end all lines of SQL/PSM code with a semicolon. You can also declare multiple variables of the same type in the same DECLARE statement:

```
DECLARE min_passing_grade, page_num_records INT;
```

As you might have guessed, the generic syntax is:

```
DECLARE <variable name> <variable type>;
```

in which *<variable type>* can be either an SQL data type or a user-defined data type, created by a CREATE TYPE statement. If you're not familiar with this statement, don't worry, as I'll explain CREATE TYPE later.

Variable Assignment

Now that you know how to declare your own variables, let's see how you can assign values to them. There are two ways to assign a value to a variable in SQL/PSM: SET and INTO. You've probably used SET before, on UPDATE statements. The syntax here is similar. You just write:

```
SET <variable name> = <value to assign>;
```

Let's say I wanted to assign a value of 50 to a variable named min_passing_grade. To do that I'd write:

```
SET min_passing_grade = 50;
```

You can also assign the result of a query to a variable. For instance, imagine I wanted to store the highest salary paid to the university's teachers in a variable called max_salary. I'd have to write:

```
SET max_salary = (SELECT MAX(SALARY) FROM TBL_TEACHERS);
```

Now let's complicate things a bit. You can use a single SET statement to perform multiple assignments. In other words, you can do this:

```
SET min_passing_grade = 50, max_salary = (SELECT MAX(SALARY) FROM TBL_
TEACHERS)
```

However, the variables' new values are not available until the statement is executed. This means that if you try this:

```
SET page_num_records = 0;
SET page_num_records = 1, total_records = page_num_records + 4;
```

you'll see that page_num_records does not contain 5, as you'd expect, but 4. This happens because immediately before the second SET statement, the page_num_records variable contained 0, not 1. The value is changed to 1 within the second SET statement, but the total_records assignment ignores that value change, because it happens in the same SET. Because I prefer to keep my code as clear as possible, I prefer to stick to one assignment per SET statement.

If you've ever embedded SQL into RPG programs, you surely have seen the other assignment statement. The INTO statement can be used in a couple of different ways, using VALUES or using a SELECT statement. In this particular case, it's easier to see an example to better understand the syntax. Let's use the same examples as before. First I'll assign 50 to min_passing_grade:

```
VALUES(50) INTO min_passing_grade;
```

Now let's see the other possible syntax, using the highest teacher salary example:

```
SELECT MAX(SALARY) INTO max_salary FROM TBL_TEACHERS;
```

From these examples, it should be possible to infer that the syntax is as follows:

```
VALUES(<value to assign>) INTO <variable name>;
```

and

```
SELECT <value to assign> INTO <variable name> FROM <table name>;
```

Note that you can assign multiple values to multiple variables, just as you could do with the SET statement. Similarly, the values are not assigned to the variables until the statement ends, so what I've mentioned before in the page_num_records example also applies here. However, in this case, the multiple variable assignment can be useful when you want to store more than one resulting column from a single SELECT statement. Just be sure to have the same number of values and variables! Technically, INTO is not part of SQL/PSM. However, it's so commonly used when SQL is embedded in high-level languages that it should be mentioned when referring to variable assignment.

Flow Control

It's simply not possible to implement validations without some sort of conditional control. In SQL/PSM, this comes in two flavors: IF (in its multiple forms) and CASE (in its two forms). I've already used the simplest form of CASE in the previous chapter, so I'll cover just the other one here. But let's start with the IF statement. As in most programming languages, SQL/PSM's IF can be an extremely simple and single IF-THEN structure or something more complex, like a multiple-cascaded IF-THEN-ELSEIF structure. Let's start with an example of the simple form and then look at the more convoluted form.

Imagine I want to assign a value of 'PASSED' to a variable called exam_result whenever the student_grade variable's value is at least 50. I just need to write the following statement:

```
IF student_grade >= 50 THEN
SET exam_result = 'PASSED';
```

Now let's take it up a notch and evolve this to an IF-THEN-ELSE structure. Let's change the statement, so that 'FAILED' is assigned to exam_result if the student_grade contains a value below 50:

```
IF student_grade >= 50 THEN
SET exam_result = 'PASSED'
ELSE
SET exam_result = 'FAILED';
```

This gets even more complicated if you have more than one condition. For instance, let's say that students who get a grade between 45 and 50 are required to make an oral presentation in order to determine the exam result:

```
IF student_grade >= 50 THEN
SET exam_result = 'PASSED'
ELSEIF student_grade >= 45 THEN
SET exam_result = 'REPORT FOR ORAL PRESENTATION'
ELSE
SET exam_result = 'FAILED';
```

Even this more complex structure is similar to RPG's version of the IF construct. Personally, I prefer to use a CASE structure instead of nested IFs and ELSEIFs. Speaking of which, let me refresh the CASE statement's two possible syntaxes:

```
CASE (<variable or expression>)
WHEN <value> THEN <statement(s) to execute>;
WHEN <other value> THEN <other statement(s) to execute>;
...
        ELSE <statement(s) to execute when none of the values are matched>;
END CASE;
```

Note that when there's more than one statement to execute, an additional construct is required. I'll talk about this "thing", called a *compound statement*, later. For now, let's try and make this clearer with a couple of examples, recycling the IF statement scenario:

```
CASE student_grade
WHEN 100 THEN SET exam_result = 'PASSED'
WHEN 99 THEN SET exam_result = 'PASSED';
        (...)
WHEN 50 THEN SET exam_result = 'PASSED';
WHEN 49 THEN SET exam_result = 'REPORT FOR ORAL PRESENTATION';
WHEN 48 THEN SET exam_result = 'REPORT FOR ORAL PRESENTATION';
        (...)
WHEN 45 THEN SET exam_result = 'REPORT FOR ORAL PRESENTATION';
ELSE SET exam_result = 'FAILED';
END CASE;
```

This is how the simplest form of CASE handles ranges of values; it's definitely not pretty or useful. But it can be made simpler, by using CASE's other syntax:

```
CASE
WHEN <condition> THEN <statement(s) to execute>;
WHEN <other condition> THEN <other statement(s) to execute>;
...
ELSE <statement(s) to execute when none of the conditions are met>;
END CASE;
```

Using this syntax, the statement is crystal clear:

```
CASE
WHEN student_grade >= 50 THEN
SET exam_result = 'PASSED';
WHEN student_grade BETWEEN 45 AND 49 THEN
SET exam_result = 'REPORT FOR ORAL PRESENTATION';
ELSE SET exam_result = 'FAILED';
END CASE;
```

This is a simple example, with just two comparisons, but things can get complex sometimes, so it's important to know how this flow-control structure works.

When multiple WHEN/THEN clauses are specified in a given CASE, the order of processing is left to right and top to bottom, until a WHEN clause's condition is found to be TRUE. If there are multiple WHEN conditions that would evaluate to TRUE, the THEN of the first WHEN condition that is TRUE is executed and the rest of the WHEN/THENs are skipped.

Often having flow control is not enough, because you might need to repeat a similar operation or set of operations over and over again. That's what loops are for.

Loop Control

Every decent programming language has a looping structure or two. SQL/PSM has four: LOOP, WHILE, REPEAT, and FOR. I'll cover only the first three now, because the FOR loop requires additional information. I'll talk about it later in this chapter.

Let's start with the most basic of the looping statements: LOOP. This is a bare-bones looping structure, which will run endlessly if you don't issue a statement to end it. Everything between the LOOP and END LOOP statements will be executed until a LEAVE or RETURN statement is issued. (I'll explain RETURN later in this chapter, and LEAVE in a moment.) Let's say I want to increment a variable by 1 until it reaches 10, starting at zero (yes, it's a silly example, but its aim is only to demonstrate LOOP's syntax):

```
DECLARE my_counter INT;
SET my_counter = 0;
my_loop:
LOOP
        SET my_counter = my_counter + 1;
        IF (my_counter >= 10) THEN
                LEAVE my_loop;
        END IF;
END LOOP my_loop;
```

In this piece of code, I start by declaring an integer variable named my_counter and assign it a value of zero. Then I declare a tag (my_loop:) by giving it a name followed by a colon (:). Finally, I start the loop, which will increment the my_counter and check if its value has reached or surpassed the value of 10. If it has, a LEAVE statement is issued to break the otherwise infinite loop. Personally, I dislike this looping structure, because it's very easy to accidentally create an infinite loop. Depending on the loop's objective—run until a condition is met, or run a predefined number of times, I prefer to use WHILE and FOR, respectively.

WHILE is a very well-known looping structure, and because SQL/PSM follows industry standards, its WHILE implementation is similar to that of many programming languages. Let's use the same "dumb" example to illustrate WHILE in action:

```
DECLARE my_counter INT;
SET my_counter = 0;
WHILE (my_counter < 10) DO
        SET my_counter = my_counter + 1;
END WHILE;
```

Note that you can also use a LEAVE statement to break a WHILE loop. You just need to declare and use a tag, as I showed in the previous example, to do so. In the WHILE looping structure, the exit condition is checked first, and the code within the loop is executed if the condition is met.

REPEAT, another looping structure in SQL/PSM, works in reverse: the code is executed first, and then the exit condition is checked. Let's analyze an example to make this clearer:

```
DECLARE my_counter INT;
SET my_counter = 0;
DO
        SET my_counter = my_counter + 1;
UNTIL (my_counter >= 10)
END REPEAT;
```

WHILE and REPEAT are particularly useful when you have complex conditions or an unknown or unpredictable number of iterations.

There's another statement that I have to mention because it usually confuses programmers: ITERATE. This SQL/PSM statement is also common among programming languages (in RPG it's called ITER) and is somewhat similar to LEAVE. However, instead of breaking the loop and continuing the code execution after the END of the loop statement, ITERATE makes the code execution resume at the top (as opposed to the bottom, the END statement) of the loop. Here's an example, using the REPEAT loop:

```
DECLARE my_counter INT;
SET my_counter = 0;
my_loop:
DO
        IF my_counter = 5 THEN
                SET my_counter = my_counter + 2;
                ITERATE my_loop;
        END IF;
        SET my_counter = my_counter + 1;
UNTIL (my_counter >= 10)
END REPEAT my_loop;
```

In this case, the my_counter variable's value will "jump" from 5 to 7, because I added an IF statement that adds 2 instead of 1 and skips back to the top of the loop, without executing the SET my_counter = my_counter + 1; line of code. Also, note the usage of the tag, similar to the LEAVE statement.

As I mentioned earlier, explaining the FOR loops requires that you know a thing or two about cursors and procedure calls. I'll cover procedure calls next and discuss cursors later.

Calling Other SQL Routines, FOR Loops, and Cursors

I briefly mentioned that we'll use SQL/PSM code to create stored procedures (SPs), user-defined functions (UDFs), and triggers. However, I neglected to mention how all these SQL routines are invoked. In short, SPs are callable from other SPs using a CALL statement, which I'll explain in a moment; UDFs can be used in a DML statement, just as if they were a regular SQL function; and triggers are activated by the database engine when certain actions over the tables are performed (more about this later).

For now, let's imagine that I want to send an email to all the teachers inviting them to the university's Christmas party. I won't explain in detail how the email-sending SP works; let's simply assume it takes as input parameters the teacher's name and email address and sends the necessary email message. All I have to do is go through all the teachers records, or in other words, loop through the entire Teachers table, and send an email for each record. I've dropped a few hints on how this is done, so please reread the last sentence carefully before looking at the next piece of code.

```
my_loop: FOR each_teacher AS
        my_cursor CURSOR FOR
            SELECT          PERSONS.NAME AS Teacher_Name
, PERSONS.EMAIL_ADDRESS AS Teacher_Email
            FROM            TBL_TEACHERS TEACHERS
            INNER JOIN TBL_PERSONS PERSONS
ON PERSONS.PERSON_ID = TEACHERS.TBL_PERSONSPERSON_ID
            DO
                    CALL send_invitation(each_teacher.Teacher_Name
, each_teacher.Teacher_Email);
END FOR;
```

Because there's a lot of new stuff here, let's analyze the code block by block, starting with the FOR loop declaration. The first couple of lines define a FOR loop with a cursor named my_cursor:

```
my_loop: FOR each_teacher AS
        my_cursor CURSOR FOR
```

But the cursor is not an abstract "thing"; it will point to a result set, in this case, a query over the Teachers and Persons tables, which returns the teachers' names and email addresses:

```
            SELECT          PERSONS.NAME AS Teacher_Name
, PERSONS.EMAIL_ADDRESS AS Teacher_Email
            FROM            TBL_TEACHERS TEACHERS
            INNER JOIN TBL_PERSONS PERSONS
ON PERSONS.PERSON_ID = TEACHERS.TBL_PERSONSPERSON_ID
```

In other words, on each iteration of our FOR loop, a line of the result set of this query will be returned and made available to the FOR loop body of statements, which I'll explain next. This is similar to a FOR EACH loop in Java or C#, where you loop through the elements of a list, working with the details of each element on an iteration of the loop. Perhaps the most similar RPG construct would be a WHILE NOT %EOF(SOME_FILE) loop that performs a set of operations using the fields of each record of SOME_FILE. In SQL/PSM's FOR loop, this set of operations is delimited by the DO and END FOR statements:

```
            DO
                        CALL send_invitation(each_teacher.Teacher_Name
, each_teacher.Teacher_Email);
END FOR;
```

Note that I'm calling another stored procedure, named send_invitation, to send the invitations for the university's Christmas party. It's like calling a program in RPG and passing parameters: in this case, the teacher's name and email address of the record of the result set to which the cursor is currently pointing. Notice, however, that I don't use the cursor name, but the FOR loop "name" to refer to each element: each_teacher.Teacher_Name and each_teacher.Teacher_Email. Additionally, I could have an output parameter in my send_invitation stored procedure to indicate whether the email was sent successfully and update a file with that piece of information. In this case, the DO and END FOR block would look something like this:

```
DO
                        CALL send_invitation(each_teacher.Teacher_Name
, each_teacher.Teacher_Email
, invite_sent_boolean);
                UPDATE TBL_INVITE_LIST
                SET INVITE_SENT = invite_sent_boolean
                WHERE TEACHER_NAME = each_teacher.Teacher_Name;
END FOR;
```

Naturally, I'd need to declare the invite_sent_boolean variable before entering the loop. This is just to remind you that it's possible to mix "pure" SQL—an UPDATE statement, in this case—with SQL/PSM code in an SQL routine. This will be made clearer with the examples provided later in this chapter.

Dynamic SQL

So far, I've been using static SQL. It's true that I used some variables in SQL statements, but the statements themselves, mainly SELECT and UPDATE statements, have been hard-coded. For simple SQL routines, this is more than enough. However, if the goal is to move business rules and validations to the database, static SQL won't do.

Sometimes the statement is only known at run time, as when a statement is built up from business logic. SQL/PSM offers the necessary flexibility in the form of dynamic SQL statements. As you'll see later, you can dynamically write SELECT, UPDATE, DELETE, CREATE, and even BEGIN/END code blocks (compound statements, which I'll discuss in a little while) using logic, local, global, and parameter variables. The nicest part is that you can compose your dynamic SQL statement as if it were a text string, using placeholders (formally named parameter markers) to indicate where the variables should be. Then, when the time comes to run the statement, you simply provide the necessary values to fill those placeholders. This added feature provides a "write once/use many times" reusability and flexibility that you'll soon learn to appreciate.

Dynamic SELECTs

I'll start by showing you how to create and use dynamic SELECT statements. The DECLARE and SET statements shown before are used together when working with dynamic SELECT statements that are declared as cursors, similar to the one I used in the FOR loop example. Although not required, a SELECT statement is typically constructed as a text string and stored in a variable. In order to use a dynamically prepared SELECT statement, a few steps must be followed. You need to declare the cursor and prepare it, in no particular order, as either statement can precede the other. However, since the DECLARE CURSOR statement must be defined in the DECLARE section of a compound statement, as you'll see later, it normally comes before the PREPARE statement in the same compound statement. If the PREPARE statement comes first, the DECLARE CURSOR must be specified in a subsequent nested compound statement. Then you must open the cursor, so that the data is made available.

The DECLARE CURSOR statement associates a SELECT statement with a cursor, which can be used to read the resulting rows from the SELECT statement. The syntax of the statement is as follows:

```
DECLARE <cursor name> CURSOR FOR <prepared statement name>
```

The *<cursor name>* identifies the cursor that is subsequently used for the OPEN, FETCH, and CLOSE statements. The prepared statement name must match the name used in the PREPARE statement.

The PREPARE statement prepares an SQL SELECT statement for execution. The most common syntax is as follows:

```
PREPARE <statement name> FROM <variable or expression>
```

The statement name provides an identifier that is used to associate the statement to a cursor. Naturally, the prepared statement name must match the DECLARE CURSOR prepared statement name in order to successfully pair the two together. The PREPARE statement creates an executable form of an SQL statement from a text string form of the statement. The text string form is called a *statement string*, and the executable form is called a *prepared statement*.

During the PREPARE, the statement is validated, and all referenced objects, such as tables, are checked. Any syntax problems with the statement text or unresolved objects will cause an error. In short, the PREPARE statement takes the dynamically built SELECT statement and turns it into bits and bytes that the database engine can handle. Then the cursor can use the statement to fetch the data that matches the SELECT. However, this requires a few more steps, which I'll explain next.

Once the cursor has been declared and the respective statement prepared, it can be opened. The OPEN statement is really simple:

```
OPEN <cursor name>
```

However, if parameter markers (the placeholders for variables I mentioned earlier) were used in the SELECT statement, the OPEN statement will take a slightly different form to accommodate them:

```
OPEN <cursor name> USING <1st variable>, <2nd variable>, <3rd variable>
...
```

After successfully opening the cursor, you can get the output of the SELECT statement using the FETCH statement, the same way you'd use a READ*xx* instruction in RPG. You can read the next or the previous row. It can also do other neat tricks, like "jumping" to a particular row, like the first, last, or *n*th row. However, unlike RPG's READ*xx*, FETCH can read multiple rows at a time and load the result directly into an array-like data structure. Let's go over the different syntax possibilities.

```
FETCH FROM <cursor name> INTO <1st output variable>, <2nd output
variable> ...
```

This is the simplest form, and it will read (or fetch) the next row of the cursor's execution result set into the indicated variables. It's actually doing a FETCH NEXT, which is the default operation and can be omitted, but there are other possibilities:

```
FETCH PRIOR FROM <cursor name> INTO <1st output variable>, <2nd output
variable> ...
FETCH FIRST FROM <cursor name> INTO <1st output variable>, <2nd output
variable> ...
FETCH LAST FROM <cursor name> INTO <1st output variable>, <2nd output
variable> ...
FETCH RELATIVE <variable or integer> FROM <cursor name> into <1st output
variable>, <2nd output variable> ...
```

In a way, all these possibilities are similar, in the sense that they simply navigate to a certain position of the result set and return the respective row. Even RELATIVE does this, but with a twist, because you can use RELATIVE to emulate some of the other keywords:

RELATIVE +1 is the same as NEXT, and RELATIVE -1 is the same as PRIOR. Then there's also a way to reread the last-fetched row:

```
FETCH CURRENT FROM <cursor name> INTO <1st output variable>, <2nd output
variable> ...
```

Finally, if you tweak the FETCH syntax a bit, you can fetch multiple rows into a data structure:

```
FETCH NEXT FROM <cursor name> FOR <variable or integer representing the
number of rows to fetch> INTO <array data structure>
```

Once you're done with the cursor, you must explicitly close it. How? Well, as easily as you opened it: by issuing a CLOSE statement containing the name of the cursor, as shown next.

```
CLOSE <cursor name>
```

Let's stop for a moment and analyze an example to consolidate all this new information. Imagine the university wants to award a 10 percent bonus to all the teachers who hold a certain rank. Our job is to write a dynamic SQL set of statements—not a full procedure yet (we'll get to that later)—to calculate the total cost for the university. In this shortened and simplified example, the rank's name will be stored in a local variable, but it could easily be received as an input parameter, as the calculated cost could also be "exported" as an output parameter.

```
DECLARE w_calculated_cost DECIMAL(11, 2) DEFAULT 0;
DECLARE w_teacher_rank VARCHAR(50) DEFAULT 'Dark Master';
DECLARE w_sql_stmt VARCHAR(2000);
DECLARE teacher_cursor CURSOR FOR teacher_stmt;
SET w_sql_stmt = 'SELECT SUM(TEACHERS.SALARY * .1) FROM UMADB_CHP5.TBL_
TEACHERS TEACHERS';
```
Continued

```
SET w_sql_stmt = TRIM(w_sql_stmt) CONCAT ' INNER JOIN UMADB_CHP5.
TBL_TEACHER_RANKS RANKS ON TEACHERS.TBL_TEACHER_RANKSTEACHER_RANK_ID =
RANKS.TEACHER_RANK_ID';

SET w_sql_stmt = TRIM(w_sql_stmt) CONCAT ' WHERE RANKS.NAME = ' CONCAT
TRIM(w_teacher_rank);

PREPARE teacher_stmt FROM w_sql_stmt;

OPEN teacher_cursor;

FETCH teacher_cursor INTO w_calculated_cost;

CLOSE teacher_cursor;
```

All the steps I described previously regarding the creation, preparation, and use of a cursor were taken here. Let's analyze this piece of code, line by line, to see how that was achieved.

The first four lines contain DECLARE statements, but not "regular" ones: the two lines include a DEFAULT keyword, similar to the one used in a CREATE statement, to provide a default value for the variables. This is the same as RPG's INZ keyword in a variable declaration. The third line defines a 2,000-character VARCHAR. Why so big, you ask? Well, dynamic SELECT statements, particularly in databases with complex structures, can get pretty long. In our case, 2,000 characters is overkill, but sometimes it's not enough. Just so you know, you're allowed to use up to 2Mb to write a "text string version" of a dynamic SQL statement.

Finally, the fourth line defines the cursor. Note that it mentions a teacher_stmt, which I haven't defined. This may seem a little odd at first, but it's related to the PREPARE statement. I mentioned earlier that the order of the DECLARE CURSOR and PREPARE statements is irrelevant, as long as they use the same names. In this case, the PREPARE statement, almost at the bottom of this piece of code, defines the prepared statement as teacher_stmt, so this would work just fine.

The next three lines, containing the SET statements, are used to compose the dynamic SQL statement. Since I can't use my regular indentation in a string, I prefer to use several SET statements to separate the different parts of the SELECT statement. This way it's easier to find and change the FROM or WHERE clauses without having to change the whole thing. Note that the last of the three lines ends with the concatenation of the w_teacher_rank variable to the statement. I'm actually concatenating the value of the variable, so I could use 'Dark Master' instead of TRIM(w_teacher_rank). This is just to show you one way to use variables in dynamic SQL statements. The other way involves parameter markers and is shown in the next example.

Before getting to that, let's finish examining our current example. The next two lines of this code sample—the PREPARE and OPEN lines—follow the generic syntax mentioned earlier. The PREPARE statement transforms the text string version of the dynamic statement into something the database engine can work with. The OPEN statement simply takes the compiled SQL cursor and "opens it for business." Then the FETCH line reads the sum into the w_calculated_cost local variable, and the CLOSE line simply closes the cursor, freeing up the allocated resources.

Now let's change the scenario a bit. Imagine that I have a baseline for the bonus, created dynamically using a certain teacher rank, defined and stored in a w_base_rank variable, and I want to use the same statement to calculate the bonus for several different teacher ranks, using input parameters or local variables. Instead of creating and preparing several cursors, I can reuse the same one as in the previous example, with a minor change: I'll simply replace the variable name (the last concatenation of the third SET line) with a parameter marker and use the appropriate variable in the OPEN statement. Here's a shortened version of how it could be done:

```
DECLARE w_calculated_cost DECIMAL(11, 2) DEFAULT 0;
DECLARE w_base_cost DECIMAL(11, 2) DEFAULT 0;
DECLARE w_base_rank VARCHAR(50) DEFAULT 'Assistant Teacher';
DECLARE w_teacher_rank VARCHAR(50) DEFAULT 'Dark Master';
DECLARE w_sql_stmt VARCHAR(2000);
DECLARE teacher_cursor CURSOR FOR teacher_stmt;
SET w_sql_stmt = 'SELECT SUM(TEACHERS.SALARY * .1) FROM UMADB_CHP5.TBL_
TEACHERS TEACHERS';
SET w_sql_stmt = TRIM(w_sql_stmt) CONCAT ' INNER JOIN UMADB_CHP5.
TBL_TEACHER_RANKS RANKS ON TEACHERS.TBL_TEACHER_RANKSTEACHER_RANK_ID =
RANKS.TEACHER_RANK_ID';
SET w_sql_stmt = TRIM(w_sql_stmt) CONCAT ' WHERE RANKS.NAME = ?';
PREPARE teacher_stmt FROM w_sql_stmt;
```

Continued

```
OPEN teacher_cursor USING w_base_rank;

FETCH teacher_cursor INTO w_base_cost;

CLOSE teacher_cursor;

/* Reuse the cursor, by opening it again using a different variable */

OPEN teacher_cursor USING w_teacher_rank;

FETCH teacher_cursor INTO w_calculated_cost;

CLOSE teacher_cursor;
```

You'll notice similarities to the previous example: the declarations are nearly the same, and the composition of the SELECT statement's text is almost the same; the only difference is in the final part, in which I've replaced the variable name with a parameter marker. But there are also a couple important differences: I've added a second OPEN/FETCH/CLOSE set of operations, and the OPEN statements now include a USING keyword (because of the parameter marker in the SELECT statement). This is a simple example of the "write once/use many" flexibility I mentioned earlier: by using a parameter marker and two sets of OPEN/FETCH/CLOSE operations, I was able to reuse the same dynamic SELECT statement.

Dynamic UPDATE and DELETE Statements

With a little help from cursors, I've shown you how to create and use dynamic SELECT statements, so now let's do the same for other SQL statements. Even though I'll provide examples of UPDATE and DELETE statements, you can use this technique with nearly all non-SELECT SQL statements. The SELECT is the most complicated because it requires using a cursor. Other statements don't need the whole DECLARE/PREPARE/OPEN/FETCH/CLOSE sequence of operations. Instead of that long and sometimes hard-to-follow structure, you just need to prepare and execute the SQL statement, using (you guessed it) SQL/PSM's PREPARE and EXECUTE statements.

You already know the PREPARE statement from the previous section, so I'll just focus on the EXECUTE. Its syntax is somewhat similar to the OPEN statement, in the sense that it can include the USING keyword to handle parameter markers:

```
EXECUTE <prepared statement name>
```

Or, if the prepared statement includes parameter markers:

```
EXECUTE <prepared statement name> USING <variable 1>, <variable 2> ...
```

However, if the SQL statement you want to run doesn't require the flexibility provided by the parameter markers functionality, you can even use a single SQL/PSM statement to run it. The EXECUTE IMMEDIATE statement combines the functions associated with PREPARE and EXECUTE statements into a single step. EXECUTE IMMEDIATE's syntax is as follows:

```
EXECUTE IMMEDIATE <variable>
```

Or, if you're running on IBM i 7.2 or later:

```
EXECUTE IMMEDIATE <expression>
```

The *<variable>* this statement is expecting is the text string version of the statement, whereas the *<expression>* is the text of the statement itself. Perhaps it's best to look at an example of both EXECUTE and EXECUTE IMMEDIATE and their variations. Let's start with the EXECUTE:

```
DECLARE w_sql_stmt VARCHAR(2000);
SET w_sql_stmt = 'UPDATE TBL_CLASS_DEFINITION';
SET w_sql_stmt = TRIM(w_sql_stmt) CONCAT ' SET DESCRIPTION = ''A
description for this class will be provided later'' ';
SET w_sql_stmt = TRIM(w_sql_stmt) CONCAT ' WHERE DESCRIPTION = ''N/A''
AND CLASS_ID = 1';
PREPARE class_update FROM w_sql_stmt;
EXECUTE class_update;
```

In this example, I'm issuing an UPDATE statement that could be hard-coded. I could have created a more complex composition, resorting to IF or CASE statements to implement some logic. However, that's not the point of the example; I'll get to that sort of thing later.

I'm simply showing how to use the PREPARE/EXECUTE set of operations without parameter markers. Here's another example of this same set of operations, now using the parameter markers:

```
DECLARE w_sql_stmt VARCHAR(2000);
DECLARE w_class_id INT DEFAULT 1;
SET w_sql_stmt = 'UPDATE TBL_CLASS_DEFINITION';
SET w_sql_stmt = TRIM(w_sql_stmt) CONCAT ' SET DESCRIPTION = ''A
description for this class will be provided later'' ';
SET w_sql_stmt = TRIM(w_sql_stmt) CONCAT ' WHERE DESCRIPTION = ''N/A''
AND CLASS_ID = ?';
PREPARE class_update FROM w_sql_stmt;
EXECUTE class_update USING w_class_id;
```

The main difference is the declaration and use of the w_class_id variable and the slight change in the text-string version of the statement. As I said before, if you don't need parameter markers, you can use the simpler EXECUTE IMMEDIATE SQL/PSM statement. Here's the same example using the EXECUTE IMMEDIATE statement:

```
DECLARE w_sql_stmt VARCHAR(2000);
SET w_sql_stmt = 'UPDATE TBL_CLASS_DEFINITION';
SET w_sql_stmt = TRIM(w_sql_stmt) CONCAT ' SET DESCRIPTION = ''A
description for this class will be provided later'' ';
SET w_sql_stmt = TRIM(w_sql_stmt) CONCAT ' WHERE DESCRIPTION = ''N/A''
AND CLASS_ID = 1';
EXECUTE IMMEDIATE w_sql_stmt;
```

This piece of code uses a variable to compose and store the SQL statement to be executed. However, because there's no need to use a cursor, a much simpler statement is required to actually execute the composed statement. But if you're running V7.2 or later, this can get even shorter, because you're allowed to place the text string directly in the execution statement:

```
EXECUTE IMMEDIATE 'UPDATE TBL_CLASS_DEFINITION SET DESCRIPTION = ''A
description for this class will be provided later'' WHERE DESCRIPTION =
''N/A'' AND CLASS_ID = 1';
```

There's something I've neglected to mention, but it's kind of important, particularly in this last example: if you need to include single quotes in the middle of the text version of the SQL statement, you can do so by using two single quote characters (") instead of just one. This will be automatically converted when the statement is prepared.

Compound Statements

SQL/PSM's standards specify that an SQL routine (a user-defined function or a stored procedure) consist of a single SQL statement. However, as you've probably realized by now, SQL/PSM has so much to offer that it would be a waste to try to write SPs with a single line. A compound statement is another way to write an SQL routine. Instead of having a single SQL statement, a compound statement is more like a structured, high-level language program, with several sections, delimited by the BEGIN and END statements.

Let's start by reviewing the structure of a compound statement:

```
BEGIN <atomic setting>
<variable declarations>
<cursor declarations>
<condition handler declarations>
<SQL statement list/procedure logic>
END
```

As I said before, the compound statement is delimited by the BEGIN and END statements. Note that the BEGIN line has an additional *<atomic setting>* specification. The possible values are NOT ATOMIC, which is the default value, and ATOMIC. When you specify ATOMIC, the whole compound statement will be placed in a kind of all-or-nothing execution mode. In other words, if the compound statement includes DML lines, such as INSERT, UPDATE, or DELETE statements, they take effect in the database only if all are executed without producing errors. If just one of them produces an error, the database engine simply wipes clean the changes performed thus far. It's an all-or-nothing execution: either all statements are executed successfully, or all of them are undone and the database is returned to its state before the compound statement was executed. Just so you know, the proper name for this mechanism is *commitment control*. I won't discuss commitment control in this book, but there's a lot of good literature about it, such as Jim Cooper's *Database Design and SQL for DB2* (*https://www.mc-store.com/products/ database-design-and-sql-for-db2*).

The *<variable declarations>* section represents the several DECLARE statements used to define local variables. I explained the syntax of the DECLARE statement in the Variable Declaration section earlier in this chapter, so I won't go over that again. Similarly, I won't go into details about the *<cursor declarations>* section, which represents the cursor declarations needed for your dynamic SELECT statements, as I discussed it a couple of sections ago. However, the *<condition handler declarations>* refers to something I haven't explained yet; actually, I'll discuss it in the next section. For now, I'll tell you that it is related to SQL/PSM's error handling. You'll know more in a while .... Finally, the *<SQL statement list/procedure logic>* section corresponds to the "regular" SQL statements (DML and DDL) and the SQL/PSM-specific statements discussed earlier in this chapter.

Together, these sections form the body of the SQL/PSM routines I'll discuss in the next chapters: stored procedures, user-defined functions, and triggers. Before getting to that, though, I need to discuss a fundamental but unfortunately often-neglected part of the SQL/PSM language: error handling.

Error Handling

SQL/PSM statements are incredibly powerful and flexible, but they are not entirely "safe": a typing error or database problem will cause your beautiful code to blow up in your face, unexpectedly and uncontrollably. Even though it's fairly easy to test a compound statement's instructions one by one (they are mostly "regular" SQL statements, after all), things might not go according to plan when the said statements are executed together, inside a compound statement. That's why you need error handling. SQL/PSM's error handling is peculiar and takes a bit of time to get used to, but it's flexible enough. Let's explore its components, starting with a few basic notions.

SQLSTATE and SQLCODE

The SQLCODE and SQLSTATE global variables provide the same information, but in different ways and data formats: SQLCODE is an INTEGER, whereas SQLSTATE is a CHAR(5). While it is not necessary to know all the possible SQLSTATE and SQLCODE values, it is important to understand their general format and which of the codes represent the most common set of errors. These variables' values are automatically updated by the database engine after the execution of each statement.

If you've ever used embedded SQL in RPG programs, you're probably no stranger to SQLCODE, and you know that if everything goes according to plan (without any errors or warnings), when the embedded statement is executed, SQLCODE is set to 0. Otherwise, depending on the type of occurrence, SQLCODE will be a positive or negative number. Negative numbers indicate errors, while positive numbers are used to represent warnings. The same happens during the execution of an SQL/PSM routine: after each statement is executed, both SQLCODE and SQLSTATE are updated.

Each SQLCODE that the database engine is able to recognize has a corresponding message in the message file QSQLMSG. The message identifier for any SQLCODE is constructed by appending the absolute value (five digits) of the SQLCODE to SQ and changing the third character to L if the first character of the SQLCODE is 0. For example, if the SQLCODE is 40050, the message identifier is SQ40050. If the SQLCODE is -0321, the message identifier is SQL0321. Finally, if the SQLCODE is a three-digit positive number, a zero is added before the first digit to make the necessary four-digit code. For example, if the SQLCODE is 123, the message identifier is SQL0123. This will allow you to rapidly identify the message associated with an SQLCODE.

SQLSTATE is not a DB2 for i–specific variable; quite the contrary: the SQLSTATE definitions are the same for all databases and are based on the ISO/ANSI standards, thus providing portability. SQLSTATE is also the basis for the error handlers in SQL/PSM, which makes them more important for this discussion.

Within the SQLSTATE definition is a set of reserved areas of class codes (the first two characters) that can be used by applications, allowing some degree of communication and control over the application-wide error handling. However, this doesn't mean that you can go ahead and define whichever SQLSTATE values you'd like for your application.

Remember that SQLSTATE is CHAR(5). SQLSTATE's internal structure is comprised of classes, represented by the first character, and subclasses, represented by the last three characters. Naturally, some of these are reserved for internal use of the database manager. Even so, this still allows for a large number of possible combinations, but there are a couple rules that you must follow:

- Classes with the characters 7 through 9 or I through Z can be defined for use in your application. Any subclass for these classes can be defined by the programmer. For example, SQLSTATEs '70000' and '98765' could be defined to convey a certain meaning to the application.

- SQLSTATE classes that begin with the characters 0 through 6 or A through H are reserved for the database manager. Within these classes, subclasses that begin with the characters 0 through H are also restricted. This means that the remaining subclasses (those that begin with the characters I through Z) can be defined by you.

You can find the complete list of SQLSTATE codes for version 7.2 at *http://www.ibm.com/support/knowledgecenter/ssw_ibm_i_72/rzala/rzalaclass.htm*. Beware, it's a long table! However, in general terms, an SQLSTATE that starts with '00' represents success, while '01' is a warning, and '02' means no data.

Handling SQLSTATEs and SQLCODEs Dynamically with Condition Handlers

As a programmer, you know that the perfect program is a utopian idea. The more complex a program gets, the better the chances of something having undesired behaviors. SQLSTATEs and SQLCODEs allow you to "catch" these unexpected situations and act accordingly. This is achieved using two SQL/PSM constructs: condition declarations and condition handlers.

A *condition declaration* provides a way to declare a meaningful condition name for a corresponding SQLSTATE value. Sometimes the person in charge of maintaining the SQL/PSM routine doesn't need to know what SQLSTATE "22003" means (actually, it means that a numeric value is out of range). Instead of forcing people to refer to that huge SQLSTATE codes table I mentioned earlier, you can provide a nice, descriptive name for the codes you want to handle. In order to do that, you need to declare a *condition handler*. The syntax of this statement is quite simple:

```
DECLARE <name> CONDITION FOR '<SQLSTATE>';
```

where *<name>* is a meaningful name given to the condition and <SQLSTATE> is the five-character SQLSTATE value. This means that declaring a condition handler for my numeric value out-of-range condition would be something like this:

```
DECLARE Number_Out_Of_Range CONDITION FOR '22003';
```

This solves half the problem: a nice name doesn't actually do anything by itself. The next step is writing the condition handler: the piece of code that will be executed whenever a statement's execution in the SQL/PSM routine set the SQLSTATE to the declared value. I'll get to that in a minute; first let's review the condition handler syntax:

```
DECLARE <type> HANDLER FOR <condition> <statement>
```

This is slightly more complex than the condition definition, so let's dissect it bit by bit. The *<condition>* is the name that was previously defined in a condition declaration, and the *<statement>* is the code to be executed. You can use a single statement or a compound statement to properly handle the SQLSTATE that triggered the condition handler. Condition handlers are very important to a fully functioning SQL/PSM object, such as a procedure. In fact, whenever an error occurs, the running SQL/PSM object will terminate, and control is passed to the calling application, unless a condition handler is defined—a bit like a *PSSR subroutine in an RPG program, or a try/catch block in Java.

What happens after the *<statement>* is executed depends on the *<type>* defined for the condition handler. There are three possibilities:

- CONTINUE—When this condition is specified, after the *<statement>* section of the handler is successfully executed, control is returned to the SQL statement following the one that raised the exception.

- EXIT—EXIT has a similar behavior to CONTINUE, except it terminates the execution and, you guessed it, leaves the compound statement instead of resuming on the next instruction.

- UNDO—When UNDO is specified, all the statements already executed within the current compound statement are undone. Naturally, this is only possible if the compound statement is defined with the ATOMIC keyword.

Continuing with our little example, if I wanted to log the numeric range error to a hypothetical table named TBL_ERROR_LOG and exit the compound statement, I'd write something like this:

```
DECLARE EXIT HANDLER FOR Number_Out_Of_Range
INSERT INTO TBL_ERROR_LOG
VALUES('Numeric out of range at xxxx');
```

Note that I could reuse the same handler for multiple conditions, assuming that they were previously defined. Simply write them next to each other in the correct place of the condition handler, separated by commas. For instance, if I wanted to define a more or less generic condition handler to log invalid input values, something that would catch not only numbers out of range but also invalid dates, I'd write the following code:

```
DECLARE Number_Out_Of_Range CONDITION FOR '22003';
DECLARE Invalid_DateTime CONDITION FOR '22008';
DECLARE EXIT HANDLER FOR Number_Out_Of_Range, Invalid_DateTime
INSERT INTO TBL_ERROR_LOG
VALUES('Invalid input on xxx');
```

It's also important to mention that you can write condition handlers for the existing general condition values provided by the database. These will "kick in" if the SQLSTATE value wasn't "caught" by a previously defined handler in the compound statement:

- SQLWARNING—which is used to catch any warnings, meaning all SQLSTATE values starting with '01'

- NOT FOUND—useful for catching "not found" conditions, which are the SQLSTATE values that start with '02'

- SQLEXCEPTION—this one is the general "catch-all condition" for any errors, which are SQLSTATE values starting with anything other than the previously mentioned

SQLSTATEs starting with '01', '02', and the SQLSTATE corresponding to a successful operation ('00').

If I wanted to write a simple, generic handler for all the SQL errors, I could write a condition handler similar to the following:

```
DECLARE EXIT HANDLER FOR SQLEXCEPTION
INSERT INTO TBL_ERROR_LOG
VALUES('An error occurred on routine xxx');
```

If you think this is too generic, which makes it basically useless, think again: there's a way to retrieve additional information about the statement that triggered the SQLEXCEPTION using another SQL/PSM statement: GET DIAGNOSTICS.

Using GET DIAGNOSTICS to Retrieve Additional Data About an SQLSTATE

GET DIAGNOSTICS is like the old lady in the neighborhood, who spends her days by the window and knows everything about everyone. Except that this "old lady" has a goldfish memory: it only knows everything about what just happened. This statement can be used to retrieve a world of information (I'm not exaggerating, as you'll see in a minute) about the statement that was executed before it, or, as shown in the last example of the previous section, about the statement that triggered a condition handler. This statement has a peculiar syntax, because you need to specify a variable name for each piece of information you want to retrieve:

```
GET DIAGNOSTICS <type of information> <variable name> = <keyword>
```

The *<type of information>* may be optional depending on the keyword (more about that shortly), but the variable name and keyword are mandatory. Note that the variable or variables used in the statement must be defined prior to the execution of the statement and must match the keyword output. As you'll see in the first GET DIAGNOSTICS example, presented shortly, a specific keyword requires the receiving variable to have a specific data type and sometimes even a specific size. You can find the complete list of data types for GET DIAGNOSTICS items in table 83 of the *DB2 for i Reference* manual. You'll find a link to the current online version of this manual near the end of this section.

It's also possible to use GET DIAGNOSTICS to obtain information about the connection to the database and even specific information about the condition (SQLSTATE) returned by the statement. I know this may sound confusing, so let's look at an example. Imagine I want to update a teacher's salary, giving him/her a 10 percent raise, and check whether the update was successful, all in one compound statement:

```
BEGIN ATOMIC
        DECLARE REC_COUNT INT DEFAULT 0;
        UPDATE TBL_TEACHERS
            SET SALARY = SALARY * 1.1
            WHERE TEACHER_ID = 123;
        -- Use GET DIAGNOSTICS to check how many rows were affected
        GET DIAGNOSTICS REC_COUNT = ROW_COUNT;
        -- If no row was affected, an error occurred
        IF (REC_COUNT = 0) THEN
            SIGNAL SQLSTATE '75000'
                SET MESSAGE_TEXT = 'Teacher Id not found';
        END IF;
END;
```

In this example, I'm using one of GET DIAGNOSTICS' statement-related keywords—ROW_COUNT—to determine whether an update actually occurred. Note that the statement-related keywords allow me to omit the *<type of information>*. If the variable that stores the row count (REC_COUNT) is equal to zero, that means the update failed. Then an error is raised and the appropriate error text set within the IF statement. I'll explain these error-signaling statements in detail on the next section, so just ignore these two lines for now. The important part is to understand how GET DIAGNOSTICS is being used to retrieve a piece of information—the number of rows affected by the UPDATE statement, in this particular case—and store it in a variable with which you can do a number of things. ROW_COUNT is an example of statement-related information, but there are many others. Here are a few of them:

- COMMAND_FUNCTION—returns the name of the previous SQL statement, using a shortened version of the command name. For instance, a FETCH statement will be returned either as FETCH (for a static SQL FETCH) or DYNAMIC FETCH.

- DB2_GET_DIAGNOSTICS_DIAGNOSTICS—For programmers who are suspicious of everything, DB2_GET_DIAGNOSTICS_DIAGNOSTICS returns any errors or warnings that occurred during the execution of the GET DIAGNOSTICS statement as textual information about the errors or warnings.

- DB2_SQL_ATTR_CURSOR_CAPABILITY—for an OPEN statement, indicates the capability of the cursor (i.e., whether a cursor is read-only, deletable, or updatable) via the following codes:

  ○ R indicates that this cursor can only be used to read.

  ○ D indicates that this cursor can be used to read as well as delete.

  ○ U indicates that this cursor can be used to read, delete, and update.

Although this seems like a lot of information, it's just a tiny bit of what GET DIAGNOSTICS has to offer. These are the statement-related keywords, but there are two other types of information: *connection-related* and *condition-related* data. I have never used the connection-related data in a real-life scenario, so I can't share any practical insights about it. The condition-related data is much more interesting, because it allows you to "look inside" the condition that resulted from the last-executed statement, beyond the SQLSTATE.

For instance, imagine I know that a certain INSERT statement might violate a database constraint (such as a foreign key or unique constraints) and, if that violation occurs, I want to know the name of the constraint that caused it. SQLSTATE doesn't provide this type of information. You'll see an SQLSTATE of class 23 (Integrity Constraint Violation) or 27 (Triggered Data Change Violation), depending on the type of constraint, but that's about it. With the GET DIAGNOSTICS statement shown below, you can store the name of the constraint in a variable and then decide how to proceed. For instance, you can retry the statement with a different value for the offending column or simply log the error and continue:

```
GET DIAGNOSTICS CONDITION 1 VIOLATED_CONSTRAINT = CONSTRAINT_NAME;
```

The CONDITION 1 part is required to specify that the diagnostic information retrieved corresponds to the condition indicated by the SQLSTATE value actually returned by the execution of the previous SQL statement (other than a GET DIAGNOSTICS statement). In other words, it indicates that I'm retrieving information about the first condition that occurred before the GET DIAGNOSTICS statement. Then VIOLATED_CONSTRAINT = CONSTRAINT_NAME tells the database manager that you want to store the name of the constraint that was violated (assuming the SQLSTATE belongs to one of the classes I mentioned earlier) in the VIOLATED_CONSTRAINT variable.

Just like the statement-related diagnostics, the condition-related information "menu" is also vast. That's why I won't list it all here. I'll just mention the options I usually use:

- COLUMN_NAME—If the returned SQLSTATE belongs to class 42 (Syntax Error or Access Rule Violation) and the error was caused by an inaccessible column, the name of the column that caused the error is returned. Otherwise, an empty string is returned.

- CONDITION_IDENTIFIER—If the value of the returned SQLSTATE is 45000, which corresponds to an unhandled user-defined exception, then the condition name of the user-defined exception is returned.

- CONSTRAINT_CATALOG—This is similar to the CONSTRAINT_NAME keyword I mentioned before, but it returns the name of the server that hosts the table containing the constraint that caused the error. Otherwise, an empty string is returned.

- CONSTRAINT_SCHEMA—Similarly, CONSTRAINT_SCHEMA returns the name of the schema of the constraint that caused the error. Otherwise, an empty string is returned.

- CURSOR_NAME—If the returned SQLSTATE is class 24 (Invalid Cursor State), the name of the cursor is returned. Otherwise, the empty string is returned. This is used mainly in error-handling SQL routines to track and log cursor errors for further investigation.

- DB2_MESSAGE_ID1—returns the underlying IBM i CPF escape message that originally caused the error. If an error didn't occur (i.e., a warning SQLSTATE was issued), then an empty string is returned.

- DB2_RETURNED_SQLCODE—returns the corresponding SQLCODE

- MESSAGE_TEXT—contains the message text of the error, warning, or successful completion returned by the last-executed SQL statement. However, if SQLCODE is 0, then an empty string will be returned, even if SQLSTATE contains a warning code.

- RETURNED_SQLSTATE—returns the corresponding SQLSTATE

- TABLE_NAME—This is a tricky one. If the SQLSTATE belongs to classes 09 (Triggered Action Exception), 23 (Integrity Constraint Violation), or 27 (Triggered Data Change Violation) and the constraint that caused the error is a referential, check, or unique constraint, the table name where the constraint resides is returned. Otherwise, if SQLSTATE belongs to classes 42 (Syntax Error or Access Rule Violation) or 44 (WITH CHECK OPTION Violation), then the name of the table that caused the error is returned. For any other SQLSTATE, an empty string is returned.

Finally, you can also retrieve a complete diagnostics string, which indicates that all items that are set for the last SQL statement executed should be combined into one string. The format of this string is a semicolon-separated list of all the available information in the form:

```
item-name=character-form-of-the-item-value;
```

It's important to mention that only items that contain actual diagnostic information are included in the string. There are also no entries in this string for the DB2_GET_DIAGNOSTICS_DIAGNOSTICS and DB2_SQL_NESTING_LEVEL items.

You can find detailed explanations about each of these keywords (and all the others I didn't mention) in the *DB2 for i Reference* manual, available at *http://www.ibm.com/support/knowledgecenter/ssw_ibm_i_72/db2/rbafzintro.htm*.

The Final Piece of SQL/PSM's Error Handling: SIGNAL, RESIGNAL, and RETURN

Now that you know how to retrieve SQLSTATEs and SQLCODEs, and retrieve detailed information about what happened with GET DIAGNOSTICS, it's time to learn how to generate your own SQLSTATEs, thus providing the application with a powerful error-handling mechanism. Let's return to the example from the beginning of the previous section:

```
BEGIN ATOMIC
        DECLARE REC_COUNT INT DEFAULT 0;
        UPDATE TBL_TEACHERS
                SET SALARY = SALARY * 1.1
                WHERE TEACHER_ID = 123;
        -- Use GET DIAGNOSTICS to check how many rows were affected
        GET DIAGNOSTICS REC_COUNT = ROW_COUNT;
        -- If no row was affected, an error occurred
        IF (REC_COUNT = 0) THEN
                SIGNAL SQLSTATE '75000'
                    SET MESSAGE_TEXT = 'Teacher Id not found';
        END IF;
END;
```

You should know by now how most of the compound statement works, so let's just focus on the SIGNAL statement:

SIGNAL SQLSTATE '75000' SET MESSAGE_TEXT = 'Teacher Id not found';

The SIGNAL statement is used to create your own SQLSTATEs or simply set the condition-related items for later retrieval via a GET DIAGNOSTICS statement. In the example above, I'm using both possibilities, by changing whichever error or warning SQLSTATE was set by the UPDATE statement (assuming it failed and resulted in a ROW_COUNT not equal to zero) to '75000', a user-defined code.

I'm also setting the message text for this error to something that can be shown to the user. This is particularly important for inter-application error handling, where routines call other routines and eventually one of them communicates with the "outside world." It's not helpful to send back a bland and undecipherable technical message or a five-character code that holds no meaning to the end user. Using SIGNAL, you can control the code that's sent back and, most importantly, the additional information that might be used by the calling program to better react to the current state of affairs.

Before I get to that, though, let's look at SIGNAL's generic syntax:

```
SIGNAL <SQLSTATE>
SET <one or more condition-related items, separated by commas>;
```

Note that not all GET DIAGNOSTICS condition-related items are available here. You can only set the following items:

- MESSAGE_TEXT—the text message to send back, limited to 1,000 characters
- CONSTRAINT_CATALOG—the name of the database that contains a constraint related to the signaled error or warning
- CONSTRAINT_SCHEMA—the name of the schema that contains the previously mentioned constraint
- CONSTRAINT_NAME—the name of the previously mentioned constraint
- CATALOG_NAME—the name of the database that contains a table or view related to the signaled error or warning
- SCHEMA_NAME—the name of the schema that contains the previously mentioned table
- TABLE_NAME—the name of the previously mentioned table
- COLUMN_NAME—the name of a column in the previously mentioned table
- CURSOR_NAME—the name of a cursor related to the signaled error or warning
- CLASS_ORIGIN—the string that indicates the origin of the SQLSTATE class related to the signaled error or warning
- SUBCLASS_ORIGIN—the string that indicates the origin of the SQLSTATE subclass related to the signaled error or warning

Of all these, I usually use the MESSAGE_TEXT, CONSTRAINT_NAME, TABLE_NAME, and CURSOR_NAME. Just a final note regarding the value of these items: you can also use a variable instead of a fixed value, as long as it has the appropriate data type and size.

Let's look at another example, this time including a variable and the RESIGNAL statement, which I'll explain in a minute:

```
BEGIN
DECLARE not_found_text CHAR(70);
DECLARE CONTINUE HANDLER FOR SQLSTATE '38TNF' 1
BEGIN
INSERT INTO TBL_ERROR_LOG
 VALUES('Error found on xxxx');
RESIGNAL SQLSTATE '38TNF'
 SET MESSAGE_TEXT = not_found_text;
END;
SET not_found_text = 'Part number not found!';
INSERT INTO TBL_ERROR_LOG
 VALUES('Routine xxx starting');
SIGNAL SQLSTATE '38TNF';
END;
```

In this compound statement, I'm inserting a control record into my error log table, indicating that a certain routine has started. Then I'm raising an error, as the database manager would do if something had gone wrong. I'm signaling a user-defined SQLSTATE, which will be caught by the handler defined in the declarations section of the compound statement. Because I defined a CONTINUE handler specifically for my user-defined SQLSTATE, the "error" is caught and processed there. What will happen is that a statement named RESIGNAL, similar to the SIGNAL statement (RESIGNAL can only be used within condition handlers and can only set the MESSAGE_TEXT), is used to change the message text to the contents of the not_found_text variable, while maintaining the original SQLSTATE. Note that this is an over-simplified example, not really useful in real life. You'll have the opportunity to see the SIGNAL and RESIGNAL statements in action in the next chapters.

In short, you need to remember that the RESIGNAL statement is only allowed inside of a condition handler. It is used to re-signal the error or warning condition that triggered the handler. It returns the SQLSTATE and the message text to the caller.

If the caller is an external program, which will happen many times if you're opening your database to the "outside world," it's common that the external program expects a return code from the call. When a program terminates, it usually returns a code indicating the success (a value of zero) or failure (a negative value, typically -1) of the call. This concept also exists in SQL/PSM, materialized by the aptly named RETURN statement. RETURN's syntax is as simple as it gets:

```
RETURN <integer value>;
```

Easy enough, right? You'll see examples of RETURN, used in stored procedures, in the next chapter. It makes more sense to show examples of this statement in its proper context.

In This Chapter, You've Learned ...

This chapter was a bit different from the previous ones, as it introduced a lot of new concepts almost without hands-on practice. It was a necessary approach, in order to explain the SQL/PSM building blocks that will be used in the next few chapters. Here's a summary of what I've covered here:

- The concept of data-centric programming, which consists of bringing as much code as possible to near or inside the database, making it easier to "open the database to the outside world," as the Dean requested
- SQL/PSM's most important statements, namely:
  - ○ Variable declaration and assignment, using DECLARE and SET, respectively
  - ○ Flow control, resorting to IF and CASE structures
  - ○ Loop control, with LOOP, WHILE, REPEAT, FOR, and the "bail-out" statements ITERATE and LEAVE
  - ○ Dynamic SELECT statements, using cursors and the related statements (DECLARE, OPEN, PREPARE, FETCH, and CLOSE)
  - ○ Other dynamic statements, also using DECLARE and PREPARE, but also EXECUTE and EXECUTE IMMEDIATE
  - ○ Compound statements, one of the most important concepts in SQL/PSM
- Finally, I discussed error handling, using SQLSTATE, SQLCODE, and the creation of more complex handling structures, with the help of condition declarations and handlers, supported by the GET DIAGNOSTICS, SIGNAL, RESIGNAL, and RETURN statements.

7

Creating and Using Stored Procedures

This chapter explains how to use the SQL/PSM building blocks from the previous chapter to create and use stored procedures (SPs). It explains the structure of an SP, its parameters, and their usage, then uses that information to explain how to create cursor-returning SPs. This chapter also explains how to use SPs, particularly those that return cursors. This will require applying most of the concepts from the previous chapter, so it's highly recommended that you read it thoroughly, or reread it, before advancing to this chapter.

Now that we've learned a lot about SQL/PSM, let's put that knowledge to work in our effort to open the database to the outside world! We'll begin by creating a procedure to register a new student. It's simple: the procedure will receive all the necessary data and create two records: a Persons record (if a matching name is not found) and a Students record. You'll see later that there's another way to do this, using a trigger, but for now, an SP will do. However, before we start writing code, there are a few things to talk about. Let's start with a simple way to determine which SQL routine to use in each situation.

SPs, UDFs, and Triggers: When to Use Each

SPs, user-defined functions (UDFs), and triggers are all SQL routines. As such, they share certain similarities, and much of what's said in this chapter about SPs also applies to

UDFs and triggers. This might add to the confusion and leave you wondering why there are three different types of SQL routines. Mainly, it has to do with the way these routines are called:

- *SPs* are called from other programs (for instance, other SPs or external programs, such as a client/server application invoking database code, using the CALL statement). You can't call an SP directly from a "regular" SQL statement, such as a SELECT, INSERT, or UPDATE statement. However, you can call SPs from SQL/PSM code, using the aforementioned CALL statement. SPs are mostly used to return data sets, in the form of cursors, but they can return data as output parameters.

- *UDFs* are almost the exact opposite of SPs: you can only call them from "regular" SQL statements. UDFs return a value themselves (if you remember the canonical definition of procedure versus function, you'll know what I mean) and are typically used to perform complex calculations or check complicated business rules.

- *Triggers* are not like SPs and UDFs—you can't call them directly. They are activated by database events, such as a record insertion, update, or delete. They don't return anything, and they have a very special set of input parameters, as you'll see in a later chapter.

Having said that, let's refocus our discussion on the topic of this chapter and take a look at the SP's structure.

Analyzing the SP's Structure

An SP is SQL's equivalent to an RPG program, in the sense that it can have input and output parameters, it can be called from within another program or from the command line, and, as you'd expect, the structure of an SP is very similar to an RPG program, with some interesting additions. It includes the following components:

- A name
- A set of parameters, although it's possible to create SPs without parameters
- A set of properties, which define the language the procedure is written in and the type of access to data it has, among other things
- A set of options, which define how the procedure is created
- And finally, the body of the procedure, where the actual code resides

What's in a Name?

Let's start with the name. Because SPs are SQL objects, they're not limited to the system's 10-character name limit. The name can be almost as long as you'd like (the maximum length is 128 characters). You can also use the SPECIFIC option to declare a shorter, system-recognizable name, up to 10 characters. This is particularly important because some IBM i products can't handle the SQL name and rely on the system name instead. Short names are also a factor to consider when accessing the system's catalog information. If you have no idea what I'm referring to, don't worry—an entire chapter (Chapter 11) will discuss in depth the trove of information found in the system catalog.

Procedure Parameters

Just like any other program, SPs can have parameters, up to a maximum of 1,024. To define a parameter, you must specify a data type, which can be an SQL or user-defined data type; a name, up to 128 characters; and a type of parameter. The parameter name can be up to 128 characters in length and must be unique within the procedure. A good practice to ensure this uniqueness is to use a naming convention that prevents the possible duplication of the parameter name with a declared variable or table column name. For instance, appending a prefix such as the generic "p_" or the letters "i", "o", or "io" to designate the parameter type is a well-known practice. Imagine a scenario in which a table column named Student_Id is passed as a parameter to the procedure. However, the parameter name could be p_Student_Id, thus avoiding duplication. Even though it's not mandatory, it's a good practice to identify the parameter type upon declaration.

There are three parameter types you can choose: IN, OUT, and INOUT. Here's how they work:

- IN identifies the parameter as an input parameter to the procedure, which means that any changes made to the parameter within the procedure are not available to the calling application when control is returned. If you don't specify a parameter type when declaring it, the default is IN. Speaking of defaults, it's possible to make an input parameter optional, by defining a default value for it, as you'll see later.

- OUT, as the name implies, identifies an output parameter that is returned by the procedure. If a value is not set for the parameter, the null value will be returned.

- Finally, INOUT is a mix of the previous two. If the parameter is not set within the procedure, its input value is returned. However, if a procedure is called using the default value for an INOUT parameter, no value for the parameter is returned.

Using what we've discussed this far, I can write the first few lines of our first procedure:

```
CREATE OR REPLACE PROCEDURE Register_Student (
    -- Mandatory Parameters
    IN p_Name char(60),
    IN p_Date_of_Birth decimal(8, 0),
    IN p_Home_Address char(60),
    IN p_Mobile_Nbr char(15),
    IN p_Email_Address   char(60),
    IN p_Drivers_License char(20),
    IN p_Social_Sec_Nbr   char(11),
    -- Optional Parameters
    IN p_Home_Phone_Nbr char(15) DEFAULT 'N/A'
)
```

This piece of code, together with the SPECIFIC property (that I'll discuss next), defines the *signature* of the procedure, specifying its name and parameters. This concept of procedure signature is important, because you can have different procedures with the same name, as you'll see later.

Now note that there are only input parameters, and one of them is optional. How do I know that? Well, the way to make a parameter optional is to provide a default value for it. In this case, only the p_Home_Phone_Nbr parameter has a default value. If the caller program doesn't provide a value for this parameter in the CALL instruction (as you'll see in the next code example), the 'N/A' value is used, because that's the default defined for the p_Home_Phone_Nbr parameter.

Let's analyze a couple of ways to call this procedure. First, let's omit the optional parameter:

```
CALL Register_Student ( 'Jake Jacobs', 19560101, 'Atlantic Ocean', '555-
123-456', 'jjacobs@gmail.com', 'N/A', '1234567890');
```

If you count the number of parameters in the CALL instruction, you'll see that there's one missing. That's our optional parameter. This is why it's handy to "push" an optional parameter to the end of the list: you can simply omit it in the CALL instruction. However, you can place the optional parameters anywhere in the parameter list, which may cause a problem ... or not?

Imagine for a minute that the home phone number parameter remains optional, but it's now placed in its "natural" position—that is, right after the home address parameter. If I simply omit the home phone number parameter, the database engine will try to use the value specified for the mobile phone number to fill the home phone number parameter, thus "pulling" all parameters back one slot. This will cause an error, because the CALL instruction will be one parameter short. How to circumvent this problem? Use the DEFAULT keyword. This keyword tells the database engine to use the respective parameter's default value, so that you can get away with mixing mandatory and optional parameters.

Here's how the CALL instruction would look if I moved the optional home phone number next to the home address and used the DEFAULT keyword in its place:

```
CALL Register_Student ( 'Jake Jacobs', 19560101, 'Atlantic Ocean',
DEFAULT, '555-123-456', 'jjacobs@gmail.com', 'N/A', '1234567890');
```

This is particularly handy when you can have more than one optional parameter, either at the end or somewhere in the middle of the parameter list. DEFAULT allows you to skip parameters and let the procedure provide a value for them at run time.

But there's yet another way to handle optional parameters mixed with mandatory ones in a parameter list: you can explicitly name some of the parameters with the corresponding parameter name and omit unused parameters. To provide an example for this possibility, let's imagine that all of this procedure's parameters are optional except the student name, date of birth, and email address (I know it's strange, but bear with me). I could call the procedure and provide a boatload of DEFAULTs, or I can use the email address parameter name (p_Email_Address) and specify its value in the CALL instruction, like this:

```
CALL Register_Student ( 'Jake Jacobs', 19560101, p_Email_Address =>
'jjacobs@gmail.com');
```

Note that I provided only the parameter name for the email address parameter, because the other two parameters are "where they should be"—that is, in the proper order in the parameter list. However, because the email address is not the third parameter, I have to explicitly provide its name in the CALL instruction. This provides us with a manageable way to call SPs with multiple optional parameters, regardless of their position in the parameter list. Although this method is not immediately obvious to understand, it's very useful once you get used to it.

Procedure Properties

Now let's take a look at the properties you can use to shape how the procedure will be created. I prefer to call them *properties*, to distinguish this group from the options you can specify on the SET OPTION keyword, which I'll discuss next, but some authors join both the procedure properties and the SET OPTION possible choices under the same hat and call the whole thing *procedure options*. Anyway, I already mentioned the SPECIFIC property, which allows you to indicate a "secondary" name for the procedure, but there's more ... not much more, but several interesting choices:

- LANGUAGE—allows you to specify the programming language used to code the procedure. SQL is the default choice, which means that you can omit this property when creating SQL SPs. I'm saying this because you can create SPs using any high-level programming language supported by the IBM i. My book, *Evolve Your RPG Coding* (*https://www.mc-store.com/products/evolve-your-rpg-coding-move-from-opm-to-ile-and-beyond*), explains how to create RPG SPs and many other related topics in detail.

- SPECIFIC—A specific name may be used in conjunction with the procedure name to uniquely identify the procedure. I explained why this is important earlier in this chapter (read: procedure signature), but note that this can also be helpful when defining multiple procedures with the same name and schema but with a different number of parameters. This is known as "overloading," and I'll discuss it later.

- Also note that when using the OR REPLACE option to replace an existing procedure, as shown in this example, the specific name and procedure name of the new definition must be the same as the specific name and procedure name of the old definition. If they don't match, the database manager won't recognize the procedure you're replacing and will create a new one. Finally, this property provides a system-friendly name for the procedure, so it's important to specify it at all times.

- DETERMINISTIC or NOT DETERMINISTIC—You're probably familiar with the mathematical definition of a deterministic function: given the same input, it always produces the same output. That's also the idea here. The default is NOT DETERMINISTIC, which in practice means given the same input, it's not guaranteed that the same result will be returned. This may sound strange, but keep in mind that a database is a living, constantly changing "thing," which makes it is unlikely that, even with the same inputs the same results would be returned every time.

However, it's important to mention that there's a performance gain when DETERMINISTIC is used, because the database manager doesn't have to call the procedure repeatedly if the parameters' values don't change, because it can "remember" the last answer—and not call your procedure, thus improving performance. If what you need is something that applies a formula to a set of input parameters and returns the result, then a function, discussed in the next chapter, is more suitable.

- SQL DATA properties—These properties specify which SQL statements this and any other routine it calls can execute. These restrictions are also applicable to the expressions used on the DEFAULT keyword. There are four "levels," presented from the most to the least restrictive:

  - MODIFIES SQL DATA—This is the most "liberal" property, as it allows you to execute all the SQL statements supported within a CREATE PROCEDURE statement.

  - READS SQL DATA—As the name implies, only the SQL statements that read data are allowed.

  - CONTAINS SQL—Only simple local statements, such as DECLARE and SET, are allowed.

  - NO SQL—This doesn't quite make sense on an SQL SP. It's used by external SPs, such as the ones created using RPG, to indicate that there's no SQL code in, or called by, the procedure.

- DYNAMIC RESULT SETS *<integer>*—For now, let's just say that this specifies the number of dynamic results sets a procedure can return. The *<integer>* in the definition can assume a number between 0 (the default) and 32,768. I'll discuss result sets and how to use them later in this chapter.

- DEBUG MODE properties—There are several debug modes available, and you can limit their usage with this group of properties. Note that specifying a debug mode requires setting the DBGVIEW option, which can be found under the SET OPTION group (discussed next). The choices at your disposal are the following, from the most to the least restrictive:

  ○ DISABLE DEBUG MODE—Using this property prevents the procedure from being debugged.

  ○ DISALLOW DEBUG MODE—As the name implies, this property prevents the procedure from being debugged, at least until the debug mode is changed.

  ○ ALLOW DEBUG MODE—This means that the procedure is debuggable, at least until the debug mode is changed.

There are a few more, mainly related to commitment control, which I won't discuss at this time. If you're curious and can't wait, check out *Database Design and SQL for DB2* (*https://www.mc-store.com/products/database-design-and-sql-for-db2*), or refer to the *DB2 for i Reference* manual for the rest of the story.

After this subsection, I can add a few more lines of code to our procedure:

```
CREATE OR REPLACE PROCEDURE Register_Student (
    -- Mandatory Parameters
    IN p_Name char(60),
    IN p_Date_of_Birth decimal(8, 0),
    IN p_Home_Address char(60),
    IN p_Mobile_Nbr char(15),
    IN p_Email_Address  char(60),
    IN p_Drivers_License char(20),
    IN p_Social_Sec_Nbr  char(11),
    -- Optional Parameters
                                              Continued
```

```
      IN p_Home_Phone_Nbr char(15) DEFAULT 'N/A'
)
    MODIFIES SQL DATA
    ALLOW DEBUG MODE
    SPECIFIC AddStudent
```

Now the procedure signature is complete, with the procedure name, parameter list, and specific name.

Procedure Options

The procedure options are a group of processing options you can set to change the way the procedure is handled by the pre-compiler during the generation of the program. You have many options at your disposal, but I'll stick to the most commonly used ones. Before explaining what those are, let me take a moment to discuss the syntax. Unlike the procedure properties, which exist "on their own," the procedure options require a SET OPTION prefix. Note that you only need to specify this prefix once, regardless of the number of options you're declaring. Here's the generic syntax:

```
SET OPTION <option 1 name> = <option 1 value>, <option 2 name> = <option
2 value>, ... , <option n name> = <option n value>
```

Personally, I prefer to write one option per line and indent the group, like this:

```
SET OPTION    <option 1 name> = <option 1 value>
, <option 2 name> = <option 2 value>
, ...
, <option n name> = <option n value>
```

Now that that's out of the way, let's take a look at the most commonly used options:

- DBGVIEW—Arguably the most often-used option, DBGVIEW determines the type of debug view that will be made available when you try to debug this SP. Just like its RPG counterpart, it gives you a few choices:

○ *NONE—as the name implies, this means that a debug view will not be generated.

○ *SOURCE—means that the resulting program or service program can be debugged using the SQL statement source. If *SOURCE is specified, the modified source is stored in source file QSQDSRC in the same schema as the created SP, UDF, or trigger.

○ *STMT—indicates that the resulting program or service program can be debugged using program statement numbers and symbolic identifiers.

○ *LIST—specifies that the listing view for the program or service program should be generated.

- USRPRF—Sharing the podium with DBGVIEW, USRPRF is used to specify the user profile that will be used when the SP, UDF, or trigger (in short, the program object) is executed. There are a couple of independent choices available plus a third one that depends on the next option I'll discuss:

○ *USER—The profile of the user running the program object is used.

○ *OWNER—The user profiles of both the program owner and the program user are used when the program is run.

○ *NAMING—The value chosen for this option is based on the previous options, and depends on the naming convention used. If the naming convention is IBM i's native, then the assumed value for the user profile is *USER; if the naming convention is SQL's standard, then the assumed value is *OWNER. Note that you're not allowed to specify the NAMING option on SQL routines, only on external SPs.

- DYNUSRPRF—This can be seen as an extension of USRPRF, because it extends the authorities defined by the USRPRF option to dynamic SQL statements. DYNUSRPRF's choices are very similar to USRPRF, with the exception of the *NAMING choice, which doesn't exist for this option.

- DATFMT—If you work in an international environment, such as a multinational company, date and time formats can be a nightmare. This option allows you to take control of how the date result columns are output. I'll be talking about the time result columns in a minute. Note that DATFMT also impacts the way the date format validation works for input date strings, because it's used to determine whether the specified date is in a valid format. The following choices are available:

- ○ *JOB—The format specified for the job is used. Use the DSPJOB (Display Job) CL command to determine the current date format for the job.

- ○ *ISO—The International Organization for Standardization (ISO) date format (yyyy-mm-dd) is used.

- ○ *EUR—The European date format (dd.mm.yyyy) is used.

- ○ *USA—The United States date format (mm/dd/yyyy) is used.

- ○ *JIS—The Japanese Industrial Standard date format (yyyy-mm-dd) is used.

- ○ *MDY—The date format (mm/dd/yy) is used.

- ○ *DMY—The date format (dd/mm/yy) is used.

- ○ *YMD—The date format (yy/mm/dd) is used.

- ○ *JUL—The Julian date format (yy/ddd) is used.

- DATSEP—To further customize the date format of the outputted date columns, DATSEP offers a handful of choices you can select in order to indicate which separator character will be used:

  - ○ *SLASH or '/'—a slash character (/) is used.

  - ○ *PERIOD or '.'—a period (.) is used.

  - ○ *COMMA or ','—a comma (,) is used.

  - ○ *DASH or '-'—a dash (-) is used.

  - ○ *BLANK or ' '—a blank space ( ) is used.

  - ○ *JOB—The job's date separator is used. As mentioned before, you can check which character is used in this case via a CL command.

- TIMFMT—specifies the format used when accessing time result columns. All output time fields are returned in the specified format. For input time strings, the specified value is used to determine whether the time is specified in a valid format. The available choices are somewhat similar to the ones DATFMT offers:

  - ○ *ISO—The International Organization for Standardization (ISO) time format (hh.mm.ss) is used.

  - ○ *EUR—The European time format (hh.mm.ss) is used.

- ○ *USA—The United States time format (hh:mm *xx*) is used, where *xx* is AM or PM.

- ○ *JIS—The Japanese Industrial Standard time format (hh:mm:ss) is used.

- ○ *HMS—The (hh:mm:ss) format is used.

- TIMSEP—Just as DATSEP allows you to specify which separator character should be used for date output columns, TIMSEP does the same for time output columns. The choices it offers are also similar:

- ○ *COLON or ':'—a colon (:) is used;

- ○ *PERIOD or '.'—a period (.) is used.

- ○ *COMMA or ','—a comma (,) is used.

- ○ *BLANK or ' '—a blank space ( ) is used.

- ○ *JOB—The job's time separator is used. As mentioned before, you can check which character is used in this case via a CL command.

There are many more options, which will not be covered by this book. Others, like CLOSQLCSR, for instance, will be explained later in this chapter, along with examples of cursor-returning SPs. You can access the full list of procedure options in the *DB2 for i Reference* manual.

It's now time to update our little SP example with a few options:

```
CREATE OR REPLACE PROCEDURE Register_Student (
    -- Mandatory Parameters
    IN p_Name char(60),
    IN p_Date_of_Birth decimal(8, 0),
    IN p_Home_Address char(60),
    IN p_Mobile_Nbr char(15),
    IN p_Email_Address   char(60),
    IN p_Drivers_License char(20),
    IN p_Social_Sec_Nbr  char(11),
                                                    Continued
```

```
    -- Optional Parameters
    IN p_Home_Phone_Nbr char(15) DEFAULT 'N/A'
)
    MODIFIES SQL DATA
    ALLOW DEBUG MODE
    SPECIFIC AddStudent
    SET OPTION USRPRF = *OWNER
```

Procedure Body

Finally, the last and probably the most important part of a SP's structure, the *procedure body* can be composed of a single SQL statement, such as SELECT, UPDATE, or DELETE, or a compound statement instead, as discussed in Chapter 6. The other option is to create an external SP—a SP written in RPG, C, or another supported high-level language. This last option is discussed at length in the book *Evolve Your RPG Coding*, so I won't go into details about it here. Instead, let's apply the SQL/PSM goodies explained in Chapter 6 to create a proper Register_Student SP.

Creating Your First Stored Procedure

Now that you know the structure of a SP, let's build upon the example from the previous section, by providing a simple two-table insertion. As you might recall from Chapter 5, the student data is actually distributed between the Students table, which contains the ID column that provides the key to link to other tables, and the Persons table, which contains the students' personal data. If you were creating a student's data "by hand," you'd simply insert a record in the Persons table, make a note of the newly generated Person_Id, and use it to create a new Students table record.

From this point on, I'll be using the schema created for Chapter 5 as the base upon which the successive versions of the SPs, UDFs, and triggers will be built. If you want to follow along using a hands-on approach, be sure to download and restore the appropriate source code (you can download the code on the book's page at *https://www.mc-store.com/ products/sql-for-ibm-i-a-database-modernization-guide*). Having said that, we're ready to start, now with a full-fledged procedure:

```
CREATE OR REPLACE PROCEDURE UMADB_CHP5.Register_Student_v1 (
   -- Mandatory Parameters
   IN p_Name char(60),
   IN p_Date_of_Birth decimal(8, 0),
   IN p_Home_Address char(60),
   IN p_Mobile_Nbr char(15),
   IN p_Email_Address   char(60),
   IN p_Drivers_License char(20),
   IN p_Social_Sec_Nbr  char(11),
   -- Optional Parameters
   IN p_Home_Phone_Nbr char(15) DEFAULT 'N/A'
)
   MODIFIES SQL DATA
   ALLOW DEBUG MODE
   SPECIFIC AddStudent
   SET OPTION USRPRF = *OWNER

   BEGIN

      DECLARE W_PERSON_ID integer;
      -- Create the Persons' record
      INSERT INTO UMADB_CHP5.TBL_PERSONS
         (NAME, DATE_OF_BIRTH, HOME_ADDRESS, HOME_PHONE_NBR, MOBILE_NBR,
EMAIL_ADDRESS, DRIVERS_LICENSE, SOCIAL_SEC_NBR)
         VALUES (P_NAME, P_DATE_OF_BIRTH, P_HOME_ADDRESS, P_HOME_PHONE_
NBR, P_MOBILE_NBR, P_EMAIL_ADDRESS, P_DRIVERS_LICENSE, P_SOCIAL_SEC_NBR)
         ;

      -- Retrieve the newly created Person_Id
      SELECT PERSON_ID INTO W_PERSON_ID
        FROM UMADB_CHP5.TBL_PERSONS
        WHERE NAME = P_NAME
        ;
```

Continued

```
     -- Create the Students' record
     INSERT INTO UMADB_CHP5.TBL_STUDENTS
       (TBL_PERSONSPERSON_ID)
       VALUES (W_PERSON_ID)
     ;


   END;
```

This will create a new record in the Persons table, retrieve the newly created person ID, and use it to create the new Students table record. In other words, this will create the Jake Jacobs person and student records. Even though this works, it's not very safe, as I'll explain in a minute. Now I can call it from an SQL command line, filling in the necessary information, like this:

```
CALL UMADB_CHP5.Register_Student_v1 ( 'Jake Jacobs', 19560101, 'Atlantic
Ocean', '555-123-456', 'jjacobs@gmail.com', 'N/A', '1234567890', 'N/A');
```

Just try to call the SP twice with the same parameters, and you'll get errors. This happens because I'm not checking whether a person with that name already exists in the Persons table. (Recall that I defined the Name column of the Persons table as unique, back in Chapter 5.) As you should know by now, I can use "regular" SQL statements along with SQL/PSM statements, which means I can count how many records with a certain name exist in the Persons table, and, if the result is zero (or in other words, a record with that name doesn't exist), I can safely insert the Persons record.

Even though there's no check in place to prevent the creation of two student records for the same person (not yet, anyway, because I'll address this problem later), I can apply the same reasoning and also check, via a count, whether a student record already exists. This may sound a bit confusing, so it's best to take a look at the code below and then reread the last few lines:

```
CREATE OR REPLACE PROCEDURE UMADB_CHP5.Register_Student_v2 (
   -- Mandatory Parameters
                                                          Continued
```

```
   IN p_Name char(60),
   IN p_Date_of_Birth decimal(8, 0),
   IN p_Home_Address char(60),
   IN p_Mobile_Nbr char(15),
   IN p_Email_Address   char(60),
   IN p_Drivers_License char(20),
   IN p_Social_Sec_Nbr  char(11),
   -- Optional Parameters
   IN p_Home_Phone_Nbr char(15) DEFAULT 'N/A'
)
   MODIFIES SQL DATA
   ALLOW DEBUG MODE
   SPECIFIC AddStudent
   SET OPTION USRPRF = *OWNER

   BEGIN

      DECLARE W_PERSON_ID integer;

      -- Check if a Persons record exists for this student's name
      IF (SELECT COUNT(*) FROM UMADB_CHP5.TBL_PERSONS WHERE NAME = P_
NAME) = 0 THEN
      -- If it doesn't, create the Persons record
         INSERT INTO UMADB_CHP5.TBL_PERSONS
            (NAME, DATE_OF_BIRTH, HOME_ADDRESS, HOME_PHONE_NBR, MOBILE_
NBR, EMAIL_ADDRESS, DRIVERS_LICENSE, SOCIAL_SEC_NBR)
            VALUES (P_NAME, P_DATE_OF_BIRTH, P_HOME_ADDRESS, P_HOME_PHONE_
NBR, P_MOBILE_NBR, P_EMAIL_ADDRESS, P_DRIVERS_LICENSE, P_SOCIAL_SEC_NBR)
            ;
      END IF;

      -- Retrieve the Person_Id for the input parameter P_NAME
      SELECT PERSON_ID INTO W_PERSON_ID
       FROM UMADB_CHP5.TBL_PERSONS
```

Continued

```
        WHERE NAME = P_NAME

    ;


    -- Check if a Students record exists for this person's id
    IF (SELECT COUNT(*) FROM UMADB_CHP5.TBL_STUDENTS WHERE TBL_
PERSONSPERSON_ID = W_PERSON_ID) = 0 THEN
        -- If it doesn't, create the Students' record
        INSERT INTO UMADB_CHP5.TBL_STUDENTS
        (TBL_PERSONSPERSON_ID)
        VALUES (W_PERSON_ID)
        ;
    END IF;


END;
```

This new version of the SP is slightly safer than the previous one: at least you don't get
duplicate records in the Persons table. However, if something goes wrong with the SELECT
COUNT... statements, the SP will still return errors. I discussed a better way to handle
errors in Chapter 6: using error conditions and handlers. Let's put them into practice, with
a very simple check. I'll look for duplicate records in the Persons table, by defining a
condition for the duplicate key error (SQLSTATE '23505') and writing a condition handler
for that error, stating that the execution should continue after the statement that produced
the error. Here's version three of the SP with these changes:

```
CREATE OR REPLACE PROCEDURE UMADB_CHP5.Register_Student_v3 (
    -- Mandatory Parameters
    IN p_Name char(60),
    IN p_Date_of_Birth decimal(8, 0),
    IN p_Home_Address char(60),
    IN p_Mobile_Nbr char(15),
    IN p_Email_Address   char(60),
    IN p_Drivers_License char(20),
    IN p_Social_Sec_Nbr   char(11),
                                                    Continued
```

```
    -- Optional Parameters
    IN p_Home_Phone_Nbr char(15) DEFAULT 'N/A'
)

    MODIFIES SQL DATA
    ALLOW DEBUG MODE
    SPECIFIC AddStudent
    SET OPTION USRPRF = *OWNER

    BEGIN
        DECLARE DuplicateKey CONDITION FOR SQLSTATE '23505';
        DECLARE DUMMY_VAR INTEGER DEFAULT 0;

        DECLARE W_PERSON_ID integer;

        DECLARE CONTINUE HANDLER FOR DuplicateKey SET DUMMY_VAR = 0;

        -- Create the Persons record without prior checks
        -- If a duplicate key error occurs, the continue handler will take
care of it
        INSERT INTO UMADB_CHP5.TBL_PERSONS
        (NAME, DATE_OF_BIRTH, HOME_ADDRESS, HOME_PHONE_NBR, MOBILE_NBR,
EMAIL_ADDRESS, DRIVERS_LICENSE, SOCIAL_SEC_NBR)
        VALUES (P_NAME, P_DATE_OF_BIRTH, P_HOME_ADDRESS, P_HOME_PHONE_
NBR, P_MOBILE_NBR, P_EMAIL_ADDRESS, P_DRIVERS_LICENSE, P_SOCIAL_SEC_NBR)
        ;

        -- Retrieve the Person_Id for the input parameter P_NAME
        SELECT PERSON_ID INTO W_PERSON_ID
        FROM UMADB_CHP5.TBL_PERSONS
        WHERE NAME = P_NAME
        ;

        -- Checking for duplicate keys won't work here, because the
foreign key doesn't have to be unique
        -- Check if a Students record exists for this person's id
```

Continued

```
        IF (SELECT COUNT(*) FROM UMADB_CHP5.TBL_STUDENTS WHERE TBL_
PERSONSPERSON_ID = W_PERSON_ID) = 0 THEN
        -- If it doesn't, create the Students' record
            INSERT INTO UMADB_CHP5.TBL_STUDENTS
            (TBL_PERSONSPERSON_ID)
            VALUES (W_PERSON_ID)
            ;
        END IF;

    END;
```

The DuplicateKey condition in conjunction with the continue handler defined near the top of the procedure ensure that all duplicate key (and similar) errors are caught. I could define a global error handler, but that would require further analysis and careful implementation. I'll leave that for later. Instead, let me explain why I still need the second IF statement.

At this moment, if I insert a second student record with the same person ID, no errors will occur. This is not what we'd expect, because from a logical point of view, it doesn't make sense to have more than one student record for each person record. However, we didn't "tell" the database that this one-to-one relationship has to be enforced. This is something we'll do in a later chapter. For now, we must live with the IF statement check.

I'm bringing this up again because it's a very common situation that I've encountered many times. It's usually supposed to be a temporary measure, but it has a way of becoming permanent—and this is a risk. The bottom line here is simple: using SELECT statements to do this type of check is "a" solution; it's not "the" solution. Proper database design, with relationship enforcement via constraints, is the only way to ensure that you'll have no surprises when it comes to this type of thing.

Time for Some Practice

Now that you've seen how to create an SP, it's your turn to create one from scratch. Well, not exactly from scratch, because I'll provide the procedure signature, and you can use the Register_Student_v3 as a template.

I'd like you to create a procedure to register courses, similar to the Register_Student_v3. The SP should create a Course record, if the course name doesn't exist already in the Courses table. But that's not all! Courses belong to Departments, so you'll need to get the Department ID from the Departments table, using the department name provided in the input parameters. If the provided department name doesn't exist, return the user-defined SQLSTATE '70000' with the MESSAGE_TEXT = 'Invalid Department Name'.

Here are a few hints. The first relates to the use of user-defined SQLSTATES: I explained them in Chapter 6, where you'll find a SIGNAL instruction example that fits like a glove in this SP.

Second, here are the SP's signature and properties:

```
CREATE OR REPLACE PROCEDURE UMADB_CHP5.Register_Course (
    -- Mandatory Parameters
    IN p_Name char(60),
    IN p_Description char(100),
    IN p_Course_Director_Teacher_Id integer DEFAULT 0,
    IN p_Course_TA_Teacher_Id integer DEFAULT 0,
    IN p_Department_Name char(60)
)
    MODIFIES SQL DATA
    ALLOW DEBUG MODE
    SPECIFIC AddCourse
    SET OPTION USRPRF = *OWNER
```

Finally, a couple of CALL examples:

```
CALL UMADB_CHP5.Register_Course ('MODERN PHYSICS', 'A masterclass on
modern physics and its implications for the world today', DEFAULT,
DEFAULT, 'Physics');
```

This should fail, producing the '75000' SQLSTATE code with the message 'Invalid Department Name' because there's no 'Physics' department, whereas the next one should work, because the 'Creative Management' department already exists in the Departments table:

```
CALL UMADB_CHP5.Register_Course ('Tax Loophole hopping', 'A masterclass
on exploiting the tax system loopholes', DEFAULT, DEFAULT, 'Creative
Management');
```

This may seem daunting, but take it slowly; reread the previous chapter and this one thus far. You should be able to make it work. In the downloadable source code for this chapter there's a possible solution (note that there's more than one way to solve the problem, as is often the case in programming—and life).

Remember, this is not a "perfect" solution, but it's a good start. Feel free to improve it by accepting the Course Director and TA names instead of their IDs, look up those names in the Persons table, and use the respective teacher IDs when inserting the record in the Courses table, for example. After that, try to create the Register_Teacher SP, again using the Register_Student as a starting point. Practice is essential before jumping into real-life SP development.

Data-returning Stored Procedures

As I said at the beginning of the chapter, data insertion can be performed via a trigger instead of an SP. The most common and practical use for SPs is in returning cursors or, more accurately, result tables associated with the cursors opened in the SP. These data sets, called *result sets* in SQL lingo, usually aggregate information from one or more tables, in a way that makes sense from a business point of view, as opposed to a database point of view. For instance, it makes sense to return Person and Student data as one result set, even though they exist in two separate tables in the database. The interesting part of data-returning SPs is that business logic can be applied in the construction of the returned data sets. Yes, plural: data sets, because you can return more than one data set from the call to a data-returning SP. First, I'll explain how to create these SPs and then how to call them.

Creating Data-returning Stored Procedures

Creating a data-returning SP is an easy task. You simply create an SP that declares and opens a cursor. However, this is no more than a simple SELECT statement, and it doesn't take advantage of the power of SQL/PSM. Even so, I'll start with a simple SP, to help you get the hang of it, before moving to business logic–infused SPs.

Let's say I want to return the student information: student ID, name, home address, and so on, for another program to use. As you probably recall, the student data is spread across a couple of tables, which complicates things a bit. Still, it's a simple SELECT statement within an SP with a few extra lines of code, as you can see in this example:

```
CREATE OR REPLACE PROCEDURE UMADB_CHP5.Get_Student_Data (
    -- Parameters
    IN p_Name char(60)
)
    RESULT SETS 1
    READS SQL DATA
    ALLOW DEBUG MODE
    SPECIFIC GetStud1
    SET OPTION USRPRF = *OWNER

    BEGIN
        -- Declare the cursor with the appropriate SELECT statement
        DECLARE GetStudentData_C1 CURSOR WITH RETURN FOR
            SELECT      STUDENT.STUDENT_ID
            , PERSON.NAME
            , PERSON.HOME_ADDRESS
            , PERSON.MOBILE_NBR
            , PERSON.EMAIL_ADDRESS
            , PERSON.DRIVERS_LICENSE
            , PERSON.SOCIAL_SEC_NBR
            FROM UMADB_CHP5.TBL_PERSONS PERSON
                INNER JOIN UMADB_CHP5.TBL_STUDENTS STUDENT
                                                        Continued
```

```
                                  ON PERSON.PERSON_ID = STUDENT.TBL_
PERSONSPERSON_ID
        WHERE         PERSON.NAME = P_NAME
     ;

     -- Open the cursor
     OPEN GetStudentData_C1;
  END;
```

When compared with the previous SP, this one presents a few noteworthy differences. There's a new property, RESULT SETS 1, which indicates that this SP will return a single result set. Then there's also a different setting for the SQL DATA property: it is now READS SQL DATA instead of the previously used MODIFIES SQL DATA. It's important to keep the properties aligned with the purpose of the SP because, among other things, this serves as documentation. If you're reading this SP's code, you'll soon realize that the SP is not supposed to change SQL data in any way. Finally, there's the declaration of a cursor, albeit a simple one, and the respective OPEN instruction. You may find it strange that the code ends with the OPEN instruction, but before I explain why, let's analyze the DECLARE CURSOR statement.

The DECLARE CURSOR Syntax

The version of the DECLARE CURSOR statement used in this SP is the absolute minimum possible. This statement provides a lot of flexibility, allowing you to customize the way data is retrieved from the database and provided to the program that calls the SP. Because the complete syntax is long and a bit confusing, I'll break it down into chunks and review their syntax, step by step:

```
DECLARE <cursor name> <SENSITIVITY> <SCROLLABILITY> CURSOR <HOLDABILITY>
<RETURNABILITY> <EXTENDED INDICATORS USAGE> FOR <SELECT-Statement or
Prepared statement name>
```

Even a small section like this may seem like a lot, so let's start with the cursor sensitivity to changes in the database. There are three possibilities:

- SENSITIVE—indicates that changes made to the database after the cursor is opened are visible in the result table. This means that with this keyword you get the latest available state of the data. The cursor is always sensitive to changes (UPDATE/ DELETE statements) performed using the same cursor, as you might expect, but also to the changes performed outside this cursor. If the database manager cannot make changes visible to the cursor, then an error is returned.

- INSENSITIVE—It's the exact opposite of SENSITIVE. The data made available is a frozen image of the database at the time the cursor is opened. By the way, the cursor will be opened as read-only, so the SELECT statement cannot contain an UPDATE clause.

- ASENSITIVITY—In this case, it's the optimization of the SELECT statement that determines the sensitivity of the cursor, which can be either of the previously mentioned.

Scrollability, or the ability to scroll, is just a fancy name to group the two different possibilities:

- SCROLL—indicates that you can "navigate" freely on the cursor, retrieving the next, previous, or a specific row of the result set. If you're an RPG programmer, it might help if I tell you that file access in RPG programs is achieved via scrollable cursors. This is the feature that allows you to use stuff like READ, READP, READEQ, SETLL, and SETGT. If this doesn't ring a bell, reread the section of Chapter 6 that discusses the FETCH statement.

- Basically, scrollable cursors reduce the amount of time and effort required to move backward and forward through the result set. But as helpful as scrollable cursors are, do not make every cursor a scrollable cursor. Scrollable cursors require substantially more overhead than a traditional, non-scrollable cursor. Analyze the requirements of the application and deploy scrollable cursors only where it makes sense to do so.

- NO SCROLL—As you might have gathered, it's the opposite of SCROLL.

Note that if a prepared statement is used, the default is the corresponding prepare attribute of the statement. Otherwise, NO SCROLL is the default.

The next group of keywords is probably not so obvious, because it is related to commitment control. I'll just provide a brief overview of the available choices.

HOLDABILITY hides a couple of keywords that are fairly easy to understand, even if you don't know a thing about commitment control:

- WITHOUT HOLD—As the name implies, this keyword doesn't "hold the cursor hostage" or lock the cursor, which is the same as saying that it allows the cursor to be closed as a result of a commit operation. For now, let's just say that a commit operation is making a bunch of changes to the database permanent and visible to other running processes.

- WITH HOLD—If this keyword is specified, the cursor can't be changed by a commit operation. When WITH HOLD is specified, a commit operation makes all the changes in the current unit of work permanent and visible in the database and releases all locks, except those that are required to maintain the cursor position. Afterward, a FETCH statement is required before a positioned UPDATE or DELETE statement can be executed. If you're feeling a bit frustrated by this explanation, don't despair! Commitment control is not important at this time, and it's something you can tackle later on, after finishing this book.

Just as happens with the scrollability when a prepared statement is specified, the default is the corresponding prepare attribute of the statement. If you use a SELECT statement directly in the cursor definition, WITHOUT HOLD is the default.

The next item in the DECLARE CURSOR syntax requires some contextualization. Creating SPs is a simple way to encapsulate business rules and database logic in a kind of "black box" that other applications, internal or external to the IBM i, will be able to use. It's common to have applications that are composed of multiple programs or routines that serve a specific purpose and, in doing so, call other programs and routines. Eventually, one of these programs or routines, somewhere on the call stack, will call your SP. You may or may not want your result set to be available outside a certain context, or call stack level. *Returnability* is the group of keywords that allows you to control just that. There are two possible options:

- WITHOUT RETURN—specifies that the result set produced by the cursor is intended to be used as a procedure result set—that is, the result set will not be made available *outside* the procedure.

- WITH RETURN—This is the exact opposite of WITHOUT RETURN, and it requires an additional definition, to indicate how far up on the call stack the result set can be used:

    o TO CALLER—indicates that the cursor can return a result set to the caller of the procedure, or in other words, to the program or routine immediately above the SP on the call stack

    o TO CLIENT—specifies that the cursor can return a result set to the client application (the program/routine that sits at the top of the call stack to which the SP call belongs). Note, however, that this cursor is invisible to any intermediate nested procedures. If a function or trigger called the SP (directly or indirectly), its result sets cannot be returned to the client and the cursor will be closed after the SP finishes. It's also important to mention that TO CLIENT may be necessary if the result set is returned from an ILE program with multiple modules.

Note that the returnability of the cursor is influenced by the type of statement used, similarly to the previously discussed keyword groups. If a prepared statement is used, the corresponding prepare attribute is used as default. If you're using a SELECT statement, then the default is WITHOUT RETURN.

The EXTENDED INDICATOR USAGE group is used to indicate whether these special variables are available when the SP is called. If you have no idea what I'm talking about, here's a quick refresher: host variables with indicator variables can be used with the CALL statement to pass additional information to and from a procedure. To indicate that the associated host variable contains the null value (which is something that some programming languages such as RPG can't handle properly), the indicator variable is set to a negative value of -1, -2, -3, -4, or -6. A value of -5 indicates that the DEFAULT value should be used, and a value of -7 specifies that the value returned is UNASSIGNED (just in case you don't know, this means it will remain unchanged during an UPDATE).

A CALL statement with indicator variables is processed as follows: if the indicator variable is negative, a default value is passed for the associated host variable in the CALL statement and the indicator variable is passed unchanged. Otherwise, if the indicator variable is not negative, the host variable and the indicator variable are passed unchanged, which can lead to problems with mishandling of NULL values in languages like RPG. When a native SP that was compiled without the *EXTIND option is called, the extended indicator values of -5 and -7 cannot be passed, because they'll cause an error on the CALL statement. If the *EXTIND option was specified at compilation time, then the error won't occur.

Now that we're all on the same page (pun intended), I can explain the available choices:

- WITH EXTENDED INDICATORS—specifies that extended indicator variables are enabled, and non-updatable columns are allowed in the implicit or explicit UPDATE clause of the SELECT statement.

- WITHOUT EXTENDED INDICATORS—As you probably guessed, this is the opposite of the WITH EXTENDED INDICATORS keyword.

Finally, the <SELECT-*Statement or Prepared statement name*> bit is the easiest part of the DECLARE CURSOR syntax. It contains either a SELECT statement, as is the case in this first cursor-returning SP example, or the name of a prepared statement. In the latter case, the attributes used in the respective PREPARE statement will influence the behavior of the cursor, as I mentioned, on each of the keyword groups.

I'll provide a few more cursor-returning SP examples sporting different DECLARE CURSOR configurations, but keep in mind that the objective of these SPs is to supply data to another program, not to process the data on this SP. That's why the SP ends with the OPEN operation. By returning an open cursor to another program, you centralize the business logic and fine-tune the security of your database at the same time.

Let's imagine that this SP is going to be used by a Web application. You can keep the business logic within the database, which allows the Web application to ignore all the rules and peculiarities of the business and the data. Additionally, by granting access to the SP but not the tables it uses, you create an additional security layer between the "outside world" and your database. The option SET OPTION USRPRF = *OWNER will provide the SP with the necessary authority to read data from the tables it needs, even if the user profile used to call the SP doesn't have access to those tables.

However, there's no actual business logic in this SP, and it doesn't provide a lot of flexibility. It's a simple two-table query that requires an exact match with the student name to return results. Let's spruce it up a bit! I'll improve this SP's flexibility by adding a second (optional) parameter, the student ID, and by allowing a less restrictive name search. But the inclusion of the second parameter will force us to use a dynamic SELECT statement, because searching by student ID is very different from searching by person name. If you recall what you read in the previous chapter about cursors (if you don't, just go back and take a peek; I'll wait), you'll know that you can declare a cursor that uses a dynamic statement. That's what will be used on this occasion. If the student ID is not supplied, a slightly modified version of the SELECT statement used in the previous version of the SP will be used; otherwise, a brand-new WHERE clause will replace the "old" one.

Because the procedure is a bit long, I'll show and comment on it, section by section, from top to bottom:

```
-- Version 2: additional (and optional) input parameter for the student
ID and name-matching using the LIKE operator on the query
CREATE OR REPLACE PROCEDURE UMADB_CHP5.Get_Student_Data (
    -- Parameters
    IN p_Name char(60),
    IN p_Student_Id Integer DEFAULT -1
)
    RESULT SETS 1
    READS SQL DATA
    ALLOW DEBUG MODE
    SPECIFIC GetStud2
    SET OPTION USRPRF = *OWNER
```

A couple of notes regarding this bit of code: you might have noticed that I used the same procedure name, Get_Student_Data, but with different parameters (I added p_Student_Id). This didn't replace the existing version of the SP. Why? Well, because I used a different SPECIFIC name, which is used by the database engine to determine which procedure I'm referring to, as I explained earlier in this chapter. If you use PDM or RDi to explore the content of the UMADB_CHP5 library after the creation of the procedure (which you'll be able to do in a little while), you'll find the following:

GETSTUD1	*PGM	CLE	SQL PROCEDURE	GET_STUDENT_DATA
GETSTUD2	*PGM	CLE	SQL PROCEDURE	GET_STUDENT_DATA

Yes: two SQL procedures with the GET_STUDENT_DATA name, but with different system names. Remember, the SPECIFIC name is used by the operating system instead of the longer, potentially problematic SQL name of the procedure. This allows the consumers of the SP to call it using different parameter sets, which in turn are linked to different SPs with the same name, but diverse functionality.

This might sound strange to an RPG programmer, but it's a very common practice among Java and C# developers. In object-oriented programming languages, this concept of having more than one procedure with the same name but different parameters and functionality is called *overloading*. You can argue that neither the parameters nor the functionality is very different between these two SPs—and you're right. I chose to implement slight changes instead of a total revolution to keep things as simple as possible at this time. I'll revisit the overloading topic in the next chapter with more complex examples.

Let's continue to examine this new version of the SP, by looking at the next chunk of code, which contains the declaration "section" of the procedure:

```
BEGIN
    DECLARE w_sql_stmt VARCHAR(2000);
    -- Declare the cursor with the appropriate SELECT statement
    -- This now depends on the input parameters
    DECLARE GetStudentData_C1 CURSOR WITH RETURN FOR StudentData_
Statement;
```

Again, a couple of changes here: I added the w_sql_stmt variable, which I'll use in the next bit of code. The cursor declaration no longer includes a SELECT statement. Instead, it makes reference to a prepared statement, named StudentData_Statement. I mentioned earlier that cursors can use either a SELECT statement or a prepared (read: potentially dynamic) statement in their declaration. It may seem weird that I'm referring to something that doesn't exist at this time (until I issue a PREPARE statement, StudentData_ Statement is simply a placeholder), but the database engine doesn't mind, as long as somewhere in the SP's code you materialize the prepared statement.

The next part of the SP will do just that, but before showing the code, I'll remind you of the desired functionality of this procedure: if the student ID is supplied, I'd like the procedure to return a cursor containing the records that match that ID—in this case, it will be a single record, because the studentID is the primary key of the Students table. Otherwise, I'd like the result to be a list of all students whose names contain the value passed on the P_NAME parameter. For instance, if P_NAME is equal to 'Chris', student names like 'Christopher', 'Christine', and 'John Christopherson' will be included in the returned result set, assuming that these names exist in the Persons table. In short, I want to implement different SELECT statements, depending on the value of the input parameters of the SP. Here's how it's done:

```
    -- Set up the constant part of the SELECT statement (everything up
to the WHERE clause)
    -- Set the SELECT clause
    SET w_sql_stmt = 'SELECT STUDENT.STUDENT_ID, PERSON.NAME, PERSON.
HOME_ADDRESS, PERSON.MOBILE_NBR, PERSON.EMAIL_ADDRESS, PERSON.DRIVERS_
LICENSE, PERSON.SOCIAL_SEC_NBR';
    -- Set the FROM clause
    SET w_sql_stmt = TRIM(w_sql_stmt) CONCAT ' FROM UMADB_CHP5.TBL_
PERSONS PERSON';
    SET w_sql_stmt = TRIM(w_sql_stmt) CONCAT ' INNER JOIN UMADB_CHP5.
TBL_STUDENTS STUDENT ON PERSON.PERSON_ID = STUDENT.TBL_PERSONSPERSON_
ID';
    -- If the student ID was not supplied, build the SELECT statement
using PERSON.NAME LIKE %P_NAME%
    IF (P_STUDENT_ID = -1) THEN
        -- Set the appropriate WHERE clause, using P_NAME
        SET w_sql_stmt = TRIM(w_sql_stmt) CONCAT ' WHERE PERSON.NAME
LIKE ''%' CONCAT TRIM(P_NAME) CONCAT '%''';
    ELSE
        -- Set the appropriate WHERE clause, using P_STUDENT_ID
        SET w_sql_stmt = TRIM(w_sql_stmt) CONCAT ' WHERE STUDENT.
STUDENT_ID = ' CONCAT P_STUDENT_ID;
    END IF;
```

At this time, my SELECT statement is simply a string, dynamically composed and stored in the w_sql_stmt variable. Most of the statement doesn't really depend on the input parameter's value—just the WHERE clause, so I can set up that part before checking whether the P_STUDENT_ID parameter was passed. How do I do that? I check whether it contains its default value. If it does, this means that a value for parameter was not passed on the call to the SP. In other words, it means that I should use the P_NAME to set up the WHERE clause, as explained before. Otherwise, I need to build a different WHERE clause that uses the P_STUDENT_ID to find a matching record.

Let me try to clarify this explanation with a couple of examples. First, let's imagine that the SP is called using ar in the first parameter (P_Name) and DEFAULT in the second (P_Student_Id). This causes the procedure to produce the following WHERE clause for the SELECT statement:

```
WHERE PERSON.NAME LIKE '%a%'
```

If the SP is called with something other than the default value for the P_Student_Id parameter (assuming that a value is provided at all), let's say 4, for instance, then the WHERE clause will be different:

```
WHERE STUDENT.STUDENT_ID = 4
```

This happens because there's an IF statement controlling the formation of the WHERE clause, based on the input parameters. After dynamically composing the statement according to the "business logic" defined for this SP, I simply need to prepare the statement and open the cursor:

```
    -- Prepare the statement, using w_sql_stmt
    PREPARE StudentData_Statement FROM w_sql_stmt;


    -- Open the cursor
    OPEN GetStudentData_C1;
END;
```

This ends the procedure's code. If you don't want to type it all, you'll find the complete source code in the downloadable files for this chapter. However, even if you compile these SPs, you won't be able to test them. I'll explain how to do that in a while. Before moving to that part, let me show you how to create a SP that returns more than one cursor.

Creating More Complex Data-returning Stored Procedures

You might find the notion a bit strange, but its potential is huge: for instance, you can return an invoice and its details with a single call to an SP from a Web application. In one step, you can return a complete and complex multi-table structure, such as a customer relationship management (CRM) system's information about a client: all its purchases, invoices, complaints, interactions with the company, and so on. It's a very effective way to "hide" the database complexity and business rules, because you can tailor each result set (i.e., each cursor) to the exact specification of the calling application or to the output data model that was defined by the analysts.

Returning more than one cursor is not difficult. You simply adjust the RESULT SETS 1 procedure property to whichever number of cursors you're returning, declare and open the cursors, and you're done. However, returning multiple cursors that present different perspectives of the same "thing" is slightly more complex. This is a typical master-detail context (or an invoice header/invoice lines scenario, if you prefer a more concrete example).

If I were writing an SP to return invoice data in two cursors, the first would contain the invoice header information—stuff like invoice number, client identification, and invoice total amounts—and a second cursor would contain the invoice lines, with columns such as item identification, price, discount, and so on. The link between the two cursors would be the invoice ID. It's important to mention this, because using a common ID between the several types of information is directly linked to the reusability of the code. What I mean by this is that if I wanted to add a third cursor, I could keep it in sync (i.e., make it return contextualized information) with the other two cursors simply by using the same ID. For instance, if the data in the first cursor includes information about the header of the invoices with the IDs 1, 2, and 3, it's fairly easy (as you'll see in a minute) to get the second cursor to produce data about the detail lines of the same invoices. This is also applicable to a third, fourth ... *n*th cursor, as long as there's a common link between all of them.

OK, it might be a bit hard to picture a third set of information about an invoice, but try to picture client data instead: it's possible to have different perspectives (or result sets) about a client—identification data, order history, payment history, and so on. In short, what I'm trying to say is that if there's a way to keep the data synchronized between the different cursors, find it, isolate it in your code, and reuse it. In this type of context, it's important to reuse as much code as possible, to keep future maintenance of the code as simple and inexpensive as possible. This discussion will start to make (more) sense in a minute, with the example from the student contact information and grades.

Before diving into the details, let's take a moment to find and understand where the student contact information and grades exist in our database. Figure 7.1 shows the current UMADB entity relationship diagram (ERD).

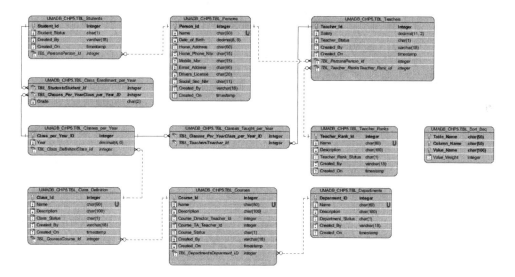

Figure 7.1: Current UMADB ERD

A brief analysis leads us to the conclusion that we'll need all the left-side tables to retrieve information about the students' grades. To include the students' contact information, we'll have to add the Persons table as well. Actually, the second version of the SP we've been building already uses the Students and Persons table, so that problem is solved. All we need to do is create a SELECT statement that returns the information relevant to the students' grades. To keep it "human-readable," we'll have to add the class name and year. There's no actual need to include student contact data other than the student ID on the second cursor, because the first cursor, which will work in tandem with the one we'll trying to build here, already provides it. After careful consideration of the information provided by the ERD and of the particular demands of this situation, I wrote the following SELECT statement:

```
SELECT TBL_STUDENTSSTUDENT_ID STUDENT_ID
       , NAME CLASS_NAME
       , YEAR CLASS_YEAR
       , GRADE FINAL_GRADE

FROM   UMADB_CHP5.TBL_CLASS_DEFINITION CLASS_DEFINITION
            INNER JOIN UMADB_CHP5.TBL_CLASSES_PER_YEAR CLASSES_PER_YEAR
                 ON CLASS_DEFINITION.CLASS_ID = CLASSES_PER_YEAR.
TBL_CLASS_DEFINITIONCLASS_ID
            INNER JOIN UMADB_CHP5.TBL_CLASS_ENROLLMENT_PER_YEAR CLASS_
ENROLLMENT
                 ON CLASSES_PER_YEAR.CLASS_PER_YEAR_ID = CLASS_
ENROLLMENT.TBL_CLASSES_PER_YEARCLASS_PER_YEAR_ID
```

It starts from the bottom left corner of the ERD and moves up, joining the tables by following the relations between them, to list the student ID, class name, class year, and the grade the student achieved in each class. However, this will list every single record of the Class Enrollment per Year table, because there's no WHERE clause in this statement. This is where the talk about keeping the cursors in sync comes into play. The way to do it is to use the same selection of student IDs in both cursors.

How do we do that? Well, the link between the students' contact information and the students' grades is the student ID, so I just need to restrict the SELECT statement above to the student IDs listed by the first cursor, using an IN predicate. In other words, if I strip the first cursor, which will be the same as in the previous version of the SP, of every column except the student ID, I have a fairly easy and manageable way to keep the cursors in sync. But there's a catch: the first cursor is dynamic. Its WHERE clause depends on which input parameters are passed, as I explained near the end of the previous sub-section. In this improved version of the SP, I can reuse the code to do the same for the

WHERE clause of the new cursor, slightly modified to use different variables, instead of repeating the same code.

In short, here's what will be done to create the improved, two-cursor version of the SP:

- Having two cursors instead of one implies that I'll have to use two text variables to temporarily store the SELECT statements and I'll have to declare one additional cursor. I'll use w_sql_stmt_C1 and w_sql_stmt_C2 for the statements and GetStudentData_C2 as the new cursor.

- Because of what I just explained regarding the reuse of a significant part of the SELECT statement of the first cursor, an additional variable will be required. I'll use w_sql_stmt_reusable.

- Two dynamically prepared cursors also mean two prepared statements. I'll use keep using StudentData_Statement and create StudentGradesData_Statement.

- Finally, I'll compose the second cursor's statement using the SELECT that joins all the class-related tables and add a WHERE statement that will use the code contained in w_sql_stmt_reusable to assure flexibility and reusability.

It's now time to look at the code itself. I'll use the same chunk-by-chunk approach to present the code, and I'll comment on each chunk as needed. Let's start with the procedure parameters and properties:

```
-- Improved Version 2: using the same "business logic," the SP now
returns a second cursor with the students' grades
CREATE OR REPLACE PROCEDURE UMADB_CHP5.Get_Student_Data (
    -- Parameters
    IN p_Name char(60),
    IN p_Student_Id Integer DEFAULT -1
)
    RESULT SETS 2
    READS SQL DATA
    ALLOW DEBUG MODE
    SPECIFIC GetStud2
    SET OPTION USRPRF = *OWNER
```

The only difference here is the RESULT SETS property, now set to 2, because I'll return two cursors. I kept the same SPECIFIC name because I want to improve version 2, not create a version 3. All in all, only minor changes occurred on this piece of code. The next one, however, was heavily modified:

```
    BEGIN
        -- variable to hold the SELECT statement of the primary cursor
(C1)
        DECLARE w_sql_stmt_C1 VARCHAR(2000);
        -- variable to hold the SELECT statement of the secondary cursor
(C2)
        DECLARE w_sql_stmt_C2 VARCHAR(2000);
        -- variable to hold the reusable part of the first SELECT
statement
        DECLARE w_sql_stmt_reusable VARCHAR(2000);
        -- Declare the cursors with the appropriate SELECT statement
        -- This now depends on the input parameters
        DECLARE GetStudentData_C1 CURSOR WITH RETURN FOR StudentData_
Statement;
        DECLARE GetStudentData_C2 CURSOR WITH RETURN FOR
StudentGradesData_Statement;
```

If you go back a bit and reread the list of changes, you'll find the explanation for the modifications performed here. They're all linked to the introduction of the second cursor and the link between it and the one that was already there. The next block of code performs the same function as before—dynamically composing the SELECT statement of the first cursor, but it was changed to use the variable w_sql_stmt_reusable in order to reuse a large part of the SQL statement later.

```
        -- Set up the constant part of the SELECT statement of the primary
statement (everything up to the WHERE clause)
        -- Set the SELECT clause
        SET w_sql_stmt_C1 = 'SELECT STUDENT.STUDENT_ID, PERSON.NAME,
PERSON.HOME_ADDRESS, PERSON.MOBILE_NBR, PERSON.EMAIL_ADDRESS, PERSON.
DRIVERS_LICENSE, PERSON.SOCIAL_SEC_NBR';
                                                        Continued
```

```
        -- Set the FROM clause and store it in the reusable part of the
first SELECT statement
        SET w_sql_stmt_reusable =  ' FROM UMADB_CHP5.TBL_PERSONS PERSON';
        SET w_sql_stmt_reusable = TRIM(w_sql_stmt_reusable) CONCAT ' INNER
JOIN UMADB_CHP5.TBL_STUDENTS STUDENT ON PERSON.PERSON_ID = STUDENT.TBL_
PERSONSPERSON_ID';


        -- If the student ID was not supplied, build the SELECT statement
using PERSON.NAME LIKE %P_NAME%
        IF (P_STUDENT_ID = -1) THEN
            -- Set the appropriate WHERE clause, using P_NAME
            SET w_sql_stmt_reusable = TRIM(w_sql_stmt_reusable) CONCAT '
WHERE PERSON.NAME LIKE ''%' CONCAT TRIM(P_NAME) CONCAT '%''';
        ELSE
            -- Set the appropriate WHERE clause, using P_STUDENT_ID
            SET w_sql_stmt_reusable = TRIM(w_sql_stmt_reusable) CONCAT '
WHERE STUDENT.STUDENT_ID = ' CONCAT P_STUDENT_ID;
        END IF;

        -- Take the SELECT clause of the first statement and add the
reusable part (FROM and WHERE clauses)
        SET w_sql_stmt_C1 = TRIM(w_sql_stmt_C1) CONCAT ' ' CONCAT TRIM(w_
sql_stmt_reusable);
```

The code, along with the line-by-line comments, speaks for itself. I could have used
a single variable assignment (that's the SET instruction) to fill the "fixed" parts of the
statement. However, I found that separating the different clauses (SELECT, FROM, and
WHERE) in separate assignments improves readability and future maintenance of the code.
The composition of the second cursor's SQL statement follows the same principles, as
you can see in the next piece of code:

```
        -- Set up the secondary cursor's SELECT statement
        -- Set the SELECT clause
        SET w_sql_stmt_C2 = 'SELECT TBL_STUDENTSSTUDENT_ID STUDENT_ID,
NAME CLASS_NAME, YEAR CLASS_YEAR, GRADE FINAL_GRADE';
```
Continued

```
      -- Set the FROM clause, starting with the Class Definition table
      SET w_sql_stmt_C2 = TRIM(w_sql_stmt_C2) CONCAT ' FROM UMADB_CHP5.
TBL_CLASS_DEFINITION CLASS_DEFINITION';
      -- Join with the Classes per Year table
      SET w_sql_stmt_C2 = TRIM(w_sql_stmt_C2) CONCAT ' INNER JOIN
UMADB_CHP5.TBL_CLASSES_PER_YEAR CLASSES_PER_YEAR';
      SET w_sql_stmt_C2 = TRIM(w_sql_stmt_C2) CONCAT ' ON CLASS_
DEFINITION.CLASS_ID = CLASSES_PER_YEAR.TBL_CLASS_DEFINITIONCLASS_ID';
      -- Join the Class Enrollment per Year table
      SET w_sql_stmt_C2 = TRIM(w_sql_stmt_C2) CONCAT ' INNER JOIN
UMADB_CHP5.TBL_CLASS_ENROLLMENT_PER_YEAR CLASS_ENROLLMENT';
      SET w_sql_stmt_C2 = TRIM(w_sql_stmt_C2) CONCAT ' ON CLASSES_PER_
YEAR.CLASS_PER_YEAR_ID = CLASS_ENROLLMENT.TBL_CLASSES_PER_YEARCLASS_PER_
YEAR_ID';

      -- Set the WHERE clause
      -- The WHERE uses a simplified version of the primary SELECT
statement, using only the student ID
      SET w_sql_stmt_C2 = TRIM(w_sql_stmt_C2) CONCAT ' WHERE TBL_
STUDENTSSTUDENT_ID IN (SELECT STUDENT.STUDENT_ID';
      SET w_sql_stmt_C2 = TRIM(w_sql_stmt_C2) CONCAT ' ' CONCAT TRIM(w_
sql_stmt_reusable) CONCAT ')';
```

The most important differences are the last two assignments. They are used to include
the WHERE clause that keeps both cursors in sync. The link between the statements is the
student ID, so the WHERE clause uses a modified version of the first cursor's statement to
restrict the results of the second cursor's SELECT statement to the IDs included in the first
statement. The rest of the procedure wraps things up, by creating the prepared statements
from the text versions of the SELECT statements and opening the cursors:

```
      -- Prepare the primary statement, using w_sql_stmt_C1
      PREPARE StudentData_Statement FROM w_sql_stmt_C1;
```

Continued

```
    -- Prepare the secondary statement, using w_sql_stmt_C2
    PREPARE StudentGradesData_Statement FROM w_sql_stmt_C2;

    -- Open the primary cursor
    OPEN GetStudentData_C1;

    -- Open the secondary cursor
    OPEN GetStudentData_C2;
END;
```

Time for Some (More) Practice

Now that you know how to create cursor-returning SPs, try to create one yourself. The idea is to create a SP that returns two cursors: the first with teacher contact information and the second with the classes that teacher taught through the years, for a given teacher name or ID. Just as in the previous SP, the name passed as a parameter can be simply a fragment of the name. I'll help you with the SELECT statements, which should always be the first step of cursor-returning SPs.

Let's focus on the first cursor; it's supposed to return the teacher's contact information, based on one of two inputs: either a part of the name of the teacher or his/her teacher ID. As before, there are two options, but the statements are almost identical; only the WHERE clause changes, depending on which input parameter is filled. Let's build the common part of the statements first and then think about the WHERE clause later.

If you look at Figure 7.1, you'll see that the link between the Teachers and Persons tables is similar to the one used in the previous SP (if you replace the Students table with the Teachers table), which means that building the first part of the statement is fairly easy:

```
SELECT TEACHER.TEACHER_ID
     , PERSON.NAME
     , PERSON.HOME_ADDRESS
     , PERSON.MOBILE_NBR
     , PERSON.EMAIL_ADDRESS
                                                    Continued
```

```
          , PERSON.DRIVERS_LICENSE
          , PERSON.SOCIAL_SEC_NBR
  FROM    UMADB_CHP5.TBL_PERSONS PERSON
          INNER JOIN UMADB_CHP5.TBL_TEACHERS TEACHER
  ON PERSON.PERSON_ID = TEACHER.TBL_PERSONSPERSON_ID
```

This will provide the teacher's contact information. If you want a little extra practice, figure out how to add the teacher's rank as well. Now let's build the two possible WHERE clauses, starting with the teacher ID:

```
  WHERE TEACHER.TEACHER_ID = <input parameter P_Teacher_Id goes here>
```

I started with the teacher ID WHERE clause, because the other one is exactly the same as before. Remember, it's based on the PERSONS record, not the TEACHERS, which means that the one used in the previous SP can be used here without any changes:

```
  WHERE PERSON.NAME LIKE '%<input parameter P_Name goes here>%'
```

To use these WHERE clauses in the Get_Teacher_Data SP, just replace the comments between the left and right angle brackets (< and >) with the appropriate code.

Now let's move to the second cursor. The idea is to return the list of classes the teacher taught through the years. A quick look at Figure 7.1 will tell you that table TBL_CLASSES_TAUGHT_PER_YEAR contains the necessary information. However, this is an intermediate table that sits in the middle of a many-to-many relationship. In other words, it only contains ID data—the class per year ID and the teacher ID, which is not very useful for humans (regular humans, anyway). From the teacher side of things, the problem is solved because the first cursor provides all the necessary information. The class side of things is a bit different: just the ID won't do, but if we add the class name and year, things start to make sense.

Based on this line of thought, I created the SELECT statement for the second cursor:

```
SELECT        TBL_TEACHERSTEACHER_ID TEACHER_ID
         , NAME CLASS_NAME
         , YEAR CLASS_YEAR


FROM     UMADB_CHP5.TBL_CLASS_DEFINITION CLASS_DEFINITION
            INNER JOIN UMADB_CHP5.TBL_CLASSES_PER_YEAR CLASSES_PER_YEAR
               ON CLASS_DEFINITION.CLASS_ID = CLASSES_PER_YEAR.
TBL_CLASS_DEFINITIONCLASS_ID
            INNER JOIN UMADB_CHP5.TBL_CLASSES_TAUGHT_PER_YEAR CLASSES_
TAUGHT_PER_YEAR
               ON CLASSES_PER_YEAR.CLASS_PER_YEAR_ID = CLASSES_
TAUGHT_PER_YEAR.TBL_CLASSES_PER_YEARCLASS_PER_YEAR_ID
```

However, note that there's no WHERE clause. This will list all the classes taught that are on file, which is not the objective. I need to restrict the list to the teacher IDs' list produced by the first cursor, thus linking the two cursors together:

```
WHERE TBL_TEACHERSTEACHER_ID IN
(SELECT TEACHER.TEACHER_ID
 FROM UMADB_CHP5.TBL_PERSONS PERSON
INNER JOIN UMADB_CHP5.TBL_TEACHERS TEACHER
ON PERSON.PERSON_ID = TEACHER.TBL_PERSONSPERSON_ID
 WHERE PERSON.NAME LIKE '%<input parameter P_Name goes here>%'
);
```

Note that this statement is using the P_Name version of the WHERE clause. You need to build it dynamically in order to make it work for both P_Name and P_Teacher_Id. This may seem daunting, but it's actually quite easy. Study the Get_Student_Data SP carefully, and you'll see what I mean!

A couple of closing pieces of advice: you can use the Get_Student_Data SP as a guide. If you want to take things slow, try implementing a first version of the SP with a single cursor (the teacher contact information), and then evolve it to the two-cursor version.

You'll find a possible solution for this exercise in this chapter's downloadable source code. If you find this exercise too easy, try to create an SP that returns a list of courses and a sublist of classes per course, for instance. Then experiment with your own database and find how and where you can use what you've learned about cursor-returning SPs.

Using Data-returning Stored Procedures

The objective of data-returning SPs is to hide the complexity of the database and concentrate the business logic in a single point. This means that the applications that will use the SPs don't have to "know" a lot about the database. However, they still need to use the SPs in order to get the data. This section will explain how to do just that. It will do so using SQL SPs, but note that the SQL statements and working principles are the same, regardless of the programming language that will access the data.

How to Use the Result Sets Returned by a Stored Procedure

Retrieving and using a cursor (or result set, to be more accurate) produced by a SP involves more than just calling the SP. It requires a few additional steps, before and after the CALL statement itself. Let's review them one by one, with a few examples.

You need to start by defining one or more result set locators. A *result set locator* is a variable used to contain the location of a result set opened in a called SP. The calling SP (or program) must declare one or more result set locators, for each result set returned by the called SP. The syntax of the statement you need to issue to declare the result set locators is straightforward:

```
DECLARE <one or more result set locator names, separated by commas>
RESULT_SET_LOCATOR VARYING;
```

Naturally, each result set locator must have a unique name. I like to use names that are somehow linked with the called procedure and suffix the result set locators with "_L*n*", where *n* is an incremental number. In the example you'll find later in this section, I'm declaring the GetStudentData_L1 name for the first result set locator of the Get_Student_Data SP, using the following statement:

```
DECLARE GetStudentData_L1 RESULT_SET_LOCATOR VARYING;
```

To get the data, you need to call the SP that returns it. That's the first action (the previous step is just a declaration), but by no means the last one of the process. The call itself is just a regular CALL statement.

Once you've called the SP, you need to connect, or *associate*, in SQL/PSM terminology, the result set locators with the SP. How? With the ASSOCIATE LOCATOR statement. The syntax of this statement is almost plain English (if you ignore the pair of parentheses):

```
ASSOCIATE LOCATORS(<one or more result set locator names, separated by
commas>) WITH <fully qualified procedure name or SPECIFIC name>;
```

In the complete example I'll show you shortly, you'll see that I associate the GetStudentData_L1 result set locator with the Get_Student_Data SP using the following statement:

```
ASSOCIATE LOCATORS(GetStudentData_L1) WITH PROCEDURE UMADB_CHP5.GET_
STUDENT_DATA;
```

We're almost there; the result set locators are defined, the SP was called, and we've linked together the result set locators and SP with the ASSOCIATE LOCATORS statement. What's next? Because the called SP can return more than one result set, associating the list of result set locators with the SP is not enough. I need to specify which result set locator should be used for each of the returned result sets, or cursors. Let's call them cursors to avoid repeating "result set" over and over again. Anyway, that's where the ALLOCATE CURSOR statement comes in. You need to issue one ALLOCATE CURSOR statement for each pair of result set locators/cursor. This statement's syntax is also close to regular English:

```
ALLOCATE <cursor name> CURSOR FOR RESULT SET <result set locator name>;
```

I'll keep the examples consistent and show you how to associate the GetStudentData_L1 with the first cursor returned by the Get_Student_Data SP:

```
ALLOCATE GetStudentData_C1 CURSOR FOR RESULT SET GetStudentData_L1;
```

Now that everything is connected and pointing in the right direction, I can finally retrieve data from the cursor. If you recall what I explained back in Chapter 5 in regard to cursors, you already know what comes next. To read data from the cursor, I have to issue a FETCH statement. The syntax was already explained, so I won't go over it again. However, it's important to mention the logic required to read and process the data. Just as I'd do in an RPG program, I'll read the first record, check for "end of file," and keep reading/processing each row of data until "end of file" is reached. A cursor is not exactly a file, but it's close enough, so I can use the following structure:

```
-- Fetching the first row data from the cursor
    FETCH GetStudentData_C1 INTO      W_STUDENT_ID
                , W_NAME
                , W_HOME_ADDRESS
                , W_MOBILE_NBR
                , W_EMAIL_ADDRESS
                , W_DRIVERS_LICENSE
                , W_SOCIAL_SEC_NBR;
    -- Loop to retrieve additional rows
    WHILE (SQLSTATE = '00000') DO
        -- DO something with the data...
        -- (SOME CODE HERE...)
        -- Fetch the next record from the cursor
        FETCH GetStudentData_C1 INTO   W_STUDENT_ID
                , W_NAME
                , W_HOME_ADDRESS
                , W_MOBILE_NBR
                , W_EMAIL_ADDRESS
                , W_DRIVERS_LICENSE
                , W_SOCIAL_SEC_NBR;
    END WHILE;
```

When the loop ends, I simply need to close the cursor and end the SP. In summary, I need to employ the following sequence of operations to successfully read and use data from a cursor-returning SP:

1. Declare the result set locators, using DECLARE LOCATOR.

2. Call the cursor-returning SP.

3. Link the result set locator to the cursor-returning SP with ASSOCIATE LOCATOR.

4. Assign a result set locator to each of the cursor-returning SP's cursors with ALLOCATE CURSOR.

5. Read/process the data using FETCH.

6. Close the cursor(s).

Now let's review the complete example I've been promising. The scenario is quite simple: I created an SP that reads data from the first version of the Get_Student_Data SP and writes it to a temporary table. I know it sounds strange to read from one place to write it in another, but this is an over-simplified example of data processing. A more "real-life" example would do some actual processing, such as make decisions based on the data from the cursor and call programs or other SPs to actually make something happen.

Anyway, let's analyze the SP the same way we've been doing it: piece by piece, starting with the procedure signature and declarations:

```
CREATE OR REPLACE PROCEDURE UMADB_CHP5.Test_Get_Student_Data_v1 ()
  BEGIN
    DECLARE SQLSTATE CHAR(5) DEFAULT '00000';
    -- Temp variables for fetching data
    DECLARE W_STUDENT_ID INTEGER;
    DECLARE W_NAME CHAR(60);
    DECLARE W_HOME_ADDRESS CHAR(60);
    DECLARE W_MOBILE_NBR CHAR(15);
    DECLARE W_EMAIL_ADDRESS CHAR(60);
    DECLARE W_DRIVERS_LICENSE CHAR(20);
    DECLARE W_SOCIAL_SEC_NBR CHAR(11);
```

In this case, there aren't input parameters, so the procedure signature is just the first line of the SP. The declaration section is a bit larger than the previous ones because I need to declare a bunch of variables to receive the cursor columns (more about this later). There's one declaration missing here: the result set locator. I left it out on purpose, so that I could present all the cursor declaration and allocation statements together:

```
-- Cursor-related instructions
DECLARE GetStudentData_L1 RESULT_SET_LOCATOR VARYING;
CALL UMADB_CHP5.GET_STUDENT_DATA('Jake Jacobs', 4);
ASSOCIATE LOCATORS(GetStudentData_L1) WITH PROCEDURE UMADB_CHP5.
GET_STUDENT_DATA;
ALLOCATE GetStudentData_C1 CURSOR FOR RESULT SET GetStudentData_
L1;
```

As you can see from this block of code, the methodology for using cursor-returning SPs is being followed: result set locator declaration, followed by the call to the SP, which in turn is followed by the association and allocation statements. The next step would be to fetch the first row of data, but in this over-simplified example I need to create a temporary table to receive the data. This is part of the "data processing" part of the SP:

```
-- Temp table for storing the output of the cursor
CREATE OR REPLACE TABLE UMADB_CHP5.TBL_TEMP_STUDENT
(STUDENT_ID INTEGER,
 NAME CHAR(60),
 HOME_ADDRESS CHAR(60),
 MOBILE_NBR CHAR(15),
 EMAIL_ADDRESS CHAR(60),
 DRIVERS_LICENSE CHAR(20),
 SOCIAL_SEC_NBR CHAR(11)
);
```

Finally, I'm going to read and process rows of data from the cursor until a SQL state not equal to '00000' occurs. In other words, I'll keep reading and "processing" data until the cursor reaches its last row of data or an error occurs. Note that I could (and should) take more specific precautions in regard to errors. For instance, I should check for an empty cursor, a fetch error, and so on. Again, this is an over-simplified SP, intended to provide the basics.

Here's the code that loops through the cursor and "processes" its data:

```
-- Fetching the first row data from the cursor
FETCH GetStudentData_C1 INTO        W_STUDENT_ID
                , W_NAME
                , W_HOME_ADDRESS
                , W_MOBILE_NBR
                , W_EMAIL_ADDRESS
                , W_DRIVERS_LICENSE
                , W_SOCIAL_SEC_NBR;
-- Loop to retrieve additional rows
WHILE (SQLSTATE = '00000') DO
    -- Insert result set data into a temp table
    INSERT INTO UMADB_CHP5.TBL_TEMP_STUDENT
     VALUES(W_STUDENT_ID
   , W_NAME
   , W_HOME_ADDRESS
   , W_MOBILE_NBR
   , W_EMAIL_ADDRESS
   , W_DRIVERS_LICENSE
   , W_SOCIAL_SEC_NBR)
    ;
    -- Fetch the next record from the cursor
    FETCH GetStudentData_C1 INTO    W_STUDENT_ID
                , W_NAME
                , W_HOME_ADDRESS
                , W_MOBILE_NBR
                , W_EMAIL_ADDRESS
                , W_DRIVERS_LICENSE
                , W_SOCIAL_SEC_NBR;
END WHILE;
```

After all the data is processed, all that's left to do is close the cursor, in order to prevent problems and make a "clean exit" from the procedure:

```
    -- Cleanup instructions
    CLOSE GetStudentData_C1;
  END;
```

That's it! Now it's your turn ....

And There's Still Time for a Little More Practice

To make sure you understood what's going on here, I have a little exercise for you: try to create an improved version of this SP that reads and processes (and by processes, I mean write to another temporary table) the two cursors of the second version of the Get_Student_Data SP. Yup, the one that returns the student contact information and his/her grades. You'll find the solutions in the downloadable source code, as usual. If you want some extra practice, try to create a Test_Get_Teacher_Data SP that returns and "processes" the two teacher data cursors you created in the last exercise!

In This Chapter, You've Learned ...

This was a very hands-on chapter with a lot of new stuff. Here's a summary of what was discussed:

- The distinction between stored procedures, user-defined functions, and triggers was explained: it's all about how these SQL routines are called.
- The structure of an SQL procedure was explained in detail.
- The SQL/PSM statements explained in Chapter 6 were put into practice with the creation of several SPs, starting with a very simple SP and evolving to data-returning SPs.
- Examples of data-returning SPs were explained, and it was suggested to the reader to practice a bit with the creation of an additional data-returning SP that returns Teacher data.

- The methodology for using data-returning SPs was explained using an SQL SP; note that the same instructions and sequence are also applicable to embedded SQL in RPG or other programming languages.

- A complete example of a SP that reads and "processes" a cursor returned by another SP was explained in detail, and it was suggested to the reader to practice a bit with the creation of an additional SP that reads and processes Teacher data, based on the previous exercise's SP.

The fundamental tools to create SPs were explained and demonstrated here, but nothing can replace practice. I simply can't stress this enough: before trying to apply the notions discussed here to your own database, take a moment to do the exercises provided throughout the chapter. This might save you some time (and frustration) because the UMADB database is very simple and small. This makes it the perfect test bed for experiments that otherwise could become very time-consuming and confusing.

8

Exploring User-Defined Functions

This chapter will introduce the concept of the user-defined function (UDF), in its multiple forms. The chapter starts with the anatomy of a UDF, presents a few examples, and later explains how to use UDFs in your code. The chapter will discuss the use of user-defined table functions (UDTFs), an often ignored (but extremely useful) form of UDF. Note that this chapter uses what was discussed in the previous two chapters. If you haven't read them (and you're not familiar with SQL/PSM and stored procedure concepts), please take a moment to do so.

I mentioned a few pages ago that one of the differences between a stored procedure (SP) and a UDF is how you use it. Let's start by exploring the similarities between SPs and UDFs to save some time and then explain the differences. However, before we begin, it's important to mention that I'll discuss SQL functions only. It's possible (and actually quite easy) to create functions based on RPG or any other IBM i high-level programming language. Although that discussion is beyond the scope of this book, it is covered in *Evolve Your RPG Coding* (*https://www.mc-store.com/products/evolve-your-rpg-coding-move-from-opm-to-ile-and-beyond*).

Function Versus Procedure: The RETURNS Property

A UDF is another type of SQL routine, in the sense that it can be composed by "regular" SQL statements intertwined with SQL/PSM statements to form a coherent piece of code that goes way beyond what DML and DDL statements alone can achieve. UDFs share a lot of the same "DNA" with SPs:

- UDFs' structure is essentially the same as SPs, with a few minor differences that I'll explain in a minute.

- They both use SQL/PSM and "regular" SQL statements to implement whatever logic is needed, within the limits of an SQL routine.

- They can call each other, even though calling a UDF is very different from calling a SP, as you'll see later in this chapter.

You're probably wondering what the differences are between UDFs and SPs, other than in the way you call them. The differences are in the structure of the UDF, which is actually related to the way you call a UDF.

While you use the CALL statement to invoke an SP and use its parameters to get data in and out of this type of SQL routine, UDFs require a different type of approach. A function, by definition, is something that returns a value. Don't get me wrong: an SP can also return a value, but not in the SP itself. Instead, it can return values as output parameters. A UDF returns a value (or more) as the result of the call itself, not as an output parameter.

For instance, you can create a procedure to calculate the square of a number, using two parameters: one for the number you want to square (that would be your input parameter) and another to get the square of that number (the output parameter). If you implement a function to do the same, you'll need a single parameter (the input) because the output will come from the call itself. That's why you need to use UDFs in "regular" SQL statements: they can replace complex composed statements and calculations in a simple and much more readable way. Now let's see how the UDFs return the value.

It's actually quite simple: UDFs have a property that SPs don't: the RETURNS property. You use it to specify what the UDF will return. This is where a UDF diverges more from a SP. Let's take a look at the syntax of the CREATE FUNCTION statement:

```
CREATE (OR REPLACE) FUNCTION <function name>
(<function parameters, separated by commas>)
RETURNS <return data type>
```

Naturally, this will be followed by the rest of the UDF structure: properties, options, and the function body, just as I explained in the section "Analyzing the SP's Structure" in Chapter 7.

Let me step back a bit to explain a couple of things about this statement. As you already know from the discussion about the SP structure, the name of an SQL routine doesn't have to be unique within its schema, because you can overload it, by defining multiple SQL routines of the same type and different signatures. As a reminder, an SQL routine signature is composed of its name and parameter list—not so much the names of the parameters, but their type and sequence. As you might expect, this explanation fully applies to UDFs. There's just a slight difference, in regard to the parameters: you don't need to indicate which parameters are used for input and output. This means that you don't need to prefix the parameter names with the IN and OUT keywords. As you'll see in the first and second UDF examples, this can provide you with a very interesting and flexible approach to some situations.

However, the most important and interesting part of the CREATE FUNCTION syntax is the RETURNS property, because it allows you to specify what your function will return. You're probably thinking I'm talking about returning an integer or double or something else like that, right? Well, you might not be aware of this, but you can also return an entire table! Instead of creating an SP that builds a cursor according to a certain business logic, you can write a UDTF and use it directly in a SELECT statement, in the FROM clause. I'll show you examples of this later, but for now just keep in mind that this RETURNS property is very flexible and incredibly useful.

Pick Your UDF Flavor

While they're not as diverse as some ice cream shops with 31 (or many more) flavors, UDFs offer three distinct possibilities:

- *Scalar*—This is the most popular type and the one most people think of when they discuss UDFs. A *scalar function* is a UDF that produces a single value from another value or set of values. Given an input, it will produce a single value as output: in goes the pork, out comes the sausage, as Scott Klement would put it. Common examples include the calculation of mathematical or financial formulas, such as factorials or compound interest, but a scalar function can also be used for data validation or to make actual data manipulation operations.

- *Aggregate*—An *aggregate* (column) function is a UDF that uses the values of a single column and returns a single value, which generally is derived from the values of the column. You probably already use aggregate functions, such as SUM or AVG, in your code. What you possibly didn't know is that you can write your own aggregate functions to calculate values that are specific to your business needs, such as rolling average sales versus costs ratios or another convoluted operation that currently takes tons of code to produce a result. By combining the power of UDFs and SPs, you can move that code to the database so that external applications can use it seamlessly.

- *Table*—A UDTF is a function that returns a table to the SQL statement that references it. However, it doesn't do so as do the two previously mentioned "flavors." A UDTF can only be referenced in the FROM clause of a SELECT statement. In general, the returned table can be referenced in exactly the same way as any other table. Table functions are useful for performing SQL operations on non-DB2 data or moving non-DB2 data into a DB2 table, for instance.

A Couple of Simple UDFs to Get You Started

To provide you with UDF examples to get you started, I'll introduce two that will be used later in this chapter. I don't know if you ever had this experience, but whenever you select the *OUTFILE option in the OUTPUT parameter of certain CL commands, the resulting files have some really, well ... let's just say unfriendly names, such as UPDCEN or UPDDAT. There's something else that can be mind-boggling for the uninitiated: the way the century (not the century as we usually refer to it, but the two leftmost digits of the year) is represented. Usually in these system files, the date is stored in a six-digit field, and there's an additional field, containing 0 or 1, which indicates whether the first digits of the year should be 19 or 20, respectively. I guess it's a Y2K thing, but I'm not sure. Anyway, this can be a burden when you have to do something with those date fields that aren't actually dates.

A way to solve this problem and, at the same time, provide a couple more examples of UDFs, is to show how you can transform those date fields into proper dates or timestamps, depending on the information available in the system file. Later in this chapter you'll see these UDFs used with the output file generated by the DSPUSRPRF (Display User Profile) CL command, so I won't provide a complete example right now. Let's just see how the UDFs are built, starting with the simple date conversion. I'll go over the UDFs' source code, block by block as usual, starting with the function signature and RETURNS statements:

```
SET SCHEMA = UMADB_CHP5;
CREATE OR REPLACE FUNCTION IBM_Date_to_Date (
    -- Parameters
    p_Century_Ind Char(1),
    p_Date Char(6)
)
    RETURNS Date
```

This should be more or less familiar by now, assuming you already created some SPs. This block of code resembles its SP equivalent, with a few differences: the obvious and expected FUNCTION instead of PROCEDURE, the absence of the IN/OUT keywords preceding the parameters, and the RETURNS property.

The next block, containing the rest of the UDFs' properties and options, is even more SP-like:

```
    READS SQL DATA
    ALLOW DEBUG MODE
    SPECIFIC IBMD2DATE
    SET OPTION USRPRF = *OWNER
```

These properties and options are similar to the ones used in previous SP examples. Note that I'm using a unique SPECIFIC name, because you can't have duplicated SPECIFIC names, regardless of the type SQL routines. If you try to create an SP and a UDF with the same SPECIFIC name in the same schema, the database engine will complain that the name already exists, and the creation statement will fail.

Finally, here is the fun part: the function body.

```
   BEGIN
      RETURN Date(   CASE p_Century_Ind -- p_Century_Ind indicates the
   century part of the date
                     WHEN '0' THEN '19'
                     WHEN '1' THEN '20'
                 END
                 CONCAT -- p_Date contain the date in YYMMDD format
                 SUBSTR(p_Date, 1, 2)
                 CONCAT '-' CONCAT SUBSTR(p_Date, 3, 2)
                 CONCAT '-' CONCAT SUBSTR(p_Date, 5, 2)
              );
   END;
```

As shown in the function signature code snippet, the function takes two parameters: an integer field, containing a 0 or 1, and a char field that contains the date, IBM style. The code in the function's body starts by reading the value of the first field, the century indicator, and adds '19' or '20' to what will be the output value: a date field. The rest of this field is constructed by twisting the second parameter to form a string in the format 'YYYY-MM-DD', which is one of the formats that the DATE native SQL function accepts as input. Note that there aren't any validations or fail-safe measures. The objective here is to have a "quick and dirty" function to convert IBM file columns to proper dates, assuming the all the inputs (century indicator and "IBM date") are valid.

The second function is very similar, but it returns a timestamp instead of a date. To do so, it takes an additional parameter, containing the time value. Just like the date in the previous UDF, this is just a string, representing the time, without any separators. This means that our little function will have to take care of that, too. Let's see how:

```
SET SCHEMA = UMADB_CHP5;
CREATE OR REPLACE FUNCTION IBM_Date_to_Timestamp (
   -- Parameters
   p_Century_Ind Char(1),
   p_Date Char(6),
                                                   Continued
```

```
    p_Time Char(6)
)
    RETURNS Timestamp
    READS SQL DATA
    ALLOW DEBUG MODE
    SPECIFIC IBMD2TIMES
    SET OPTION USRPRF = *OWNER
    BEGIN
    RETURN  Timestamp(  CASE p_Century_Ind -- p_Century_Ind indicates
the century part of the date
                        WHEN '0' THEN '19'
                        WHEN '1' THEN '20'
                    END
                CONCAT -- p_Date contain the date in YYMMDD format
                SUBSTR(p_Date, 1, 2)
                CONCAT '-' CONCAT SUBSTR(p_Date, 3, 2)
                CONCAT '-' CONCAT SUBSTR(p_Date, 5, 2)
                CONCAT '-' -- p_Time contains the time in HHMMSS format
                CONCAT SUBSTR(p_Time, 1, 2)
                CONCAT '.' CONCAT SUBSTR(p_Time, 3, 2)
                 CONCAT '.' CONCAT SUBSTR(p_Time, 5, 2)
                    );
    END;
```

This function is very similar to the previous one, but it takes an additional parameter (p_Time) and returns a timestamp instead of a date. How does it do that? Well, notice that the word following the RETURN statement was changed to timestamp, and the p_Time parameter is being sliced into an 'HH:MM:SS' format and concatenated to the date transformation (which remains the same as it was in the previous function) in order to form a string format that the TIMESTAMP native SQL function can convert to a timestamp: 'YYYY-MM-DD-HH:MM:SS'. I'll be using these two functions later, and you'll see more contextualized examples of UDFs' usefulness.

Using Flow Control in a UDF

Let's complicate things a bit and introduce some flow control in the next UDF. This one uses the UMADB Persons table. It takes the person name as an input parameter and returns that person's student ID, if one exists. Otherwise, a value of -900 will be returned, indicating that the name was not found in the Persons table. Note that it's implied that a negative value indicates an error, because all IDs are positive numbers. This convention also allows for multiple "error codes." In this particular case, I'll use -900, as I just explained, and one other "error code." The -901 "error code" will indicate that even though a Persons record was found, there's no match in the Students table. This may result from the fact that the name passed as parameter belongs to a teacher, for instance.

Let's see how this is done in practice, starting with the function signature and options:

```
SET SCHEMA = UMADB_CHP5;
CREATE OR REPLACE FUNCTION Get_Student_Id (
    -- Parameters
    p_Name char(60)
)
    RETURNS Integer
    READS SQL DATA
    ALLOW DEBUG MODE
    SPECIFIC GetStudId1
    SET OPTION USRPRF = *OWNER
```

Nothing really new, so far. However, as you probably guessed, from the functionality described a few lines ago, that the function body is going to be very different from the previous two functions, because now there's some logic involved:

```
BEGIN
    DECLARE W_Student_Id Integer;
    IF (SELECT COUNT(*) FROM TBL_PERSONS WHERE NAME = P_NAME) > 0 THEN
        -- A Persons table record exists, so let's try to find a
Students table record with that Person_Id
                                                    Continued
```

```
        -- The COALESCE function is used to return the -901 "error
code" if the SELECT statement returns null
        SET W_Student_Id = COALESCE    ((SELECT STUDENT_ID
                 FROM TBL_STUDENTS STUDENTS
                 INNER JOIN TBL_PERSONS PERSONS
                 ON STUDENTS.TBL_PERSONSPERSON_ID = PERSONS.PERSON_ID
                 WHERE PERSONS.NAME = P_NAME)
                 , -901);
    ELSE
        -- If a Persons record was not found, return the -900 "error
code"
        SET W_Student_Id = -900;
    END IF;

    -- Finally, end the function by returning the W_Student_Id
variable's value
    RETURN W_Student_Id;
  END;
```

The function's body starts with the declaration of a work variable, used to return the result of the processing performed within the function. As I explained before, there are three possible results:

- An existing student ID, represented by a positive integer, if the name passed as parameter matches a known student name
- The -900 "error code," if the name wasn't found in the Persons table
- The -901 "error code," if the name was found in the Persons table but doesn't belong to a student

The code starts by checking whether the name exists in the Persons table and either proceeds to the Students table check or returns the -900 "error code." If a Persons record was found, then the code tries to retrieve the student ID from the Students table. The COALESCE built-in function is used to return -901 if the SELECT statement fails. In this case, the failure to produce a valid student ID is interpreted as a null output. The COALESCE will then choose between the SELECT statement result and the -901 value, returning the first (from left to right) that is not null. I could have rigged things differently here and used error handling, but I wanted to keep this first example as simple as possible. The COALESCE function provides the necessary flexibility, and this is a nice way to show a creative yet simple use of this often misunderstood and neglected built-in function.

UDF Overloading

Now let's create a modified version of this UDF that takes the Person ID as input and returns the matching Student ID, if one is found. This new version will use the same "error codes" as the previous one. The structure is exactly the same; the main differences are the input parameters and the second SELECT statement of the function's body, as you can see below:

```
-- Alternative version of the UDF, using the person ID to get the
student ID
CREATE OR REPLACE FUNCTION Get_Student_Id (
    -- Parameters
    p_Person_Id Integer
)
    RETURNS Integer

    READS SQL DATA
    ALLOW DEBUG MODE
    SPECIFIC GetStudId2
    SET OPTION USRPRF = *OWNER

    BEGIN
        DECLARE W_Student_Id Integer;
        IF (SELECT COUNT(*) FROM TBL_PERSONS WHERE PERSON_ID = P_PERSON_
ID) > 0 THEN
            -- A Persons table record exists, so let's try to find a
Students table record with that Person_Id
            -- The COALESCE function is used to return the -901 "error
code" if the SELECT statement returns null
```
Continued

```
        SET W_Student_Id = COALESCE      ((SELECT STUDENT_ID
                    FROM TBL_STUDENTS STUDENTS
                    WHERE STUDENTS.TBL_PERSONSPERSON_ID = P_PERSON_ID)
                    , -901);
      ELSE
          -- If a Persons record was not found, return the -900 "error
 code"
          SET W_Student_Id = -900;
      END IF;

      -- Finally, end the function by returning the W_Student_Id
 variable's value
      RETURN W_Student_Id;
   END;
```

This is another example of a simple UDF, and it serves as a reminder of the overloading concept: I now have two UDFs with exactly the same name in the same schema. The difference is in their signature: the UDFs have different parameters and SPECIFIC names, so they can coexist without any problems. If you're not seeing how this can be useful, reviewing the test examples in the next section should make it clearer.

Testing the Get_Student_Id UDF

Now that your UDF is up and running, let's test it! Testing a UDF is way simpler than testing an SP, because you don't need to write another SQL routine to test and analyze the results. A UDF can be called from a regular SELECT statement. To keep things as simple as possible, I'll be using a dummy table, provided by IBM (sysibm.sysdummy1) to invoke the UDF, so we can test the three possible scenarios described in the previous section. Here's the complete test code:

```
-- Testing the UDF
-- Scenario 1: testing with the name of an existing student
SELECT get_student_id('Simpson, Bart') from sysibm.sysdummy1;
```
Continued

```
-- This will return the corresponding student id

-- Scenario 2: testing with the name of an existing teacher
SELECT get_student_id('Dr. Doom') from sysibm.sysdummy1;
-- This will return the -901 error code

-- Scenario 3: testing with a name that doesn't exist in the Persons
table
SELECT get_student_id('Alice') from sysibm.sysdummy1;
-- This will return the -900 error code
```

Now let's test the second version of the UDF, with the same conditions. In my data set, 'Simpson, Bart' exists in the Persons table with the ID 3, 'Dr. Doom' also exists and has the ID 1, and 'Alice' doesn't exist at all. I've adjusted the UDF calls accordingly, as you can see in the following test code:

```
-- Testing the UDF alternative version
-- Scenario 1: testing with the name of an existing student ('Simpson,
Bart')
SELECT get_student_id(3) from sysibm.sysdummy1;
-- This will return the corresponding student ID

-- Scenario 2: testing with the name of an existing teacher ('Dr. Doom')
SELECT get_student_id(1) from sysibm.sysdummy1;
-- This will return the -901 error code

-- Scenario 3: testing with a name that doesn't exist in the Persons
table ('Alice')
SELECT get_student_id(-1) from sysibm.sysdummy1;
-- This will return the -900 error code
```

As you can see from these code samples, testing a UDF can be pretty easy. Naturally, you can use UDFs in a more complex SELECT statement and pass columns or expressions of that SELECT instead of fixed values. You can also use UDFs as parameters to other UDFs.

This may sound a bit confusing, but the UDF we'll be creating in a little while should help you understand what I mean. Before we do that, though, it's your turn to code!

Time for Some Practice

Take a moment to review the two versions of the Get_Student_Id UDF. You'll find the complete source code in this chapter's downloadable source code, as usual. Once you've done that, you should be ready for my next challenge!

It's easier than it may sound at first: I'd like you to create two versions of a Get_Teacher_Id UDF, using the Get_Student_Id UDFs as a template. These UDFs should return the teacher ID, taking the person name (in the first version) and the person ID (in the second version) as input. Because the use cases are similar, you can even return the same error codes. Go ahead, try it! If you get stuck or want to see the result without doing the coding, you'll find the solutions for this little exercise in the downloadable source code.

If you want to go a bit further, I suggest creating other UDFs that return other things such as the course director name of a given course or the department name to which a certain class belongs. The hardest part will be setting up the necessary SELECT statements, because these UDFs can also follow the business logic/template of the Get_Student_Id UDF.

A More Complex UDF: Calculating the Student GPA

It's now time for a slightly more complex UDF. Let's create a function capable of calculating a student's grade point average (GPA). GPA ranges from 0.0 to 4.0, where 0.0 is the worst possible result. It serves as a way to facilitate the comparison between students' grades and is often used as a differentiation factor in the job market. The GPA is calculated by dividing the total number of grade points earned by the total number of credit hours attempted. If you take a look at our current database model, you'll notice that we lack some information necessary to calculate the GPA. Even though we have the students' grades in the Class Enrollment per Year table, we lack the quantification of the letter-based A-to-F scale and the number of credit hours of each class. Let's solve these problems by making a few changes to our database model.

Creating a Generic "Translation" Table ...

Instead of creating a table specifically for our current need, let's create a generic table that can be used to "translate" values in a more flexible fashion. These translation tables or correspondence tables are common in many ERP solutions and come in many shapes and sizes. Let's create the table with its simplest possible form: an ID, a data identifier (the type of data being converted), an alphanumeric column, and a numeric column. You might be tempted to call them "origin" and "destination," respectively, but resist that temptation because it may not always be the case; in this particular situation, the origin is indeed the alphanumeric column and the destination is the numeric one, but it's fairly easy to conceive a scenario in which the roles are reversed.

Having said that, here's the code for the new table:

```
/* Create the table generic data conversion */
CREATE OR REPLACE TABLE UMADB_CHP5.TBL_Data_Conversion
 FOR SYSTEM NAME PFDC
 (
  Conversion_Id        FOR COLUMN DCID integer GENERATED BY DEFAULT AS
 IDENTITY,
  Data_Type            FOR COLUMN DCTP char(20) NOT NULL,
  Alpha                FOR COLUMN DCAF char(100) NOT NULL,
  Number               FOR COLUMN DCNF decimal(10, 5) NOT NULL,
  Remarks              FOR COLUMN DCRM char(100) DEFAULT '',
  Created_By           FOR COLUMN DCCU varchar(18) DEFAULT USER,
  Created_On           FOR COLUMN DCCT timestamp DEFAULT CURRENT
 TIMESTAMP,
  PRIMARY KEY (Conversion_Id))
  RCDFMT PFCDCR;
```

... And a Couple of Functions to Access It

The use of a conversion table is a double-edged sword: on one hand, it helps you figure out the meaning of coded values, such as the grades, but on the other, it adds complexity to the statements where it's used. It will require an additional INNER JOIN per each use of the conversion table. For instance, if I want to see the numeric value of the grade of a certain student (let's say, the student with student ID equal to 3) in a certain class (let's say the class with ID equal to 20), I'd have to write something like this:

```
SELECT   Data_Conversion.Number "Grade Numeric Value"
FROM     Umadb_Chp5.Tbl_Class_Enrollment_per_Year Class_Enrollment_per_
Year
         INNER JOIN Umadb_Chp5.Tbl_Data_Conversion Data_Conversion
            ON Grade = Alpha AND Data_Type = 'GRADE'
WHERE    Tbl_StudentsStudent_Id = 3
         AND Tbl_Classes_per_YearClass_per_Year_Id = 20
;
```

Now imagine that you want to use the conversion table four times in the same SELECT statement; you'd need to "pollute" your statement with four INNER JOIN sets, like the one in the sample statement just shown!

Naturally, there's a way to prevent this: you just need to create two conversion functions. Why two, you ask? Well, you might need to convert from alpha to numeric or vice-versa. Let's start with the alpha to numeric conversion:

```
SET SCHEMA = UMADB_CHP5;
CREATE OR REPLACE FUNCTION Convert_A_to_N(
   -- Parameters
   p_Data_Type char(20)
   , p_Alpha char(100)
   )
   RETURNS numeric (10,5)
   READS SQL DATA
   ALLOW DEBUG MODE
   SPECIFIC ConvAtoN
   SET OPTION USRPRF = *OWNER

   BEGIN
      DECLARE   RetVal numeric(10, 5) DEFAULT -99999.99999;
                                                   Continued
```

```
      SELECT    Number
      INTO      RetVal
      FROM      Tbl_Data_Conversion
      WHERE     Data_Type = p_Data_Type
                AND Alpha = p_Alpha
      ;
      RETURN RetVal;
   END;
```

Just a quick note: I'm using yet another way to signal possible errors. This time around, I'm defining a weird default value for my return value variable, which hopefully won't be used in any conversion, and it's easily recognizable as a conversion error. I could include some sort of error handling, just in case. I'll be discussing a possible "catch-all" error handler later in this chapter, in the section "Creating the Calculate_GPA UDF," so I'll skip that for now.

As you might have gathered, the numeric to alpha function is very similar:

```
CREATE OR REPLACE FUNCTION Convert_N_to_A(
    -- Parameters
    p_Data_Type char(20)
    , p_Number numeric (10,5)
    )

RETURNS char(100)
READS SQL DATA
ALLOW DEBUG MODE
SPECIFIC ConvNtoA
SET OPTION USRPRF = *OWNER

BEGIN
   DECLARE   RetVal char(100) DEFAULT 'N/A';
   SELECT    Alpha
   INTO      RetVal
```

Continued

```
        FROM        Tbl_Data_Conversion
        WHERE       Data_Type = p_Data_Type
                    AND Number = p_Number

        ;

        RETURN RetVal;
    END;
```

There are a few differences between the two functions. Basically, the alpha and number columns swapped places in the parameters, return value, and SELECT statement. With the help of these functions, the SELECT statement I presented before can be simplified to this:

```
SELECT   Umadb_Chp5.Convert_A_To_N('GRADE', Grade) "Grade Numeric Value"
FROM     Umadb_Chp5.Tbl_Class_Enrollment_per_Year Class_Enrollment_per_
Year
WHERE    Tbl_StudentsStudent_Id = 3
         AND Tbl_Classes_per_YearClass_per_Year_Id = 20
;
```

It's easier on the eye and, more important, doesn't clutter the statement with loads of INNER JOINs.

Finding a Place for the Credit Hours per Class

If we were to follow the strictest principles of database normalization, we'd create a new table to store this piece of information. However, let's be reasonable and keep our database model manageable. Still, we have two options: either add the new column to the Class Definition table, thus making the credit hours a "static" piece of data, or leave some wiggle room and add the new column to the Class Enrollment per Year table, which provides us with the flexibility of changing (if needed) the number of credits every school year.

I favor this second option, not only because it's more flexible, but also because this way we'll read the grade and credit information from the same place. Naturally, this new piece of information needs to be mandatory, otherwise it would be impossible to calculate the GPA. However, for that to happen, I have to specify a default value (let's say 30), which will be used by the database engine to fill the column on the existing records. Here's the statement that performs the necessary actions:

```
/* Add the Credit Hours column to the Class Enrollment per Year table
   and set a default value of 30 credit hours */
ALTER TABLE UMADB_CHP5.TBL_Class_Enrollment_per_Year
  ADD COLUMN Credit_Hours FOR COLUMN CECH
              integer
              NOT NULL
              DEFAULT 30;
```

You might argue that this indentation is a bit overkill, but it's necessary to easily identify the different characteristics of the new column.

Finally, all that's left is to insert the letter-to-number conversion for the A-to-F grade scale. It's a simple set of nearly identical 13 INSERT statements, which I won't reproduce here. You can find all of this code and the updated entity relationship diagram (ERD) in the downloadable source code for this chapter. Figure 8.1 illustrates what the UMADB's ERD looks like after these changes.

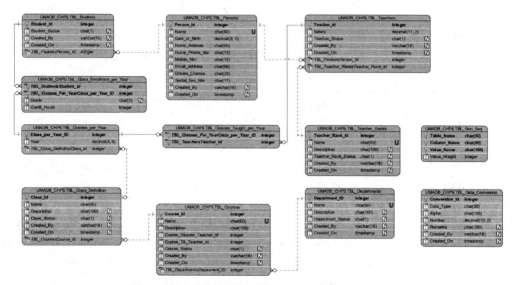

Figure 8.1: UMADB's ERD after the changes

Creating the Calculate_GPA UDF

Now let's focus on the Calculate_GPA UDF. This function will take a student ID as the input parameter and return a number between 0.0 and 4.0. The precision is important, not least because a slight increase in the GPA can mean a better job or a higher paycheck! In short, here's what the function will have to do:

1. Find all the classes the student attended.

2. For each of those classes, calculate the weighted grade, or in other words, multiply the number of credit hours of the class by the grade.

3. However, the grade is stored in an A-to-F scale, so it needs to be converted. For that, the new Data Conversion table will have to be used.

4. Finally, the sum of all the weighted grade will be divided by the sum of the credit hours, thus calculating the student's GPA. In case of error, it should return an impossible GPA, such as -1.0.

Note that the implementation doesn't need to strictly follow the order or detail of these steps. SQL statements allow us to perform several steps at once or mix their order, as you'll see in a moment. Before revealing the code for the UDF, let's take a moment to consider what can go wrong and how we'll handle it. Actually, the previous sentence hints at the solution: handle it; we'll use an error handler, in this case a generic error handler to return the error-indicating value of -1.0. It's also important to note that the return value must be in the correct format: it should have only one decimal place, which means that it needs to be properly calculated and rounded. This adds two requirements to the previously mentioned list:

- If, for some reason, it's not possible to calculate the GPA, the function should return -1.0;

- The return value needs to be accurate and rounded to one decimal place, in order to respect the 0.0 to 4.0 scale.

The code starts, as you'd expect, with the function signature, properties, and options:

```
CREATE OR REPLACE FUNCTION Calculate_GPA (
    -- Parameters
    p_Student_Id integer
                                                            Continued
```

```
)
    RETURNS numeric(2, 1)

    READS SQL DATA
    ALLOW DEBUG MODE
    SPECIFIC CalcGPA1
    SET OPTION USRPRF = *OWNER
```

There's nothing really new or surprising here. The only relevant note is the return value's format: to respect the 0.0 to 4.0 scale, the data format is numeric with only one decimal place. The next block of code encompasses all the necessary declarations:

```
BEGIN
    -- Declare a temp variable to calculate the GPA
    DECLARE W_GPA numeric(2, 1);

    -- Declare a "catch-all" error handler
    -- If an error occurs, return an impossible value to signal the
error
    DECLARE EXIT HANDLER FOR SQLEXCEPTION
    BEGIN
        RETURN -1;
    END;
```

The W_GPA variable will be used to temporarily store the calculation result, performing a similar function to the W_Student_Id from the Get_Student_ID UDF, but in a slightly different way. The exit handler used here is a generic, "catch-all" handler, designed to return the "oops-something-went-wrong" value of -1.0. In most cases, a more robust and informative error-handling solution is required. These solutions should provide additional information about the error, writing it to an error log file, for instance, before returning an error-indicating value. This is not the only bit of code that can return the -1.0 value. If the data is available but something is not exactly as expected (for example, a grade is not configured or misconfigured in the Data Conversion table), the function should also return a controlled error instead of a wrong value (which in this case, would be anything outside the 0.0 – 4.0 interval).

Before getting to that part, let's see how the necessary data is retrieved and used to calculate the GPA:

```
    -- Set the proper path to use UDFs from UMADB_CHP5
    SET PATH = UMADB_CHP5;
    -- Calculate the GPA
    SELECT CAST(ROUND(SUM(Class_Enrollment_per_Year.Credit_Hours *
Convert_A_to_N('GRADE', Grade))
                    / SUM(Class_Enrollment_per_Year.Credit_Hours),
1) as numeric(2, 1))
        INTO   W_GPA
        FROM   Tbl_Class_Enrollment_per_Year Class_Enrollment_per_Year
        WHERE  Class_Enrollment_per_Year.Tbl_StudentsStudent_Id = p_
Student_Id
               AND Class_Enrollment_per_Year.Grade <> '--';
```

Because I'm using a UDF from our schema, I need to set the proper path beforehand. It's either that or specify the schema name followed by a period (.) before the function name, like this: Umadb_Chp5.Convert_A_to_N('GRADE', Grade). I prefer setting the path beforehand, because it's easier to spot and maintain the schema name, in case it changes in the future.

As I said before, SQL allows us to perform multiple operations at once. Here, I'm using a SELECT statement to retrieve the necessary data (credit hours and the corresponding numeric value of each grade letter), calculate the GPA, and round the value in a single step. Let's dissect the statement, starting with the GPA formula:

```
SUM(Class_Enrollment_per_Year.Credit_Hours * Convert_A_to_N('GRADE',
Grade))
                    / SUM(Class_Enrollment_per_Year.Credit_Hours)
```

In the first part of this piece of code, instead of calculating the weighted grade of each class the student attended in turn, I'm doing it all at once, using the SUM scalar function to get the, well, sum of all the weighted grades. Note how the Convert_A_to_N UDF is used to convert the grade to its corresponding numeric value. Keep in mind that to get the GPA, I need to get the total credit hours and use that to transform the sum of the weighted grades into the GPA. That, too, is performed in a single step, again using the SUM scalar function. However, because of the data types and operations involved, the database engine will return a value with a lot of decimal places, which is not exactly what we want. To round it to our output format, which has only one decimal place, the ROUND function is used:

```
ROUND(SUM(Class_Enrollment_per_Year.Credit_Hours * Convert_A_
to_N('GRADE', Grade))
                    / SUM(Class_Enrollment_per_Year.Credit_Hours), 1)
```

You might think that this would be enough, but ROUND doesn't change the data type of the returned value. It just rounds it to the specified number of decimal places. In other words, if the result is 1.23456789, ROUND will change it to 1.20000000. That's what the third scalar function, CAST, is used for:

```
CAST(ROUND(SUM(Class_Enrollment_per_Year.Credit_Hours * Convert_A_
to_N('GRADE', Grade))
                    / SUM(Class_Enrollment_per_Year.Credit_Hours),
1) as numeric(2, 1))
```

After the result of the math operations is rounded, CAST will change the data format to the required by the output parameter (numeric(2, 1), in this case). Then the result is finally pumped to the W_GPA temporary variable:

```
        INTO    W_GPA
```

The rest of the SELECT statement is fairly straightforward:

```
        FROM    Tbl_Class_Enrollment_per_Year Class_Enrollment_per_Year
        WHERE   Class_Enrollment_per_Year.Tbl_StudentsStudent_Id = p_
Student_Id
                AND Class_Enrollment_per_Year.Grade <> '--';
```

Note that only the valid grades of the student indicated in the input parameter (p_Student_id) are taken into consideration. In other words, the classes in which the student is or was enrolled but didn't get a grade—the lines that have a grade of '--'—are excluded in the WHERE clause of the statement.

All that's left now is to check whether the calculated GPA is indeed valid. I could have taken the same approach as I did in the Get_Student_Id UDF and add a COALESCE function on top of the CAST, in order to provide a valid value if the result of the whole formula was NULL. However, I also need to check whether the result is within the specified boundaries, so I'll use an IF statement instead:

```
        -- Check if everything went "normally"
    IF (W_GPA < 0.0 OR W_GPA > 4.0 OR W_GPA IS NULL) THEN
        -- If the GPA is not within the expected interval (0.0 - 4.0),
 return an impossible value to signal the error
        RETURN -1.0;
    ELSE
        -- otherwise, return the calculated GPA
        RETURN W_GPA;
    END IF;
 END;
```

The code above (and the respective comments) should be clear, with the exception of the W_GPA IS NULL expression. This will evaluate to true if the "original" value of the variable remained unchanged (I declared W_GPA but didn't provide a default value, so the variable contains NULL) or if it was not possible to calculate the GPA because of a lack of data, in either the Class Enrollment per Year or Data Conversion tables, in which case the SELECT statement will also return NULL.

Having said that, let me just stress two other things: first, it's important to structure and comment your code, because you never know when and who will have to look at it to correct or improve it; second, even though I'm using the hard-coded return value of -1.0 to indicate the error (and that's OK because the function is short and simple), you should try to follow the rule of defining a variable for the error-indicating value and set that value as the default right in the declaration statement, instead of using hard-coded values all over your code.

Because this is a UDF, I can use SELECT statements to test it:

```
-- Testing the function with valid and invalid student IDs
-- Valid ID
SELECT umadb_chp5.Calculate_GPA(3) FROM sysibm.sysdummy1;
-- Invalid ID
SELECT umadb_chp5.Calculate_GPA(3000) FROM sysibm.sysdummy1;
```

Creating a Simple UDTF

You can think of UDTFs as SQL views on steroids: UDTFs also return a table-like result and can be used in the FROM clause of SELECT statements. The main difference is that you can use SQL/PSM statements in UDTFs, which provide additional flexibility.

We'll start with a simple UDTF example, which you could implement as a view and then move on to more complex scenarios. The requirement is to create a user-defined table that provides information about the classes per department. It needs to include information about the department (ID and respective name); the course (ID, name, and description); and the class (just the name). Finally, it should accept a department ID as input. Let's analyze the SQL code that implements these requirements in detail.

Anatomy of a UDTF

Because we're talking about a UDF and not a stored procedure, you probably already guessed that the "anatomy" includes a RETURNS statement. However, in this case, our function won't return a single value, as the UDFs I've show so far. Instead it returns a table. Because this may sound a bit confusing, let's analyze the code as we go along, starting with the function signature, properties, and options:

```
SET SCHEMA = UMADB_CHP5;

-- Here's a simple UDTF that returns the classes of a given department
```
Continued

```
CREATE OR REPLACE FUNCTION Department_Classes(
    -- Parameters
    p_Department_Id integer
    )

    RETURNS TABLE (
        Department_Id integer
        , Department_Name char(60)
        , Course_Id integer
        , Course_Name char(60)
        , Course_Description char(100)
        , Class_Name char(60)
        )

    READS SQL DATA
    SPECIFIC DepClass1
    SET OPTION USRPRF = *OWNER
```

The first four lines of the function's code should be familiar by now: they simply define the function's name and input parameters. As I said before, it's in the RETURNS statement that things start to get (a whole lot) different from a "regular" UDF. The RETURNS TABLE block defines the table that this UDTF will return when called. In this particular case, it returns six columns, matching the requirements described in the previous section. The properties and options block is similar to what has been shown before. The keener eye will notice the absence of the ALLOW DEBUG MODE property. This is because UDTFs can't be debugged—not in the regular way, at least; most of the UDTFs' code is pure SQL, so you can run it directly from an SQL command line. The SQL/PSM parts might be trickier to test, but there's always a way.

It's also important to mention that, just like stored procedures and UDFs, UDTFs can be written in IBM i languages, such as RPG or C. However, that topic is outside the scope of this book; I'll focus on "native" UDTFs only.

Having said that, let's continue to dissect the structure of a UDTF. Because this is a simple function that returns a set of data without any special processing, there's no BEGIN/

END block, as you've seen in all the previous SP and UDF examples; instead, there's just a RETURN statement:

```
        RETURN
            SELECT Departments.Department_Id    "Department ID"
                 , Departments.Name             "Department Name"
                 , Courses.Course_Id            "Course ID"
                 , Courses.Name                 "Course Name"
                 , Courses.Description           "Course Description"
                 , Class_Definition.Name        "Class Name"
            FROM    Tbl_Departments Departments
                    INNER JOIN Tbl_courses Courses
                        ON Departments.Department_Id = Courses.Tbl_
DepartmentsDepartment_Id
                    INNER JOIN Tbl_Class_Definition Class_Definition
                        ON Courses.Course_Id = Class_Definition.Tbl_
CoursesCourse_Id
            WHERE   Departments.Department_Id = p_Department_Id
        ;
```

You're probably wondering whether you can get the same functionality with a view—and you're right. This was just an introductory example to show the building blocks of a UDTF. In this particular case, this extremely simple UDTF's functionality can be implemented using a view. In fact, as a rule of thumb, if all the data can be accessed with a single SELECT statement, independently of the number of tables, views, or nested sub-SELECTs that are involved, creating a view instead of a UDTF is a better choice. This is mainly because using a UDTF requires more computing power than accessing a view.

Using a UDTF in a SELECT Statement

The whole purpose of creating a UDTF is to use it, instead of using a table or a view, to access data. However, writing a SELECT statement that uses a UDTF requires a bit more typing than the "regular" SELECT statements you're used to. Here's how to select all classes from department 1:

```
SELECT        *
FROM    TABLE(umadb_chp5.Department_Classes(1)) Dep_Classes;
```

Note that I'm placing the call to the UDTF inside another function, named TABLE, which basically tells the database engine to treat the output of the function as a table. It seems a bit redundant, but you'll get used to it. From this point on, you can treat a UDTF as if it were a table or view: you can join it with other UDTFs or tables, limit its result set in the WHERE clause, and so on.

Writing More Complex UDTFs

Now that you've seen how to write a simple UDTF and how to use it in a SELECT statement, let's complicate things a bit. To avoid introducing more complexity than necessary, I'll diverge from the UMADB for a while, and instead of building hypothetical scenarios, I'll try to show real-life useful examples that you can reproduce and even use in your daily work.

Scheduled User Profile Review UDTF

I'll start by presenting a UDTF I actually use to perform scheduled user profile reviews (yes, some of us actually do those). The principle is simple: using a set of predefined keywords as parameters, I produce lists of potentially problematic situations, such as users with too much authority, never-expiring passwords, and stuff like that. To keep things simple, I'll show a trimmed-down version of the actual UDTF.

The basic structure is the basically same as shown before. It starts with a header, which declares the function and its return table, followed by the body of the function. Here's where things are different. Instead of a single (and simple) RETURN statement, there's actual SQL/PSM code, enclosed in BEGIN/END instructions, ending (as you probably guessed) with a RETURN statement. That's what it looks like; now let's discuss what happens in the function's body. The sequence of actions is the same as we performed in the manual process:

1.   List all user profiles in a temporary file.

2. Run one of several of SELECT statements, each representing a potential security threat (e.g., users with too much authority, never-expiring passwords).

3. Output the results in a table, typically exported to a Microsoft Excel file.

The big difference is that by using UDTFs, you can streamline the whole process and hide all the complexity (e.g., CL commands; IBM-ish column names such as UPUPRF, UPTEXT, and UPSTAT; and so on).

This first UDTF shows the first two steps of the process. The second one will use the first to produce a summary of the issues found during the review. So, without further ado, let's start analyzing this UDTF's source code in blocks, as we've done so far, starting with the function's header:

```
SET SCHEMA = UMADB_CHP5;

CREATE OR REPLACE FUNCTION UserReview(SecChk  VarChar(10))
     RETURNS TABLE (Check_Timestamp    Timestamp,
                    System_Name        Char(10),
                    User_Name          Char(10),
                    User_Class         Char(10),
                    User_Description   Char(50),
                    Last_Sign_In       TimeStamp,
                    User_Status        Char(10),
                    Special_Auth       Char(150),
                    Limited_Cap        Char(10),
                    Start_Program      Char(10),
                    Start_Program_Lib  Char(10),
                    Start_Menu         Char(10),
                    Group_Auth         Char(10),
                    Group_Profile      Char(10),
                    Password_Exp_Int   Decimal(5, 0),
                    Password_Is_Exp    Char(4),
                    Password_Is_None   Char(4),
                    Password_Last_Chg  Timestamp,
```
                                                    Continued

```
                        Password_Exp_Date Date,
                        User_Exp_Days       Decimal(5, 0)
                     )
        LANGUAGE SQL
        MODIFIES SQL DATA
```

This is the first step in hiding the complexity: IBM-ish column names are going to be presented as user-friendly column names in the output table of this function. Also note that I'm using MODIFIES SQL DATA instead of the (so far) usual READS SQL DATA. The next part, the declarations "section," also introduces some interesting things:

```
BEGIN
    -- Variable for the DSPUSRPRF command
    DECLARE W_CmdLine VarChar(256) Not NULL Default '';
    DECLARE W_Stmt VARCHAR(2000);
```

As I said before, I'm going to use a CL command to list the user profiles data in a temporary file. In order to do that, I need a variable large enough to hold the CL command I'm going to run. In case you're wondering, yes, you can run CL commands inside SQL. First, I'll set up the command in the CmdLine variable I just defined:

```
    -- Set up the CL command that retrieves the users' information in a
physical file
    SET W_CmdLine = 'DSPUSRPRF USRPRF(*ALL) OUTPUT(*OUTFILE)
OUTFILE(QTEMP/PROFILES)';
```

I'll show you how the command is executed shortly. First, let's take a moment to see how the other variable I defined will be used. Because of the different security checks I might want to run, I also need to add some flexibility to my queries. With that in mind, I'll use the W_Stmt variable to build the statement according to the input parameter's meaning. This statement will have two parts: a first, fixed part that includes the columns I want to select, which are the same as the output table's (defined in the RETURNS statement) columns, and a second part that depends on which security check was chosen.

Let's start with the code for the first part of the statement:

```
    SET W_Stmt = 'INSERT INTO QTEMP.OUTPUT_TABLE '
              CONCAT 'SELECT umadb_chp5.IBM_DATE_TO_TIMESTAMP(UPDCEN,
UPDDAT, UPDTIM) AS Check_Timestamp,'
              CONCAT ' UPSYST AS System_Name,'
              CONCAT ' UPUPRF AS User_Name,'
              CONCAT ' UPUSCL AS User_Class,'
              CONCAT ' UPTEXT AS User_Description,'
              CONCAT ' umadb_chp5.IBM_DATE_TO_TIMESTAMP(UPPSOC,
UPPSOD, UPPSOT) AS Last_Sign_In,'
              CONCAT ' UPSTAT AS User_Status,'
              CONCAT ' UPSPAU AS Special_Auth,'
              CONCAT ' UPLTCP AS Limited_Cap,'
              CONCAT ' UPINPG AS Start_Program,'
              CONCAT ' UPINPL AS Start_Program_Lib,'
              CONCAT ' UPINMN AS Start_Menu,'
              CONCAT ' UPGRAU AS Group_Auth,'
              CONCAT ' UPGRPF AS Group_Profile,'
              CONCAT ' UPPWEI AS Password_Exp_Int,'
              CONCAT ' UPPWEX AS Password_Is_Exp,'
              CONCAT ' UPPWON AS Password_Is_None,'
              CONCAT ' umadb_chp5.IBM_DATE_TO_TIMESTAMP(UPCHGC,
UPCHGD, UPCHGT) AS Password_Last_Chg,'
              CONCAT ' umadb_chp5.IBM_DATE_TO_DATE(UPEXPC, UPEXPD) AS
Password_exp_date,'
              CONCAT ' UPEXPI AS User_Exp_Days'
              CONCAT ' FROM QTEMP.PROFILES';
```

I mentioned earlier that this was the part of the statement that was fixed. This happens because the SELECT and FROM clauses are always the same: they need to match the output table's columns (if you look closely, you'll see that the columns' types and lengths match the output table's specifications), and the file I'm using is the one I defined in my CL command.

How about the variable part of the statement? Well, that's the tricky part. My UDTF is prepared to do all kinds of checks, and it's actually quite long, so I'm presenting a shortened version for brevity's sake:

```
CASE
    WHEN SecChk = '*SPCAUTH' THEN
        SET W_Stmt = TRIM(W_Stmt)
                        CONCAT ' WHERE UPSPAU LIKE ''%*ALLOBJ%'''
                        CONCAT ' OR UPSPAU LIKE ''%*IOSYSCFG%'''
                        CONCAT ' OR UPSPAU LIKE ''%*SAVSYS%'''
                        CONCAT ' OR UPSPAU LIKE ''%*SECADM%''';
    WHEN SecChk = '*PWD' THEN
        SET W_Stmt = Trim(W_Stmt)
                        CONCAT ' WHERE UPPWEI = -1'
                        CONCAT ' AND UPSTAT <> ''*DISABLED ''';
    -- Other checks omitted here for brevity's sake
    ELSE
        SET W_Stmt = Trim(W_Stmt);
        -- Add default sorting, etc.
END CASE;
```

I'm using a CASE statement that reacts to different input parameter values to fill out the rest of the statement. In this trimmed-down version, this corresponds to the WHERE clause, but I also use customized ORDER BY clauses in the "real-life" version. After this piece of code runs, my statement is ready for execution. However, the file over which it runs doesn't exist yet, because I defined the CL command and stored it in the W_CmdLine variable but I haven't actually executed the command. Let's see how that is done:

```
    -- Executing the command, which will create and fill the PROFILES
file in QTEMP
    CALL QCMDEXC(W_CmdLine, LENGTH(W_CmdLine));
```

Yes, it's that simple! It resembles the way you can call CL commands from within an RPG program.

The next step is to create the table that will be returned by the function. Note that this step is required because I'm using a customized SELECT statement and UDTFs don't allow you to use multiple RETURN statements. So, I need this intermediate step as a workaround for that limitation.

The table definition, shown next, should look familiar:

```
CREATE OR REPLACE TABLE QTEMP.OUTPUT_TABLE
            (
            Check_Timestamp    Timestamp,
            System_Name        Char(10),
            User_Name          Char(10),
            User_Class         Char(10),
            User_Description    Char(50),
            Last_Sign_In       TimeStamp,
            User_Status        Char(10),
            Special_Auth       Char(150),
            Limited_Cap        Char(10),
            Start_Program      Char(10),
            Start_Program_Lib Char(10),
            Start_Menu         Char(10),
            Group_Auth         Char(10),
            Group_Profile      Char(10),
            Password_Exp_Int  Decimal(5, 0),
            Password_Is_Exp    Char(4),
            Password_Is_None   Char(4),
            Password_Last_Chg Timestamp,
            Password_Exp_Date Date,
            User_Exp_Days      Decimal(5, 0)
            );
```

Notice the similarities with the RETURNS statement table? This is not a coincidence. It's simply a way to avoid extra typing in the RETURN statement, which I'll show in a minute.

But before that, I need to run my customized statement, using the EXECUTE IMMEDIATE statement I mentioned a few pages ago:

```
EXECUTE IMMEDIATE W_Stmt;
```

The next step is to delete the PROFILES file, which I used to receive the output of the DSPUSRPRF CL command, because leaving that kind of information lying around, even in QTEMP, is a security risk:

```
SET W_CmdLine = 'DLTOBJ OBJ(QTEMP/PROFILES) OBJTYPE(*FILE)';
CALL QCMDEXC(W_CmdLine, LENGTH(W_CmdLine));
```

This is the final preparation step. I'm now ready to return the data I collected, using the RETURN statement:

```
        RETURN SELECT * FROM QTEMP.OUTPUT_TABLE;
END;
```

Instead of a simple SELECT * ... statement, I could use a list of columns here that matched the RETURNS table specification. However, it would be another place to change whenever I added or removed columns.

Now that we're done, let's briefly review the mechanics of this function:

1. Declare variables for the CL command and customized SELECT statement.
2. Fill these variables with the appropriate information. Note that the CL statement and a generous part of the SELECT statement are fixed, but you could easily find a scenario in which the CL command is also influenced by an input parameter.
3. Create a temporary table. As I mentioned before, this is a way to circumvent the "One RETURN statement only, please" UDTF rule.
4. Execute the CL command and the customized SELECT statement.
5. Return the temporary table, which was filled by the execution of the SELECT statement.

Now let's test the function:

```
SELECT * FROM TABLE(umadb_chp5.UserReview(' *SPCAUTH')) as UR;
```

This statement will return a table containing pertinent information about the user profiles with special authorities.

Using a UDTF's Data in Another UDTF: Introducing the User Review Report

Now that I have a working UDTF that returns a set of data related to a certain aspect of the user profile review (users with special authorities, password issues, and so on), I can perform the review of each of these aspects individually, by running SELECTs with different parameters, as shown in the last example of the previous section, or I can create another UDTF that runs all the checks for me and returns a nice table with the summary of the results. Something like "*xx* users have special authorities; *yy* users may have password issues," and so on.

The way this works is simple: I'll simply call the user review UDTF multiple times and store the output in temporary tables. Then I count how many lines those tables have, and, if there are any issues to report (hopefully there aren't), I insert a new line in my summary table.

Let's go over this UDTF, slow and easy as usual, starting with the signature, options, and properties sections:

```
SET SCHEMA = UMADB_CHP5;

CREATE OR REPLACE FUNCTION UserReviewReport()
    RETURNS TABLE (Check_Timestamp    Timestamp,
                   nbr_users          Integer,
                   Issue_Description Char(100)
                   )
    LANGUAGE SQL
    MODIFIES SQL DATA
```

If you compare this with the user review UDTF, the only differences are the name of the function and the structure of the table it returns. Remember that I'm now returning summary data instead of the details. But don't worry, because the details will also be available—that's something I'll show you later. For now, let's check out the variables and tables required for this function to do what it does:

```
BEGIN
    -- Variable for the CRTDUPOBJ commands
    DECLARE W_CmdLine VarChar(256) Not NULL Default '';

    -- Create table for this function's output
    CREATE OR REPLACE TABLE QTEMP.User_Review_Report_Table
                (Check_Timestamp     Timestamp,
                 nbr_users           Integer,
                 Issue_Description Char(100)
                );
    -- Create dummy table to collect the user review details
    CREATE OR REPLACE TABLE QTEMP.Dummy_Tbl
                (
                Check_Timestamp    Timestamp,
                System_Name        Char(10),
                User_Name          Char(10),
                User_Class         Char(10),
                User_Description   Char(50),
                Last_Sign_In       TimeStamp,
                User_Status        Char(10),
                Special_Auth       Char(150),
                Limited_Cap        Char(10),
                Start_Program      Char(10),
                Start_Program_Lib  Char(10),
                Start_Menu         Char(10),
                Group_Auth         Char(10),
                Group_Profile      Char(10),
                Password_Exp_Int   Decimal(5, 0),

                                                    Continued
```

```
                    Password_Is_Exp    Char(4),
                    Password_Is_None   Char(4),
                    Password_Last_Chg  Timestamp,
                    Password_Exp_Date  Date,
                    User_Exp_Days      Decimal(5, 0)
                );
```

Here, I start by declaring a variable to store the CL commands I'll use (shown later) and create two tables: the first to store the output of the checks and the other to serve as template to the tables in which I'll store the detailed information that is the result of the security checks. I'll run one of block of code for each of the checks that comprise my user review. For brevity's sake, the function contains only the special authorities and a partial password issues check.

Let's dissect the special authorities block in more detail. It starts by prepping the necessary object for the check. More specifically, it creates a copy of my template table and names it appropriately: I'm checking the special authorities, so the table will be called UR_SPCAUTH (user review special authorities):

```
    -- Check 1: Users with special authorities issues
    SET W_CmdLine = 'CRTDUPOBJ OBJ(DUMMY_TBL) FROMLIB(QTEMP)
OBJTYPE(*FILE) TOLIB(*FROMLIB) NEWOBJ(UR_SPCAUTH)';
    -- Duplicate the dummy table to store this type of data
    CALL QCMDEXC(W_CmdLine, LENGTH(W_CmdLine));
Then it calls the User Review UDTF, passing the appropriate parameter,
and inserts the results in the newly created table:
    -- Run the user review for this type of issue
    INSERT INTO QTEMP.UR_SPCAUTH
        SELECT * FROM TABLE(umadb_chp5.UserReview('*SPCAUTH')) as UR;
The next step is checking whether there are any issues related with the
check:
    -- Check the results; if any issues were found, report them and keep
the table
```

Continued

```
    IF (SELECT COUNT(*) FROM QTEMP.UR_SPCAUTH) > O THEN
        INSERT INTO QTEMP.User_Review_Report_Table
            SELECT   CURRENT TIMESTAMP,
                     COUNT(*),
                     'Users with potential special authorities issues.
Check QTEMP.UR_SPCAUTH for details'
            FROM QTEMP.UR_SPCAUTH;
    -- otherwise, delete the table
    ELSE
        DROP TABLE QTEMP.UR_SPCAUTH;
    END IF;
```

If one or more lines exist in the UR_SPCAUTH table, it means that there's something to report, so the UDTF will insert the number of lines that the table has (in other words, the number of issues of this type that were found) in my summary table. If there's nothing to report, the UDTF will delete the temporary table. This might be a bit of overkill, because the tables are being created in QTEMP, but because you might want to change QTEMP to another library, to facilitate the extraction of the data, it seemed a good idea to delete the table.

That's about it! This block of code is then repeated, with a few tweaks for the other checks:

```
    -- Check 2: Users with password issues
    SET W_CmdLine = 'CRTDUPOBJ OBJ(DUMMY_TBL) FROMLIB(QTEMP)
OBJTYPE(*FILE) TOLIB(*FROMLIB) NEWOBJ(UR_PWD)';
    -- Duplicate the dummy table to store this type of data
    CALL QCMDEXC(W_CmdLine, LENGTH(W_CmdLine));
    -- Run the user review for this type of issue
    INSERT INTO QTEMP.UR_PWD
        SELECT * FROM TABLE(umadb_chp5.UserReview('*PWD')) as UR;
    -- Check the results; if any issues were found, report them and keep
the table
                                                        Continued
```

```
    IF (SELECT COUNT(*) FROM QTEMP.UR_PWD) > 0 THEN
        INSERT INTO QTEMP.User_Review_Report_Table
            SELECT  CURRENT TIMESTAMP,
                    COUNT(*),
                    'Users with potential password issues. Check QTEMP.
UR_PWD for details'
            FROM QTEMP.UR_SPCAUTH;
    -- otherwise, delete the table
    ELSE
        DROP TABLE QTEMP.UR_PWD;
    END IF;

    -- Other checks omitted here --
```

As you can see from the code above, the differences are the parameter passed to the User Review function, the name of the output file and, of course, the sentence written in the summary file. I could have written yet another function to perform these actions, taking as parameters the security check code and the name of the file, which would shorten this function's code, but I decided to leave that task for you. It's a good, easy practice exercise that can help you consolidate all of this new stuff.

Anyway, back to our function! All that's left to do now is return the summary table and end the function:

```
    RETURN SELECT * FROM QTEMP.User_Review_Report_Table;
END;
```

As you've seen with previous UDTF calls, I need to run a SELECT statement to get the results from the UDTF:

```
SELECT * FROM TABLE(umadb_chp5.UserReviewReport()) as URR;
```

If you have any potential security issues, you'll see one or more lines in the resulting table. If that's the case, you can also check the details, by running SELECTs over the tables indicated in the messages, like this:

```
SELECT * FROM Qtemp.UR_SpcAuth;
SELECT * FROM Qtemp.UR_Pwd;
```

From here, you can create your own UDTFs, either based on files produced by CL commands, like these last two functions, or more complex business algorithms that you can't reproduce with views. Here are a couple of ideas:

- Cross-check users and authority lists, by creating files using the DSPAUTL (Display Authorization List) and DSPUSRPRF commands and using SQL to check the actual authority users have over the system objects (not only tables, but also programs and commands).

- Produce a database analysis impact using the DSPDBR (Display Database Relations) command to list all the relations of a specific table.

In This Chapter, You've Learned ...

I hope that this chapter has helped you to understand some of the concepts introduced in the previous two chapters, and use them to solve everyday problems. Here's a summary of the ground covered in this chapter:

- The concept of UDF, introduced in the previous chapter, was put into practice.

- The anatomy of a UDF was explained with a simple example (composing dates and timestamps using IBM-ish date fields).

- The different types of UDF (scalar, aggregate, and table) were explained, even though an aggregate UDF example was not provided.

- The use of some of SQL/PSM's control flow statements was explained and exemplified, as well as the concept of overloading (two UDFs with the same name but different parameters).

- In regard to UDTFs, I explained what makes them different from UDFs and how UDTFs can use UDFs in their inner workings.

- Finally, I showed a type of UDTF that uses CL commands to produce files that are processed with SQL/PSM statements to generate reports, namely to generate a User Review Report.

The next chapter will continue to make use of the SQL/PSM and SQL statements that I've explained and demonstrated in this and the previous chapters, but from a different point of view: it will cover triggers and what you can do with them.

9

Making a Trigger-Happy Database

This chapter will explore triggers, in their multiple forms and uses. It will start by explaining what triggers are and how they can work in a data-centric approach. Then the chapter will explore different scenarios in which you should (and shouldn't) use triggers. Finally, the chapter will also provide several examples in the UMADB context. Note that this chapter uses what was discussed in the previous three chapters. If you haven't read them (and you're not familiar with SQL/PSM concepts), please take some time to do so.

This chapter's title refers to the third and final part of the SQL routines I discussed back in Chapter 7. I mentioned that one of the differences between SQL routines is how they are called. A *trigger*, much like a tripwire, reacts automatically when certain actions are performed: if you apply too much pressure on a tripwire, it will go off or cause something else to go off. And just like the tripwire, a database trigger can make very bad things happen to your database. Don't worry, I'll explain how you can keep triggers from causing more harm than good, but that's for later in the chapter. Let's start with the basics of triggers.

Introducing Database Triggers

A trigger is a predefined event that runs automatically whenever a specified action is performed on a table. In the "smart reality" and "Internet of Things" times that we live in, it's the database equivalent of the shower turning itself on (and at the right temperature) when you enter the bathtub. The fun part is that you can be very specific about what happens when that predefined event occurs.

Before getting into the details, let me just add that there are two types of triggers: those you might already be familiar with: high-level programming language (HLL) triggers, written in RPG or one of the other languages the IBM i supports natively, and SQL triggers. I'll stick to the same guidelines followed thus far and will discuss only SQL triggers. It's true that most of the stuff I'll talk about can also be done in an RPG program. Sometimes, it might even be better to adapt an existing HLL program and link it to a trigger via the ADDPFTRG (Add Physical File Trigger) CL command, especially if complex code is involved. However, for certain tasks, an SQL-only approach is preferable for reasons of clarity and future maintenance.

Having said that, let's dissect the definition with which this section started, starting with the "specified action" part.

What Triggers a Trigger?

Going back to my bathtub analogy, imagine that you enter your bathtub with your clothes on. Turning on the shower automagically doesn't sound like a great idea now, right? Well, maybe just turning on the faucet, to start the water running, sounds better. Triggers, unlike tripwires, can be created to react only to specified actions. Because triggers are associated with tables, those actions are the I/O operations that somehow change the table: INSERT, UPDATE, and DELETE operations.

I know, you're thinking that reading the table's records also changes its state, because it can cause locks, and so on. However, it's not possible to create a trigger that goes off whenever records are read from a table, only for the three other I/O operations I mentioned. But there's more to it: you can choose when the trigger goes off: before or after the action occurs. As you'll see later in this chapter, this distinction is of paramount importance for some of the tasks you can rig a trigger to perform. Just a side note: instead of "goes off" or "is triggered," I personally prefer the expression "is activated" to refer to the moment the metaphorical tripwire is pulled. So, from this point on, I'll refer to activation to describe the moment the trigger is put to use.

*In a nutshell, here's what you need to keep in mind about triggers: they execute a piece of code (SQL or HLL) when the records of the table they're associated with are changed (via an **INSERT**, **UPDATE**, or **DELETE** operation). The execution of that piece of code can happen before or after the action that triggered it occurs.*

Why Use Triggers?

Triggers are great at making stuff happen without human intervention, because they are activated whenever the action or actions with which they're rigged happens. Yes, you read it right: it's possible to associate a trigger with more than one action. You can define a trigger that executes a piece of code upon insertion or deletion of a record, for instance, no matter where these actions are initiated. And that's the interesting part: triggers are linked to the table, not the operation's source, which means that they'll be activated no matter where the operation comes from: an RPG program, a remote ODBC call, or a DFU (remember that tool?) operation performed by you.

This "operation omniscience" makes triggers the perfect tool in a data-centric approach, because they allow you to "move" code from RPG applications to the database! Think of the possibilities: just to mention a possible scenario, you can simply rig a trigger that calls a complex (and typically old) RPG monolith instead of detailing the business logic to be rewritten in a "modern" language, in order to perform the same validations, with very little effort. You can reuse, instead of rewriting, your code by placing triggers in the appropriate tables, with the appropriate conditions, and call existing programs. Note that I do not advise perpetuating the use of old RPG monoliths. It's always better to rewrite them in smaller and more manageable chunks of code—but that's a discussion for another book.

You can also easily create audit files, validate data, and do much more—all at database level, thus making your database more "intelligent." Do you see where I'm going with this? These are just some of the reasons you should use triggers: as part of a data-centric approach, they provide an amazing level of reusability and automation.

SQL Triggers' Advantages

As I mentioned earlier, there are two types of triggers: SQL and external. You're probably familiar with the external (created using RPG or other IBM i-compatible HLL) triggers.

What you are probably not aware of is that SQL triggers offer several advantages over external triggers:

- SQL's simpler and more powerful language makes trigger development easier and faster.
- SQL triggers' activation is more precise: you can, for instance, activate the trigger only if a certain column has a certain value. This type of operation is not possible with external triggers.
- It's much easier to write an SQL trigger to handle operations that modify more than one row in the target table.
- With SQL, you can create INSTEAD OF triggers (which I'll discuss later in this chapter).
- SQL's syntax makes it easier to write and configure one trigger to process several events.

After all this discussion, you're probably itching to start coding. Well, I'll get to that in a moment. First, I'll explain how to create triggers using SQL and provide some examples to get you warmed up.

SQL Trigger Mechanics

What you've read so far hinted at (actually, it almost gave away) most of the mechanics of an SQL trigger. Let's take a moment to see how the different pieces fit in the instruction's syntax:

```
CREATE TRIGGER trigger-name
trigger-activation-time
trigger-event ON target-table
transition-variables (or transition-table)
trigger-granularity
trigger-mode
triggered-action
```

It seems like a lot but isn't that complicated, especially because I already mentioned (albeit without naming) all these different pieces. Let me go over them, one by one:

- The *trigger-name* must be unique within the schema to which it belongs. It's restricted by the same rule previously discussed in regard to SQL routines, so I won't go into details about them here.

- The *trigger-activation-time* refers to the moment in which the trigger is activated: BEFORE or AFTER the event that activated the trigger occurs (there's also another option for this parameter, named INSTEAD OF, which I'll leave for later).

- The *trigger-event* indicates with which operation(s) the trigger is associated. I mentioned the I/O operations before, but let's look at the syntax in more detail. You can choose between INSERT, UPDATE, and DELETE. It's also possible to use any combination of these three commands, separating the options with the OR keyword. For instance, a trigger that is activated by an insertion or deletion of a record will have INSERT or DELETE on the trigger-event part of its definition. By the way, the ON target-table refers to the table over which you're setting up the trigger, because unlike SPs and UDFs, triggers don't exist in a vacuum: they are always linked to a target table.

- The *trigger-granularity* is one of most interesting parts of the trigger's definition, as it allows you to decide how the trigger will be activated. You can choose between FOR EACH STATEMENT and FOR EACH ROW. This controls whether the triggered action is executed for each row or for each statement that has been changed in some way. For instance, an UPDATE operation could modify three rows, and the trigger would be activated either once or three times depending on the value defined here.

- The next item in the list, *trigger-mode*, also plays a part in the execution, but in a different way. It controls the moment in which the trigger's code is executed. If you choose MODE DB2ROW, then the trigger will be activated (in other words, its code will be executed) after each row operation. But if you choose MODE DB2SQL, then the database engine will wait until all the row operations are processed to execute all the respective trigger's actions.

- Finally, *triggered-action* is a placeholder for the actual SQL/PSM code that will run whenever the trigger is activated. It can be either a simple INSERT statement (as you'll see in one of the examples, later in this chapter), or something much more complex (such as a full-fledged SQL/PSM routine for cross-table data validation, for instance).

Keep in mind that not all these pieces are mandatory, as you'll see in a moment.

A Simple Trigger Example

To help you consolidate the syntax explanation, let's analyze a simple scenario: someone wants to keep track of how many students exist in our UMADB students table, so they asked us to create a simple counters table that stores the total number of students, teachers, and classes that exist at any moment. "It will look good on our website," they said. Note that this is a hypothetical and oversimplified scenario that ignores the fact that these three pieces of information can be obtained directly from the respective tables.

Instead of going to the RPG, Web, or any of the many simple programs or full-fledged applications that use the Students table, we'll tackle the problem at its target, rather than its source(s): We're going to create a trigger that is totally oblivious to where the student-creation request (read: the insert operation in the students table) came from, and that's it! No need to change the existing HLL (IBM i "native" or otherwise) applications. The most pressing issue here is that you need to have an exclusive lock over the table to add the trigger. There are other potential issues, which I'll address in greater depth later, but that's the most important one—for now. So, let's say we wait until a time no one is using the Students table, and we create our trigger with the following command:

```
CREATE OR REPLACE TRIGGER UMADB_CHP5.Trg_log_student_creation
    AFTER INSERT ON UMADB_CHP5.TBL_Students
    UPDATE UMADB_CHP5.TBL_Counters
        SET STUDENT_COUNTER = STUDENT_COUNTER + 1;
```

Let's dissect this statement (and please pay attention, because you're about to get some practice based on this), bit by bit. The first line (CREATE OR REPLACE TRIGGER UMADB_CHP5.Trg_log_student_creation) is quite obvious and follows the same principles of the previously presented SQL routines. It serves to identify the type and name of the SQL routine. In this case, I'm creating (or replacing, if it already exists) a trigger named Trg_log_student_creation in schema UMADB_CHP5. The second line (AFTER INSERT ON UMADB_CHP5.TBL_Students) tells us that this trigger is activated after each insert operation on table TBL_Students. So far, this follows the high-level syntax model I presented earlier.

However, I mentioned that not all the "pieces" of that model were mandatory. The next couple of lines (UPDATE UMADB_CHP5.Tbl_Counters and SET STUDENT_COUNTER = STUDENT_COUNTER + 1;) serve as an example of that statement, as they don't refer to the trigger's granularity or mode. In fact, these lines are this trigger's action: an update to another table.

But let's go back to the trigger's granularity and mode; even though it's not specified, the trigger granularity option is "still there"—its default, implicit value is the FOR EACH STATEMENT. Similarly, the trigger mode is also absent, so its default value—MODE DB2SQL—will be used, in order to keep compatibility with other DB2 implementations. Although this is a very simple trigger, I could have written the triggered action (my UPDATE statement) as a BEGIN/END block of code, because triggers are SQL routines, and SQL routines can be composed of multiple BEGIN/END blocks. I could rewrite my trigger to include the BEGIN/END lines, like this:

```
CREATE OR REPLACE TRIGGER UMADB_CHP5.Trg_log_student_creation
    AFTER INSERT ON UMADB_CHP5.TBL_Students
    BEGIN
        UPDATE UMADB_CHP5.TBL_Counters
            SET STUDENT_COUNTER = STUDENT_COUNTER + 1;
    END;
```

Testing Your First Trigger

It's now time to test this trigger. Naturally, I'll use SQL statements for that. You can either type them or use the ones provided in the downloadable source code for this chapter. The Counters table doesn't exist in the current UMADB schema, so you'll need to create it, using the following statement:

```
CREATE OR REPLACE TABLE UMADB_CHP5.TBL_Counters
    (Student_Counter    integer,
     Teacher_Counter    integer,
     Class_Counter      integer
    );
```

The next step is to add a new row, zeroing the counters:

```
INSERT INTO UMADB_CHP5.TBL_Counters
    Values(0, 0, 0);
```

Just to check whether everything is in perfect order, let's run a SELECT statement over the Counters table:

```
SELECT  *
FROM    UMADB_CHP5.TBL_Counters;
```

All the pieces are set, so let's test the trigger. This particular trigger is activated by INSERT operations in the Students table, so let's create a new student. That task is, for now, a two-step process. First, I need to create a new person record:

```
INSERT INTO UMADB_CHP5.TBL_PERSONS
    (NAME, DATE_OF_BIRTH, HOME_ADDRESS, HOME_PHONE_NBR, MOBILE_NBR,
    EMAIL_ADDRESS, DRIVERS_LICENSE, SOCIAL_SEC_NBR)
    VALUES ('David Driven', 19100301, 'London, UK', 'N/A', '333-444-
555',
            'bond@cassino_royale.007', 'N/A', '6534237890');
```

And then, using the person ID generated by the database, I can finally insert a new row in the Students table:

```
INSERT INTO UMADB_CHP5.TBL_STUDENTS
    (TBL_PERSONSPERSON_ID) VALUES (17);
```

Note that 17 is the person ID generated by the database when I inserted the record; yours will certainly be a different number, so run a quick SELECT over the Persons table, find out which is the correct number, and replace the 17 with that number. If you were expecting some sort of confirmation that the trigger was activated (or even that it exists) when the INSERT statement's execution finished, you might be disappointed, because you won't see it. To check whether the trigger was actually activated (and worked as expected), you need to check the Counters table again:

```
SELECT  *
FROM    UMADB_CHP5.TBL_Counters;
```

There you'll see the proof you were looking for: the student count's value was changed from 0 to 1, so the trigger was executed, and it performed admirably the action it was designed to perform.

Time for Some Practice

Now that you know a little more about SQL triggers and their syntax, it's time for some hands-on work. The idea is for you to create similar triggers to feed the other two columns of the Counters table—Teacher_Counter and Class_Counter—whenever new records are added to their corresponding tables (TBL_Teachers and TBL_Class_Definition, respectively). Just reread the section that dissects the trigger that keeps the Student_Counter updated, and you should do fine. If you need a little push (or get totally lost), you'll find the statement for creating the Counters table and the solutions (separate files for the two triggers) for this little practice session in this chapter's downloadable source code. If you want to check whether these two triggers work, just adapt and run the test steps mentioned in the previous section to each particular situation.

Exploring More Complex Trigger Scenarios

Now that you know how to create simple triggers, let's move on to more complex scenarios. As you probably realized by now, a trigger can be used for many different tasks. Updating a certain value each time a record is somehow created or changed is just a very small part of what you can do with a trigger. Let me take you on an exploration of a few scenarios where a properly crafted trigger can be a simple solution to a complex problem. Instead of vague and insipid scenarios, we'll return to our fictional UMADB database and its environment to provide something you can actually relate to. So, just to quickly get you back "into character": we work for ACME University's IT department, and we've been overhauling the database in order to open it to all the non-IBM i applications that need its data.

Using Triggers for Data Validation

We were called to the Dean's office (again). It seems that our good job with the database redesign and stored procedures got us on the Dean's speed-dial list. This time, the big boss is worried about data tampering and asked us to devise low-cost, low-maintenance solutions for this type of problem. The most urgent matter is related to money, naturally. More specifically, it concerns the teachers' salary data: he wants us to find a cheap way to avoid a teacher's salary being increased more than 10 percent in one update.

Now that we've helped "open up" the database to non-native applications, there are multiple points of entry from which the teacher's data can be changed. This means that an application-level change is not an option: it would be costly and time-consuming to implement, and would basically mean repeating the same business rule in multiple environments and programming languages. Our solution is to perform a database-level change, by creating a data-validity check whenever a teacher's record is changed.

However, there are many possible changes (theoretically, as many as the table's columns), so this has to be very precise. The other factor that we must take into account is that this check has to prevent the change, not find and report it after it happens. You probably already saw where this is going: we're going to set up a trigger that's activated before an update that changes a teacher's salary occurs. If, and only if, the new salary is more than 10 percent higher than the original one, we'll block the change and send an error message back to the origin of the update. This sounds tricky, but it's actually quite simple. Let's analyze the code, bit by bit, starting with the usual trigger name and even "sections":

```
CREATE OR REPLACE TRIGGER UMADB_CHP5.Trg_check_teacher_salary_update
    BEFORE UPDATE ON UMADB_CHP5.TBL_TEACHERS
```

Nothing new here: I'm just naming my trigger and saying that it will be activated before an update occurs in the Teachers table. Now I need to compare the old and new values of the salary. How can I do that, if we're talking about the same record? Well, actually the trigger's "entry parameters" are the before and after images of the records. In other words, I can access the record before its data is changed by the UPDATE statement. However, I must tell the database engine that I need both the before and after images, and

I need to define a prefix for them, because (obviously) the column names are the same in both. The following three lines of code are all that's required to do it:

```
REFERENCING NEW ROW AS UPDATED OLD ROW AS ORIGINAL
FOR EACH ROW MODE DB2ROW
WHEN (UPDATED.SALARY <> ORIGINAL.SALARY)
```

The first line tells the database engine that I'll be using both "old" and "new" records or, in other words, the original and updated records. The second line is there to guarantee that the trigger is called after each row, because the update can affect multiple rows at once. Finally, the third row tells the database engine to restrict the activation of this trigger to updates that change the salary column, because that's all I'm interested in right now. All that's left to do is check whether the change is allowed—that is, whether the new salary is within the accepted limits. That task is performed in the trigger action section:

```
BEGIN
    IF UPDATED.SALARY >= ORIGINAL.SALARY * 1.1 THEN
        SIGNAL SQLSTATE '75001'
            SET MESSAGE_TEXT = 'This teacher salary change is not
valid, because the new salary is more than 110% of the old salary';
    END IF;
END;
```

In this block of code, I'm checking whether the update (new) salary is higher than the limit: 110 percent of the original (old) salary. If it is, I'm stopping the process and sending an error message back to the caller program. If you don't recall how SIGNAL works, reread Chapter 6 to brush up on error handling and signaling. The SET MESSAGE_ TEXT sends a human-readable message that can be accessed by the caller directly (SQLCA) or via the GET DIAGNOSTICS statement, depending on the caller program's environment.

Testing the Teacher Salary Update Check Trigger

All that's left to do now is to test the trigger. This one doesn't require the creation of additional tables; all you need is a properly engineered UPDATE statement. First, let's find an appropriate teacher ID, by running a SELECT over the entire table:

```
SELECT   TEACHER_ID
         , SALARY
FROM     UMADB_CHP5.TBL_TEACHERS;
```

Let's pick one existing ID—I chose 6, but it all depends on the data—and run the following UPDATE statement:

```
UPDATE   UMADB_CHP5.TBL_TEACHERS
SET      SALARY = SALARY * 1.2
WHERE    TEACHER_ID = 6;
```

This will try to increase the salary of the teacher whose ID is equal to 6 by 20 percent. As expected, the update will fail. If you run this statement in Run SQL Scripts or a similar tool, you should receive output similar to this:

```
SQL State: 09000 Vendor Code: -723 Message: [SQL0723] SQL trigger
TRG_CHECK_TEACHER_SALARY_UPDATE of UMADB_CHP5 failed with SQLCODE
-438 SQLSTATE 75001. Cause . . . . . :   An error occurred in an SQL
instruction activated in the trigger TRG_CHECK_TEACHER_SALARY_UPDATE of
the UMADB_CHP5 schema. The SQLCODE is -438, the SQLSTATE is 75001 and
the message is This teacher salary change is not valid, because the new
salary is more than 110% of the old salary. Recovery . . :   Check the
job log for more information. Correct the error and try again.
```

With 11 lines of code, we solved a problem that would have taken several programmers quite a bit of time to solve, in their respective applications. Note that this is a very simple example of data validation, but it illustrates the foundational principles: set up the trigger to run in the appropriate event (by using the proper BEFORE/AFTER INSERT/UPDATE/DELETE combination in the trigger event section), pinpoint your target (using the WHEN clause), run the check (with one or more IF statements), and act upon it (by writing the necessary code in the trigger action section, which will either block the I/O operation entirely, as I did here, or adjust the incorrect value, for instance).

Using Triggers for Auditing

Even though this crisis was averted, somehow we find ourselves in the Dean's office (again). This time, the Dean wants us to set up history files for auditing purposes, because someone has been tampering with the grades, and no one knows how, when, who, or from where. It seems the existing auditing mechanisms, which were built in the application's RPG III days and were never properly overhauled, are not working as they should, so we got called in to save the day.

Yes, it's another trigger scenario, a bit different from the previous one. In short, we need to build something that logs all activity in the grades table (that's the TBL_Class_ Enrollment_Per_Year table, in case you don't remember), except READ operations. We're going to log all INSERT and DELETE operations, as well as all UPDATE operations that change the GRADE column.

I'll create a new table, based on the Class Enrollment per Year, with a few additional columns: EVENT, which I'll fill with the name of the operation that activated the trigger; USER (you guessed it) to contain the name of the user who initiated the operation; and TIMESTAMP to answer the "when" question. Instead of a complete CREATE TABLE statement, with all the names of the original table columns plus these three new columns, I'll use a shortcut and create the table by copying the Class Enrollment per Year table's structure and adding the new columns. Yes, that's possible and actually quite simple:

```
CREATE OR REPLACE TABLE UMADB_CHP5.TBL_class_enrollment_per_year_log AS
    (SELECT    CEM.*
              , 'OPERATION' as EVENT
              , USER as USER
              , CURRENT_TIMESTAMP as TIMESTAMP
    FROM       UMADB_CHP5.TBL_class_enrollment_per_year CEM)
    WITH NO DATA;
```

The CREATE TABLE AS statement allows you to create a new table on the fly, based on a SELECT statement. It's particularly useful in situations such as this one, because I don't have to type (or copy/paste) the complete list of columns of the original table. Finally, the WITH NO DATA line is important, because I just want the table definition, not its data. If you run a simple SELECT statement on the new table, you'll be able to confirm that it has all the necessary columns. Now I can proceed to the trigger creation.

You could write an RPG program and associate it with a trigger using the ADDPFTRG (Add Physical File Trigger) CL command, but I'll take the SQL route and use a native trigger. Just as I did before, I'll divide the trigger's code into chunks and analyze each of them separately. Let's start with the trigger name, activation, and event sections:

```
CREATE OR REPLACE TRIGGER UMADB_CHP5.Trg_log_class_enrollment_per_year_
changes
     AFTER INSERT OR UPDATE OF GRADE OR DELETE ON UMADB_CHP5.TBL_class_
enrollment_per_year
```

This looks similar to the previous trigger, but it also has some noteworthy differences. If you look carefully, you'll note that this trigger is activated after an INSERT, DELETE, or UPDATE of a record in our grades table. However, there's something special about the update: I only want the trigger to be activated if the update operation changes the GRADE column; that's why I included that OF GRADE bit after the UPDATE. This OF *some column* part only makes sense after an update, because when you insert or delete a record, you're affecting the whole record, not just one particular column or set of columns.

The next part of the statement is also similar to the previous trigger:

```
     REFERENCING OLD ROW AS OLDREC NEW ROW AS NEWREC
     FOR EACH ROW MODE DB2ROW
```

I changed the old and new record prefixes for clarity's sake, but it's basically the same as before. The difference is what I'm going to do with the records, as you'll see in the trigger action section. Remember, the objective is to keep track of all INSERT, UPDATE, or DELETE operations performed on the table where the grades are stored. It might be useful to know which row of the log file is linked to which operation. That's why the log file includes a column named EVENT. Native triggers offer us a simple way to determine which event activated the trigger. Because I want to store that information in my audit table, I'll use a variable to temporarily store the operation name:

```
BEGIN
     DECLARE W_EVENT CHAR(10) DEFAULT NULL;
```

This variable will receive different values, depending on the event that activated the trigger. Let's see this in the code, by analyzing the piece of code that's executed when an INSERT occurs:

```
IF INSERTING THEN
     SET W_EVENT = 'INSERT';
     INSERT INTO UMADB_CHP5.TBL_class_enrollment_per_year_log
         (TBL_STUDENTSSTUDENT_ID
         , TBL_CLASSES_PER_YEARCLASS_PER_YEAR_ID
         , GRADE
         , CREDIT_HOURS
         , EVENT, USER, TIMESTAMP)
         VALUES(NEWREC.TBL_STUDENTSSTUDENT_ID
                 , NEWREC.TBL_CLASSES_PER_YEARCLASS_PER_YEAR_ID
                 , NEWREC.GRADE
                 , NEWREC.CREDIT_HOURS
                 , W_EVENT, USER, CURRENT_TIMESTAMP);
```

It's that first line, IF INSERTING THEN, that does the trick. There are three such predicates: INSERTING, UPDATING, and DELETING. These keywords contain TRUE if the corresponding operation activated the trigger. When used with an IF statement, they allow you to do different things depending on the operation, instead of creating multiple triggers. In this case, I want to log when a new record is inserted, who did it, and when. Note that I'm using the "new" record for this, because there's no "old" record, in this case.

The code for the UPDATE and DELETE is similar, as you'll see in a minute, but for those scenarios I decided to log only the "old" record (that is, the image of the record before the UPDATE or DELETE operation was performed):

```
    ELSE
        IF UPDATING THEN
            SET W_EVENT = 'UPDATE';
        ELSE
            SET W_EVENT = 'DELETE';
        END IF;
        INSERT INTO UMADB_CHP5.TBL_class_enrollment_per_year_log
            (TBL_STUDENTSSTUDENT_ID
            , TBL_CLASSES_PER_YEARCLASS_PER_YEAR_ID
            , GRADE
            , CREDIT_HOURS
            , EVENT, USER, TIMESTAMP)
            VALUES(OLDREC.TBL_STUDENTSSTUDENT_ID
                , OLDREC.TBL_CLASSES_PER_YEARCLASS_PER_YEAR_ID
                , OLDREC.GRADE
                , OLDREC.CREDIT_HOURS
                , W_EVENT, USER, CURRENT_TIMESTAMP);
    END IF;
END;
```

Remember that because of that UPDATE OF GRADE bit of code, I'm only logging updates that change the GRADE column. This is another way to implement granularity, quite different from the WHEN (UPDATED.SALARY <> ORIGINAL.SALARY) used in the previous trigger. If you read carefully the documentation about triggers in the *DB2 for i Reference* manual, you'll see that there's usually more than one way to solve a problem.

Testing the Trigger

Let's test this trigger! I'll assume that you have some data in the Class Enrollment per Year table, and I'll start by updating a grade:

```
UPDATE  UMADB_CHP5.TBL_CLASS_ENROLLMENT_PER_YEAR
    SET GRADE = 'A'
    WHERE TBL_CLASSES_PER_YEARCLASS_PER_YEAR_ID = 14;
```

You might need to adjust this statement, so that the TBL_CLASSES_PER_YEARCLASS_PER_YEAR_ID matches an ID that exists in your version of the data. Now let's run an INSERT statement:

```
INSERT INTO UMADB_CHP5.TBL_class_enrollment_per_year
    (TBL_STUDENTSSTUDENT_ID
    , TBL_CLASSES_PER_YEARCLASS_PER_YEAR_ID
    , GRADE
    , CREDIT_HOURS)
    VALUES(4, 18, '--', 30);
```

Again, you might need to adjust the IDs for this to work on your system. Finally, let's delete the line we just inserted:

```
DELETE FROM    UMADB_CHP5.TBL_CLASS_ENROLLMENT_PER_YEAR
WHERE          TBL_STUDENTSSTUDENT_ID = 4
               AND TBL_CLASSES_PER_YEARCLASS_PER_YEAR_ID = 18;
```

If everything went as expected, you should have three lines in your log table. Run the following statement to check:

```
SELECT * FROM UMADB_CHP5.TBL_class_enrollment_per_year_log;
```

You should find an exact image of the record you updated, as well as two copies of the record you inserted: one for the INSERT and another for the DELETE operations. The first record is the image before the update, because I'm using the OLDREC prefix in the INSERT statement that writes data to the log table.

There you have it: a different trigger, slightly more complicated than the previous one, which you can easily adapt to create an audit/log/history table to any existing table in your database!

Using Triggers to Compose and Fill Columns

This time the request for help didn't come from the Dean's office, for a change. The manager of one of the university's Web applications (who happens to be the Dean's niece) asked for our help in preventing "that awful content" from being displayed by the application she manages. After a quick chat, we figured out that those "N/A" default values that we assigned to certain text columns were the cause of her discomfort. We could simply alter the default values and be done with it, but let's take this opportunity to do something else with triggers: we're going to compose and fill a column if, and only if, certain conditions are met. This is not a case of "change a column whenever the record is updated." It's a bit more refined than that, but still simple enough to follow and reproduce in similar (and potentially more complex) scenarios you will find in your own applications.

Let's start with something simple: the Departments table contains one of those "N/A" filled columns: the department description. Earlier in this chapter, you saw how to condition the activation of a trigger, so the code for this trigger should be fairly easy to understand:

```
-- Trigger for providing a "nice" description when one was not provided
CREATE OR REPLACE TRIGGER UMADB_CHP5.Trg_Replace_NA_Text_on_update
    BEFORE UPDATE ON UMADB_CHP5.TBL_DEPARTMENTS
    REFERENCING NEW ROW AS UPDATED OLD ROW AS ORIGINAL
    FOR EACH ROW MODE DB2ROW
    WHEN (UPDATED.Description = 'N/A')
    BEGIN
        SET UPDATED.Description = 'A description for this department was
not provided';
    END;
```

While the declaration of the trigger and the rest of the "header" should be familiar by now, the body (the line between the BEGIN and END statements) might confuse you, because you're looking at a change of a column's value. Don't worry: there's no INSERT or UPDATE action following it. That's because the INSERT/UPDATE is not necessary. Note that the trigger is activated before the update takes place. This means that any changes made to the table's columns values will be made final when the trigger ends and the actual UPDATE operation is performed. That's why there's a SET statement in the body of the trigger, but no UPDATE statement following it.

However, if this was all you could do, it wouldn't be very useful! In a real-life scenario, you might want to use more complex values—computed or composed using other columns' values, for instance.

Let's see how that works with a trigger that replaces the "N/A" of the Courses table's Description column with some nicely composed text: "A *<department name>* department course, managed by *<Teacher Rank> <Teacher Name>*." This trigger is a bit longer and complex, but it follows the same basic principles as the previous one. The difference is that there are some parts of the description that come from other tables. I'll show you how that translates to code in a moment, but first, let's look at the trigger's header part:

```
-- Trigger for providing a "nice" description when one was not provided
CREATE OR REPLACE TRIGGER UMADB_CHP5.Trg_Replace_NA_text_on_Courses_
update
    BEFORE UPDATE ON UMADB_CHP5.TBL_COURSES
    REFERENCING NEW ROW AS UPDATED OLD ROW AS ORIGINAL
    FOR EACH ROW MODE DB2ROW
    WHEN (UPDATED.Description = 'N/A')
```

It's very similar to the previous one. Actually, the only change is the table name, which went from TBL_Departments to TBL_Courses. The next part is the body of the trigger, where all the real action takes place. It starts with the declaration of the variables, which will temporarily hold the names of the department, rank, and teacher:

```
BEGIN
      DECLARE Dep_Name Char(60);
      DECLARE Rank_Name Char(60);
      DECLARE Teacher_Name Char(60);
```

Then comes the code to fill each of these variables with the necessary information, based on the Course Director and Course Department ID columns:

```
        -- Retrieve the necessary information
        -- Department Name
        SELECT   TRIM(Name)
        INTO     Dep_Name
        FROM     UMADB_CHP5.TBL_Departments Dep
        WHERE    UPDATED.TBL_DepartmentsDepartment_Id = Dep.Department_
Id;
            - Teacher Rank Name
        SELECT       TRIM(Ranks.Name)
        INTO         Rank_Name
        FROM         UMADB_CHP5.TBL_Teachers Teachers
        INNER JOIN   UMADB_CHP5.TBL_Teacher_Ranks Ranks
             ON      Teachers.TBL_Teacher_RanksTeacher_Rank_Id = Ranks.
Teacher_Rank_Id
        WHERE        UPDATED.Course_Director_Teacher_Id = Teachers.
Teacher_Id;
        -- Teacher Name
        SELECT       TRIM(Persons.Name)
        INTO         Teacher_Name
        FROM         UMADB_CHP5.TBL_Teachers Teachers
        INNER JOIN   UMADB_CHP5.TBL_Persons Persons
             ON      Teachers.TBL_PersonsPerson_Id = Persons.Person_Id
        WHERE        UPDATED.Course_Director_Teacher_Id = Teachers.
Teacher_Id;
```

Here, I'm using SELECT ... INTO statements to fill the variables with the appropriate information. I could store the teacher rank and name in the same variable, but I chose not to overcomplicate the SELECT statements.

The next step is to fill in the new description, just like I did in the previous example. The difference is this time around I'm going to compose the new value using the variables above:

```
          -- Compose the new description
               SET UPDATED.Description = 'A '
                         CONCAT TRIM(Dep_Name)
                         CONCAT ' department course, managed by '
                         CONCAT TRIM(Rank_Name) CONCAT ' '
                         CONCAT TRIM(Teacher_Name) CONCAT '.';
     END;
```

This code is available in the chapter's downloadable source code, along with working examples of both this and the previous triggers in action. Even though I didn't show it, you can also perform the same type of changes on numeric columns. You can use all of SQL's power, including UDFs, to compute or compose a column's new value.

Using what I presented in this section, you should be able to create your own column-value–changing triggers. If you need additional practice, find all the columns with the "N/A" default value and build triggers to change them appropriately!

Using INSTEAD OF Triggers to Supercharge Views

Views are a great way to hide the database complexity from the user, because they offer a much simpler structure. With a view, you can gather information from as many tables as you'd like and display them as if they all belonged to the same table. But so far, that's the only thing you can do with views: display information.

However, you can use INSTEAD OF triggers to supercharge your views, or, in other words, allow the users to use those views to insert, update, or delete records in the underlying tables. Back in Chapter 5, I created a view named Student Information View. In case you don't remember, here is its source code:

```
CREATE OR REPLACE VIEW UMADB_CHP5.VIEW_STUDENT_INFO
 FOR SYSTEM NAME V_STUDENT1
 AS
 SELECT        STUDENTS.STUDENT_ID
        , PERSONS.NAME
        , PERSONS.DATE_OF_BIRTH
        , PERSONS.HOME_ADDRESS
        , PERSONS.HOME_PHONE_NBR
        , PERSONS.MOBILE_NBR
        , PERSONS.EMAIL_ADDRESS
        , PERSONS.DRIVERS_LICENSE
        , PERSONS.SOCIAL_SEC_NBR
        , STUDENTS.STUDENT_STATUS
 FROM   UMADB_CHP5.TBL_STUDENTS STUDENTS
        INNER JOIN UMADB_CHP5.TBL_PERSONS PERSONS
             ON PERSONS.PERSON_ID = STUDENTS.TBL_PERSONSPERSON_ID
 ;
```

This view takes information from the Students and Persons tables and displays it to the user, as if all belonged to the same table. Let's start by creating a trigger that allows the user to update most of the information from the view. I say most because the majority of the columns in this view are from the Persons table. The only two that are not are the student's ID and status. An INSTEAD OF trigger can only be created over a view, and you need to specify the operation that activates the trigger.

Let's look at the source code of the trigger that will enable the UPDATE operation over this view, piece by piece, as usual, starting with the "header" part:

```
-- Create a trigger to be able to make a view updatable
CREATE OR REPLACE TRIGGER UMADB_CHP5.TRG_Update_View_Student_Info
     INSTEAD OF UPDATE ON UMADB_CHP5.VIEW_STUDENT_INFO
     REFERENCING OLD AS ORIGINAL NEW AS UPDATED
     FOR EACH ROW MODE DB2SQL
```

Apart from the INSTEAD OF UPDATE ON UMADB_CHP5.VIEW_STUDENT_INFO part, it looks pretty standard. The important thing to understand here is that this line tells the database engine to execute the code in the body of the trigger instead of (hence the name of the trigger type) failing the statement and returning an error, which would be the case in a view without such a trigger. In this particular case, what I want is that the columns from the Persons table receive the values specified in an UPDATE statement over the View_Student_Info view. For that to happen, the body of my trigger has to "tell" the database engine what to do. In this case, it must map the view columns to the respective Persons table columns in an UPDATE statement, which here is rather simple, because the columns have the same names, as you can see in the body of the trigger:

```
BEGIN
    DECLARE W_Person_Id INTEGER;
    -- Retrieve the Person ID associated with the updated Student Id
    SELECT  TBL_PersonsPerson_Id
    INTO    W_Person_Id
    FROM    UMADB_CHP5.TBL_Students STUDENTS
    WHERE   STUDENTS.Student_Id = UPDATED.Student_Id;


    -- Update the Persons table with the information coming from the
view
    UPDATE UMADB_CHP5.TBL_PERSONS PERSONS
        SET PERSONS.Name = UPDATED.Name
          , PERSONS.Date_of_Birth = UPDATED.Date_of_Birth
          , PERSONS.Home_Address = UPDATED.Home_Address
          , PERSONS.Home_Phone_Nbr = UPDATED.Home_Phone_Nbr
          , PERSONS.Mobile_Nbr = UPDATED.Mobile_Nbr
          , PERSONS.Email_Address = UPDATED.Email_Address
          , PERSONS.Drivers_License = UPDATED.Drivers_License
          , PERSONS.Social_Sec_Nbr = UPDATED.Social_Sec_Nbr
        WHERE PERSONS.Person_Id = W_Person_Id;
    END;
```

However, there is a small intermediate step: finding the right Person ID. This is necessary because the view doesn't have the Person ID, which means that I have to get it from somewhere. In this case, I'll use the Person ID from the Students table (Tbl_PersonsPerson_Id). I'll store it in a temporary variable named W_Person_Id, which I'll then use in the UPDATE statement. Also note that the UPDATE statement is simply mapping the view columns (prefixed UPDATED.) to the respective Persons table columns (prefixed PERSONS.).

In summary, what's happening here is that I'm telling the database engine that when someone tries to update a view (which is not possible under normal circumstances), it should update a table instead. More specifically, I'm telling the database engine that an UPDATE statement issued over the View_Student_Info view actually updates the TBL_Persons table, using the UPDATE statement in the trigger's body section.

Let's try it! Say I want to change the name of the student with the ID equal to 1 from "Dalton, Joe" to "Dalton, Jack". With this trigger in place, I can use the student information view to do that:

```
-- Test the trigger, by updating the view instead of the underlying
tables
UPDATE  UMADB_CHP5.VIEW_STUDENT_INFO
    SET Name = 'Dalton, Jack'
    WHERE Student_id = 1;
```

The database engine will note that I'm trying to update a view, so it will check for INSTEAD OF triggers for this operation. It will find our newly created TRG_Update_View_Student_Info trigger, which will take over and issue an UPDATE over the Persons table instead. For the end user, this is totally transparent. It's yet another way to hide complexity—and you can use it for INSERT and DELETE statements as well.

Now let's see a slightly more complex example. Chapter 5's code also included another view: Course Information. This is a more complete and complex view, spanning four tables (whereas the Teachers and Persons table are used twice), showing a lot of course-related information that is not actually part of the Courses table. Here's the view's source code:

```
CREATE OR REPLACE VIEW UMADB_CHP5.VIEW_COURSE_INFO
 FOR SYSTEM NAME V_COURSE1
 AS
 SELECT       COURSES.COURSE_ID
        , COURSES.NAME AS COURSE_NAME
        , COURSES.DESCRIPTION
        , DEPARTMENTS.NAME AS DEPARTMENT_NAME
        , DIRECTOR_PERSON.NAME AS COURSE_DIRECTOR_NAME
        , TA_PERSON.NAME AS COURSE_TA_NAME
        , COURSES.COURSE_STATUS
 FROM   UMADB_CHP5.TBL_COURSES COURSES
        INNER JOIN UMADB_CHP5.TBL_TEACHERS DIRECTOR
             ON DIRECTOR.TEACHER_ID = COURSES.COURSE_DIRECTOR_TEACHER_ID
        INNER JOIN UMADB_CHP5.TBL_PERSONS DIRECTOR_PERSON
             ON DIRECTOR_PERSON.PERSON_ID = DIRECTOR.TBL_PERSONSPERSON_ID
        INNER JOIN UMADB_CHP5.TBL_TEACHERS TA
             ON TA.TEACHER_ID = COURSES.COURSE_TA_TEACHER_ID
        INNER JOIN UMADB_CHP5.TBL_PERSONS TA_PERSON
             ON TA_PERSON.PERSON_ID = TA.TBL_PERSONSPERSON_ID
        INNER JOIN UMADB_CHP5.TBL_DEPARTMENTS DEPARTMENTS
             ON COURSES.TBL_DEPARTMENTSDEPARTMENT_ID = DEPARTMENTS.
DEPARTMENT_ID
 ;
```

Note that to display both the course director and teaching assistant's names, the SELECT statement uses the Persons and Teachers tables with different aliases. This is an important detail to consider when building the trigger, which will allow us to update that view. In the end, I want to be able to update the Courses table's Name and Description columns, or the Department's Name column, or the Teacher and TA's Name columns, stored in the Courses, Departments, and Persons tables, respectively.

Given that we're talking about quite a few tables here, it's a good idea to devise a mechanism that limits the updates to the bare minimum. In other words, it's a good idea to issue an UPDATE statement if the value of the respective table was actually changed. For instance, it doesn't make sense to execute an UPDATE statement over the Departments table if the department name wasn't changed. It's also important to mention that even though the Course ID is a column of the view, it doesn't make much sense to change it, because it's an ID column, generated automatically by the database engine.

Having said that, let's start dissecting the code! Because the header part is very similar to the previous trigger's, I'll show it with the first part of the trigger's body:

```
-- Create a trigger to be able to make a view updatable
CREATE OR REPLACE TRIGGER UMADB_CHP5.TRG_Update_View_Course_Info
    INSTEAD OF UPDATE ON UMADB_CHP5.VIEW_COURSE_INFO
    REFERENCING OLD AS ORIGINAL NEW AS UPDATED
    FOR EACH ROW MODE DB2SQL
    BEGIN
        DECLARE W_Department_Id INTEGER;
        DECLARE W_Course_Director_Person_Id INTEGER;
        DECLARE W_Course_TA_Person_Id INTEGER;
```

This piece of code is nearly the same as the previous trigger's (I actually copy-pasted it and did some changes). The main difference is that there are three temporary variables instead of just one. This is because of the tables that the trigger will have to update. Let's see how each of these variables is set:

```
        -- Retrieve the Person ID associated with the updated Student ID
        SELECT  COURSES.TBL_DepartmentsDepartment_Id
                , DIRECTOR_PERSON.Person_Id
                , TA_PERSON.Person_Id
        INTO    W_Department_Id
                , W_Course_Director_Person_Id
                , W_Course_TA_Person_Id
        FROM UMADB_CHP5.TBL_COURSES COURSES
        INNER JOIN UMADB_CHP5.TBL_TEACHERS DIRECTOR
                                                        Continued
```

```
              ON DIRECTOR.Teacher_Id = COURSES.Course_Director_Teacher_Id
      INNER JOIN UMADB_CHP5.TBL_PERSONS DIRECTOR_PERSON
              ON DIRECTOR_PERSON.Person_Id = DIRECTOR.TBL_PersonsPerson_Id
      INNER JOIN UMADB_CHP5.TBL_TEACHERS TA
              ON TA.TEACHER_ID = COURSES.COURSE_TA_TEACHER_ID
      INNER JOIN UMADB_CHP5.TBL_PERSONS TA_PERSON
              ON TA_PERSON.Person_Id = TA.TBL_PersonsPerson_Id
      WHERE   COURSES.Course_Id = UPDATED.Course_Id;
```

It's a long statement, but it's not very complicated. Still, let's review it in detail. The main table is the Courses table, which I'm accessing using the Course_Id column from the view to get the data that will let me connect to the other tables. Once I have the appropriate Courses record, I can use its TBL_DepartmentsDepartment_Id to get the link to the Departments table and store that value in the W_Department_Id temporary variable. That's the easy part.

The course director and teaching assistant (TA) names are a bit more complicated, because the Courses record only stores the respective teacher IDs. However, the names of the teachers are not stored in the Teachers table, but in the Persons table, so I need to access the respective record from the Persons table. How? Via the TBL_PersonsPerson_Id of the Teachers table. The tricky part is that I need to do this twice: for the course director and the teaching assistant. That's why I'm using the Teachers and Persons tables twice, with different aliases (DIRECTOR and DIRECTOR_PERSON for the Course Director, and TA and TA_PERSON for the Teaching Assistant). This will allow me to store the respective person IDs in the W_Course_Director_Person_Id and W_Course_TA_Person_Id temporary variables.

If you look at the previous trigger, you'll see that the next step is to perform the update. However, this situation is a bit more complex, because I have more than one table, and I want to limit the updates to the bare minimum. To do that, I'll check if the column's value was actually changed, by comparing the before and after values for the respective column. If they are different, I'll issue the respective UPDATE statement. Let's see how that translates to code, using the Department Name:

```
        -- Update the Department table if the department name changed
    IF(ORIGINAL.Department_Name <> UPDATED.Department_Name) THEN
        UPDATE UMADB_CHP5.TBL_DEPARTMENTS DEPARTMENTS
            SET     DEPARTMENTS.Name = UPDATED.Department_Name
            WHERE   DEPARTMENTS.Department_Id = W_Department_Id;
    END IF;
```

As you see in this piece of code, the before and after values are stored in the ORIGINAL
and UPDATED records, respectively. Checking whether the department name was changed
is a simple thing to do, with this statement:

```
    IF(ORIGINAL.Department_Name <> UPDATED.Department_Name) THEN
```

If this comparison returns true, then I issue my UPDATE statement, just like I did in the
previous trigger. The rest of the code is simply a rehash of this idea, with the necessary
adjustments to make it work for the rest of the columns:

```
        -- Update the tables with the information coming from the view
        -- but only if the respective values changed (ORIGINAL <>
    UPDATED)
        -- Update the Course table if the course's name or description
    changed
        IF(ORIGINAL.Course_Name <> UPDATED.Course_Name
            OR ORIGINAL.Description <> UPDATED.Description) THEN
            UPDATE      UMADB_CHP5.TBL_COURSES COURSES
                SET     COURSES.Name = UPDATED.Course_Name
                        , COURSES.Description = UPDATED.Description
                WHERE   COURSES.Course_Id = UPDATED.Course_Id;
        END IF;
        -- Update the Course Director's name, if it changed
        IF(ORIGINAL.Course_Director_Name <> UPDATED.Course_Director_Name)
    THEN
```

Continued

```
                    UPDATE UMADB_CHP5.TBL_PERSONS PERSONS
                        SET PERSONS.Name = UPDATED.Course_Director_Name
                            WHERE PERSONS.Person_Id = W_Course_Director_Person_Id;
            END IF;
            -- Update the Course TA's name, if it changed
            IF(ORIGINAL.Course_TA_Name <> UPDATED.Course_TA_Name) THEN
                UPDATE UMADB_CHP5.TBL_PERSONS PERSONS
                    SET PERSONS.Name = UPDATED.Course_TA_Name
                        WHERE PERSONS.Person_Id = W_Course_TA_Person_Id;
            END IF;
        END;
```

Here you see how and where those temporary variables are used: they serve the sole purpose of finding the right record to update in the respective tables. Keep in mind that this is not a real-life example, because I'm updating columns from other tables without performing any checks. That sort of validation will be discussed in the next chapter. For now, I just wanted to show you a more complex example of an INSTEAD OF trigger with multiple updates, performed selectively.

Use Triggers with Care

Because this last trigger probably left your head spinning, I won't hammer you with more code. Instead, I want to share a few notions about triggers that you must always remember when creating or changing existing triggers.

Triggers Are Like Salt

Triggers are like salt or any other condiment: if you use just enough it helps, but adding too much will ruin everything. This is particularly true in two different aspects: performance and control. >From a performance perspective, you have to keep in mind that a trigger is another piece of code that will be executed whenever the operation that activated runs. For instance, inserting 1,000 rows in a table with a trigger with a for each row definition will cause the execution of that trigger 1,000 times! Even worse, this trigger's actions can affect other tables, which in turn may have triggers of their own, causing "trigger storms" or "trigger cascades."

This brings us to the aspect of control. Triggers are not always obvious, and most people tend to look for problems in applications or "regular" SQL routines (read: SPs and UDFs) when something is not working as it should. Triggers can be stealthy, so it's important to have them well documented in terms of functionality and scope. My advice is that you keep your triggers' source code along with the other SQL routines' sources, preferably in a QSQLSRC file in your sources library, or whichever version of it you use.

The cascading triggers also make debugging a bit more difficult, because they might change column values in unexpected ways or, even worse, prevent modifications without warning. They can also lead to unexpectedly locked objects or, in a nightmarish scenario, unexplainable deadlocks. Keeping strict control over your triggers and, most importantly, defining a (company/shop-wide) proper and strict trigger usage policy is of paramount importance.

However, don't get me wrong: I'm not suggesting that you shouldn't use triggers. I'm just saying that you should use just enough of them—like salt.

In This Chapter, You've Learned ...

I don't know how many times I wrote the word "trigger," but it sure was a lot. I couldn't have done it any other way, because triggers were the focus of this chapter. Let's review what was discussed:

- I explained what triggers are and why you should use them.
- I explained the anatomy of a trigger, detailing each section.
- I presented a handful of "regular" trigger examples, as well as trigger usage scenarios (data validation, auditing, and automated composition/filling of information).
- Then I explained the INSTEAD OF trigger philosophy and how to use these special triggers to make views updatable.
- Finally, I presented a few reasons you should be careful with the use of triggers.

As a final note, let me add that there's a lot more to know about triggers. I barely scratched the surface. The idea was to introduce this tool without overwhelming you with all the technical details. You can consider this the minimum working knowledge you need to use triggers. However, if you really want to use them on a large scale, consider reading more about this topic. IBM has a great Redbook covering this and other SQL-related topics: *Stored Procedures, Triggers, and Functions in DB2*. Look it up: it's very informative!

Now we've explored the SQL routines trinity (SPs, UDFs, and triggers), it's time to move on to new things. The next chapter discusses SQL-based business validations, in all their forms.

10

Moving Business Validations to the Database

This chapter will present several ways to move your business validations to the database, thus making them "application independent." This will be achieved by the application of a suite of techniques grounded in the SQL routines discussed in the previous chapters and DDL constraints.

Following the data-centric approach I've been slowly introducing throughout the book, the next logical step is to leverage upon the information presented thus far to help you understand how to move your business rules (or validations, or checks, or whatever they are called in your application) to the database. This is not a universally accepted idea, as many programmers believe that it makes no sense to "reinvent the wheel" in yet another language, especially when that language is PL/SQL. I prefer a halfway solution: use SQL's constructs and features to simplify what can be simplified and keep in high-level languages what cannot be translated or makes no sense to translate to SQL. You'll see what I mean in a moment. But first, there's a little piece missing: DDL constraints.

Re-introducing DDL Constraints

SQL for i has the same set of three constraint types as standard SQL: *unique*, *referential*, and *check* constraints. It wouldn't make sense to have it any other way; if that were the case, serious problems might occur if you tried to migrate a database to (or from) DB2 for i to (or from) another database. I already covered unique and referential constraints back in Chapter 5, but here's a quick refresher that will help you to better understand the check constraints.

Unique Constraints

The unique constraints type includes the UNIQUE keyword, but also the PRIMARY KEY keyword. Although these two constraints are somewhat similar, they are different things. When you add the UNIQUE keyword to a column, you're saying that each value of that column must be different from all the others. However, unless you also specify the NOT NULL keyword, the aforementioned column accepts NULL values.

PRIMARY KEY is a bit different, because a primary key can be composed of several columns, as opposed to UNIQUE's per-column application, and it doesn't accept NULL values. Next are a couple examples of CREATE TABLE statements, retrieved from Chapter 5, which illustrate the use of UNIQUE and PRIMARY KEY. Let's start with the simpler of the two, UNIQUE, using the Departments table as an example:

```
CREATE TABLE UMADB_CHP5.TBL_Departments
  FOR SYSTEM NAME PFDPM
  (
  Department_ID        FOR COLUMN DPID integer GENERATED BY DEFAULT AS
  IDENTITY,
  Name                 FOR COLUMN DPNM char(60) NOT NULL UNIQUE,
  Description          FOR COLUMN DPDS char(100) DEFAULT 'N/A',
  Department_Status FOR COLUMN DPSC char(1) DEFAULT '1',
  Created_By           FOR COLUMN DPCU varchar(18) DEFAULT USER,
  Created_On           FOR COLUMN DPCT timestamp DEFAULT CURRENT TIMESTAMP,
  PRIMARY KEY (Department_ID))
  RCDFMT PFDPMR;
```

Even though the primary key of this table is its ID column (Department_Id), generated automatically by the database engine, it also makes sense from a "business point of view" to ensure that there aren't two departments with the same name (hence the UNIQUE keyword) or a department without a name (enforced via the NOT NULL keyword). Note that the use of these keywords is not related to the primary key in any way, although it grants this column some characteristics of a primary key.

You might be wondering: if this is not a primary key, but it could be, then why use separate keywords? Besides the obvious "maintain proper table relationships" answer, there's another one: because a primary key can be composed of several columns, it can ensure the "non-nullability and uniqueness" of those columns as a whole. In other words, if, for example, you have a table with a primary key composed of three columns, the first two columns' values can be the same in several records of the table, as long as the third one is different. The second example, the statement used to create the Classes Taught per Year table, illustrates this type of situation:

```
CREATE TABLE UMADB_CHP5.TBL_Classes_Taught_per_Year
  FOR SYSTEM NAME PFCTM
(
  TBL_Classes_Per_YearClass_per_Year_ID FOR COLUMN CYID integer NOT NULL,
  TBL_TeachersTeacher_Id                 FOR COLUMN TEID integer NOT NULL,
  PRIMARY KEY (TBL_Classes_Per_YearClass_per_Year_ID,
  TBL_TeachersTeacher_Id))
  RCDFMT PFCTMR;
```

As its name implies, this table is used to manage which teachers teach which classes, for a given school year. Because this table serves as a link between the Classes per Year and Teachers tables, its primary key is composed of the primary keys of those tables. This is a simple way to ensure that in each school year and for each class, there will be only one responsible teacher. However, the same teacher can teach another class in a different school year. Naturally, we could complicate things and introduce another table to manage additional teachers, guest lecturers, teaching assistants, and so on, but that's not the point of this discussion. The idea is to show a practical use of the PRIMARY KEY keyword with more than one column.

*In short, **UNIQUE** refers to the uniqueness of the value of a column and, unless specified otherwise, accepts **NULL** values, while **PRIMARY KEY** also ensures the uniqueness of one or more columns, treating the composition of those as a whole for the validation of its uniqueness, and cannot, by definition, accept **NULL** values.*

Referential Constraints

Constraints from this group are used to do something most IBM i programmers don't usually do: enforce the relationship between tables in the database. Most RPG programmers I know build applications that manage and enforce the relationships between the underlying tables in RPG, or in other words, at application level. This is a dangerous approach, especially now that our databases are more and more exposed to non-RPG and sometimes even non-IBM i applications. It's of paramount importance to have and maintain proper table relationships, or more formally, database referential integrity, in the database, which is where it belongs in the first place. This goes way beyond primary keys and unique values. It requires explicit rules and cross-checks that make sure a bad input, regardless of where it comes from (e.g., an internal application, an external application, SQL statements) is stopped before it causes consistency problems in the database.

As things currently stand in our UMADB database, the referential integrity would be only half assured if I had defined only the primary keys on the tables. In other words, I'm using unique IDs as primary keys to most tables, but when two tables are linked to one another, there wouldn't be anything enforcing the existence of the record with that key in the destination table if the foreign key constraints weren't in place.

This may sound a bit confusing, so let's look at an example. Take the Students table, for instance: it has a column called Tbl_PersonsPerson_Id, which supposedly contains the record that uniquely identifies the personal details of the student in the Persons table. To enforce the link between the tables, I created, with the help of Visual Paradigm, a referential integrity constraint. This can be done at design time, when you issue the respective CREATE TABLE statement, or later, using an ALTER TABLE statement, as I did here. Note, however, that the ALTER TABLE statement will fail if it finds unacceptable values in the column or columns the constraint refers to.

The following statement creates a link between the Tbl_PersonsPerson_Id and its counterpart in the Persons table (Person_Id):

```
ALTER TABLE UMADB_CHP5.TBL_Students
    ADD CONSTRAINT UMADB_CHP5.FK_TBL_Students_ TblPersonsPerson_Id
        FOREIGN KEY (Tbl_PersonsPerson_Id)
        REFERENCES UMADB_CHP5.TBL_Persons (Person_Id)
;
```

What I'm saying here is that only acceptable values for the Tbl_PersonsPerson_Id are the ones that exist in the Person_Id of the TBL_Persons table. This is achieved by adding a constraint that enforces a foreign key relationship. By the way, it's also important to mention the naming convention I'm using. The constraint can be named whatever you want, naturally. However, it's a good practice to follow a clear naming convention. This will save you a lot of time when investigating an error or writing code that manipulates data. Anyway, here's what I'm using here:

- FK indicates that this constraint is a foreign key constraint.
- Tbl_Students refers to the name of the table over which the constraint is applied.
- TblPersons Person_Id points to the column being constrained.

Note that because of the column naming convention introduced back in Chapter 5, the name of the column is composed of the names of the constraining table and column. If you use a different naming convention for the columns, you might want to change the constraint naming convention to shed some light on the relationship it enforces.

To summarize, defining foreign keys is a way to guarantee that the data links between the tables are kept consistent.

Time for Some Practice

If you didn't run the source code provided in Chapter 5's downloadable source code, take a moment to revisit the UMADB's ERD to determine where foreign key constraints are needed and write the appropriate ALTER TABLE statements. I'll provide the first one, just to get you started:

```
-- Enforcing the referential integrity between the Teachers and Persons
tables
ALTER TABLE UMADB_CHP5.TBL_Teachers
    ADD CONSTRAINT UMADB_CHP5.FK_TBL_Teachers_TblPersonsPerson_Id
        FOREIGN KEY (Tbl_PersonsPerson_Id)
        REFERENCES UMADB_CHP5.TBL_Persons (Person_Id)
;
```

Once you're done, confirm that they're working as they should, by trying to update the constrained columns with values that would damage the referential integrity of the database. For instance, due to the referential constraint introduced by the ALTER TABLE statement I just mentioned, you shouldn't be able to update the person ID of a certain teacher to 999, because that person ID doesn't exist in the Persons table. This means that if you try this statement:

```
UPDATE UMADB_CHP5.TBL_TEACHERS
    SET Tbl_PersonsPerson_Id = 999
    WHERE Teacher_Id = 1;
```

it should fail with the SQL0530 error: *Operation not allowed by the referential constraint FK_TBL_Teachers_TblPersonsPerson_Id* .... If you ran the source code supplied with Chapter 5's downloadable source code, the ALTER TABLE statements will fail because the constraints are already in place. For your convenience, I've included all those statements in this chapter's downloadable source code, as well.

Check Constraints

Now that you're up to speed on unique and referential constraints, it should be easier to understand how the check constraints work. Just like the unique and referential constraints, the check constraint is also applied via a CREATE or ALTER TABLE statement. Even the way it works is somewhat similar to what was previously presented in this chapter. The main difference resides in the type of validation performed. While unique constraints prevent data duplication and referential constraints ensure data integrity, check constraints are more malleable and "business friendly." What I mean by this is that you can use a CHECK keyword to enforce a business rule in any given column of a table.

Let's start with a very basic, almost silly example: in any order-management system, the ordered quantity must always be a positive number. For us humans, the opposite is unthinkable, but the database engine is prepared to handle both positive and negative numeric values, so it won't complain about a negative-ordered quantity unless you tell it to do so. How do we usually handle that? Collecting data is often a three-step process: collect, validate, and process. The validation in this case is (or should be) checking that the quantity is a numeric and positive number. That's typically handled at application level, with the enforcement of business rules via high-level language code. However, you can (and, in my opinion should) move this sort of trivial validation to the database. In Chapter 9, I showed how to use a trigger to prevent unrealistic variations on a teacher's salary. To enforce this "only positive quantities allowed" business rule, you could do the same sort of thing, or you could use the CHECK keyword. Assuming that the column name is OrdQty, a simple CHECK(OrdQty > 0) in a CREATE or ALTER TABLE statement would suffice to enforce the business rule. Yes, it's that simple!

Now let's see a complete statement example. The Classes per Year table contains the classes the university offers in each school year. Logically, it doesn't make sense to have records with years that are prior to the school's foundation (let's say it was founded in 1976). To enforce this business rule, I just need to issue the following statement:

```
-- Adding a constraint to enforce a simple business rule
ALTER TABLE UMADB_CHP5.TBL_Classes_per_Year
    ADD CONSTRAINT UMADB_CHP5.CHK_TBL_Classes_per_Year_Year
    CHECK (Year > 1976);
```

Just as before, the statement will fail if any of the current records of the table doesn't comply with this validation. Otherwise, it will prevent any future changes or insertions that try to set a year prior to 1976. But you can enforce other type of rules just as easily. Let's say that the university requires people (students and teachers) to provide their full name, or at least a meaningful name (that is more than three characters) for its records. Here's how this rule can be enforced:

```
-- Adding a constraint to enforce a slightly more complex business rule
ALTER TABLE UMADB_CHP5.TBL_Persons
   ADD CONSTRAINT UMADB_CHP5.CHK_TBL_Persons_Name
      CHECK (LENGTH(TRIM(Name)) > 3);
```

Note that even though this is still a single-column validation, it's slightly more complex than the previous one, as it includes calls to two built-in-functions (BIFs). But you're not limited to BIFs! You can use your own functions just as easily, as long as you provide the appropriate path (which in this case would be UMADB_CHP5., assuming the UDF you want to use resides in the schema we've been using since Chapter 5).

These are simple validations, but you can also build complex checks using a combination of conditions, chained together by AND or OR operators. For instance, if I wanted to make sure a contact number was always supplied by the people studying or teaching in the university, a CHECK constraint like this:

```
CHECK (LENGTH(TRIM(Home_Phone_Nbr)) > 3 OR  LENGTH(TRIM(Mobile_Nbr)))
```

would do the trick. It's possible to go even further using computed checks or CASE expressions—but that's something I'll show you later in this chapter.

Enforcing More Complex Sets of Business Rules

Now that you have a better knowledge of the tools at your disposal, let's go over some scenarios based on our fictional UMADB database. Even though it's a rather simple setup, we can still come up with some interestingly complex business rules, implemented by using one or several of the tools described in the last few chapters.

Keeping the Teachers' Salaries in Check

Another call, this time from the university's personnel manager (no, she's not related to the Dean). It seems that the university wants to prevent tampering with the teachers' salaries. They have presented us with a list of rules they need us to implement ASAP:

1. The salary can't be negative or zero.

2. If updated, the salary can't vary more than 10 percent in each direction (up or down).

3. The salary can't be changed if the teacher is not on active duty (in other words, the respective record is no longer active).

4. The salary can't be more than one and a half times the average of the salaries of all the active teachers.

The first rule could be easily implemented using a CHECK constraint, as discussed earlier in this chapter. However, the other rules require the sort of validations that are not possible to implement using a constraint, because constraints cannot execute queries, which means that certain things are beyond their reach. If you look closely, one of these rules is already implemented via a trigger; in the previous chapter, I implemented a trigger that prevents salary increases over 10 percent. Here's the source code of that trigger, which I'll use as a starting point to implement the rest of the teacher's salary business rules:

```
CREATE OR REPLACE TRIGGER UMADB_CHP5.Trg_check_teacher_salary_update
    BEFORE UPDATE ON UMADB_CHP5.TBL_TEACHERS
    REFERENCING NEW ROW AS UPDATED OLD ROW AS ORIGINAL
    FOR EACH ROW MODE DB2ROW
    WHEN (UPDATED.SALARY <> ORIGINAL.SALARY)
    BEGIN
        IF UPDATED.SALARY >= ORIGINAL.SALARY * 1.1 THEN
            SIGNAL SQLSTATE '75001'
                SET MESSAGE_TEXT = 'This teacher salary change is not
valid, because the new salary is more than 110% of the old salary';
        END IF;
    END;
```

The first thing to do is to remove this trigger, because the one I'll create next will replace it. This is achieved with a DROP TRIGGER statement:

```
-- Removing the "old" trigger
DROP TRIGGER UMADB_CHP5.Trg_check_teacher_salary_update;
```

Then comes the tricky part: creating the new trigger. If you read the set of rules carefully, you'll realize that there are two different operations involved: INSERT and UPDATE. Rules 1 and 4 are supposed to be enforced in both operations, while rules 2 and 3 are only for UPDATEs. I could create two triggers and repeat code, but in this instance, it's possible (and a good idea) to keep it all in one trigger. For that to work, my new trigger will have to handle INSERT and UPDATE operations. Here's the header of the trigger, specifying just that:

```
CREATE OR REPLACE TRIGGER UMADB_CHP5.Trg_check_teacher_salary
    BEFORE UPDATE OR INSERT ON UMADB_CHP5.TBL_TEACHERS
    REFERENCING NEW ROW AS UPDATED OLD ROW AS ORIGINAL
    FOR EACH ROW MODE DB2ROW
```

However, although I'm interested in all insertions, I'm not interested in UPDATEs that don't change the teacher's salary. The trick is to tweak the WHEN clause to reflect this set of criteria:

```
WHEN (INSERTING
        OR (UPDATING AND (UPDATED.Salary <> ORIGINAL.Salary)))
```

I mentioned in the previous chapter that INSERTING, UPDATING, and DELETING evaluate to true if and only if the trigger was activated by the respective operation. This allows us to create a multi-operation trigger with operation-specific code, as you'll see in a moment.

But before that, let's look at the start of the body of the trigger. I'll need only one variable, to temporarily store the "average of the salaries of all the active teachers" stated in rule 4:

```
BEGIN
    DECLARE AVG_Salary DECIMAL(11, 2);
```

It's time to start implementing the rules. I followed the order in which they were stated, but rules 1 and 4 could appear next to one another in the code. Let's start with rule 1:

```
        -- Rule 1: The salary can't be negative or zero
     IF UPDATED.Salary <= 0 THEN
         SIGNAL SQLSTATE '75001'
            SET MESSAGE_TEXT = 'This teacher salary must be greater
than zero';
     END IF;
```

The code structure is similar to the trigger I used as template: it checks a certain condition and, if true, signals an error, setting up the error's specific text. Once this happens, the code execution will stop. In other words, even if an I/O operation fails to comply with two or more rules, the error message that will be presented will be for the first rule the I/O operation didn't comply with. That was one of the reasons that led me to keep the order of the rules in the code, even though I could place rules 1 and 4 together.

A closer look at rules 2 and 3 shows that these are update-specific rules. Thankfully, the UPDATING keyword allows us to easily indicate that prerequisite:

```
        -- Update-specific validations (Rules 2 and 3)
     IF UPDATING THEN
          -- Rule 2: If updated, the salary can't vary more
          -- than 10% in each direction (up or down)
          IF UPDATED.Salary >= ORIGINAL.Salary * 1.1 THEN
              SIGNAL SQLSTATE '75002'
                  SET MESSAGE_TEXT = 'This teacher salary change is
not valid, because the new salary is more than 110% of the old salary';
              END IF;
          IF UPDATED.Salary <= ORIGINAL.Salary * 0.9 THEN
              SIGNAL SQLSTATE '75003'
                  SET MESSAGE_TEXT = 'This teacher salary change is
not valid, because the new salary is less than 90% of the old salary';
              END IF;

          -- Rule 3: The salary can't be changed if the teacher is not
on active duty
                                                        Continued
```

```
                -- (in other words, the respective record is no longer
active)
                IF UPDATED.Teacher_Status <> '1' THEN
                    SIGNAL SQLSTATE '75004'
                        SET MESSAGE_TEXT = 'This teacher salary cannot be
changed, because the teacher record is not active';
                END IF;
            END IF;
```

The first part of rule 2 is what was already implemented in the "old" trigger, while the second part is simply the opposite: the updated salary can't be less than 90 percent of the original one. Rule 3 is also plain and simple: it follows the same pattern of IF -> SIGNAL -> SET statements used thus far. Rule 4 is a bit different, because in order to check it I need to calculate the average salary of the active teachers:

```
        -- Rule 4: The salary can't be more than one and a half times
        -- the average of the salaries of all the active teachers
        -- Calculate the average salary of the active teachers
        SELECT AVG(Salary)
        INTO    W_AVG_Salary
        FROM    UMADB_CHP5.TBL_Teachers
        WHERE   Teacher_Status = '1';
```

With the correct amount stored in my temporary variable, I can once again apply my validation template to check rule 4:

```
            IF UPDATED.Salary > (1.5 * W_AVG_Salary) THEN
                SIGNAL SQLSTATE '75005'
                    SET MESSAGE_TEXT = 'This teacher salary cannot be greater
than twice the average of the active teachers' salaries;
                END IF;
        END;
```

And that's it! It's a bit of code (50 lines, including white space and comment lines), but it provides a template that you can apply to your own business rules. You'll find the complete source, along with some test statements, in this chapter's downloadable source code.

Note that you also can separate the validation code from the trigger code, by moving the checks to a stored procedure and invoking that SP in the trigger's body. Just be sure to pass all the necessary parameters to make the checks. In this case, you'd need to pass INSERTING, UPDATING, UPDATED.Salary, ORIGINAL.Salary, and UPDATED.Teacher_Status as parameters to the SP. You needn't worry about the return, because you'd only be interested in the error messages, and those would be propagated from the SP to the trigger and, because the trigger has no code to handle them, to the caller program. Putting the validation code in a SP has the advantage of not requiring an exclusive lock over the table to update (or "recompile") the business rules code. You wouldn't need to touch the trigger at all.

Finally, it's important to keep in mind that the validation SP doesn't necessarily have to be a native stored procedure; you can also use external (read high-level language–built) stored procedures to perform such tasks. I'm a big fan of modernization, but only if it's to improve something (performance, maintainability, whatever). For RPG validation code that is well-built, stable, and complex, it isn't logical to rewrite it in SQL "just because it's not native." Writing external SPs is beyond the scope of this book, but if you want to go that route, my book *Evolve Your RPG Coding* discusses the topic in reasonable depth.

Tidying Up the Personnel (Records)

Once we solved the teachers' salaries problem, the personnel manager was so happy that she called us ... not to thank us for our help, but to give us another list of rules, this time applicable to the personnel records:

- The home phone number is an optional field, but if it's filled, it must have more than 10 characters.

- The mobile number is an optional field, but if it's filled, it must have more than 10 characters.

- Even though the two fields above are optional, at least one of them must always be filled in.

- The birth date must be a valid date.
- The home address is mandatory and must be at least 10 characters long.

These rules look simple enough to enforce via CHECK constraints. However, they seemed too simple, so I called the personnel manager for a quick chat and found out that things are not so simple. Because the corresponding columns are mandatory in the database (they have the NOT NULL keyword), the Personnel department found a workaround: when they don't have data to appropriately fill these columns, they just write 'N/A'.

Also, the date of birth isn't a DATE column; it's actually a numeric, eight-digit field, inherited from the original UMA application. We can't change the data type, but the column needs to contain a valid ISO date without the separators (like 20040131, for instance). Maybe we can't check this one via a CHECK constraint, so let's leave it for last and take care of the other rules.

Rules 1 and 2 are very similar. In fact, the only difference is the name of the column involved. If it weren't for the "is an optional field, but if it's filled" part, it would be easy: CHECK(LENGTH(TRIM(Home_Phone_Nbr)) > 10) would suffice. However, that little bit of text requires some extra work. It's an excellent opportunity to show you how to build complex conditions within a CHECK constraint. I'm going to consider three possible scenarios:

- The column contains 'N/A'.
- The column doesn't contain 'N/A' and has fewer than 10 characters.
- The column doesn't contain 'N/A' and has 10 or more characters.

This looks like a chained IF scenario or, better yet, a CASE scenario, because I'm only interested in one of the three situations. As soon as the column's value matches one of the conditions, I can proceed accordingly without continuing to check the other conditions. Here's how it translates to an ALTER TABLE statement:

```
ALTER TABLE UMADB_CHP5.TBL_Persons
    -- Add a constraint to check if the Home_Phone_Nbr is valid
    ADD CONSTRAINT UMADB_CHP5.CHK_TBL_Persons_Home_Phone_Nbr
    CHECK (CASE
```
Continued

```
            WHEN Home_Phone_Nbr = 'N/A' THEN 'OK'
            WHEN LENGTH(TRIM(Home_Phone_Nbr)) < 10 THEN 'NOK'
            ELSE 'OK'
        END = 'OK')
```

Whenever a record is inserted or updated, this constraint will validate the Home_Phone_Nbr column's value according to the CASE structure I've built. Let's analyze it, line by line:

- WHEN Home_Phone_Nbr = 'N/A' THEN 'OK'—this condition is applicable when there's no value to check, because 'N/A' is equivalent to "not filled in"; in this case, the column has a NOT NULL keyword and for that reason can't be left blank. What this line means is "I can't validate, so I'll say it's OK."

- WHEN LENGTH(TRIM(Home_Phone_Nbr)) < 10 THEN 'NOK'—This is the actual validation. It means "the column is filled, so it must have more than 10 characters. If it hasn't, it's not OK."

- ELSE 'OK'—This is a "catch-all" clause that is applied when the previous conditions evaluate to false. It means "the column is filled and it has more than 10 characters, so it's OK."

- END = 'OK'—Although it seems that I'm comparing END with 'OK', that's not what's happening here. The END closes the CASE structure, and its result ('OK'/'NOK') is what's compared with the 'OK' literal you see and the end of the line.

The CHECK constraint for the Mobile_Nbr column is very similar:

```
-- Add a constraint to check if the Home_Phone_Nbr is valid
    ADD CONSTRAINT UMADB_CHP5.CHK_TBL_Persons_Mobile_Nbr
    CHECK (CASE
            WHEN Mobile_Nbr = 'N/A' THEN 'OK'
            WHEN LENGTH(TRIM(Mobile_Nbr)) < 10 THEN 'NOK'
            ELSE 'OK'
        END = 'OK')
```

As you can see, the only difference is the name of the column. Once I have those two checks in place, I can move on to rule 3 ("Even though the two fields above are optional, at least one of them must always be filled in"). This seems complicated, but it isn't. It's actually a good opportunity to present composed conditions in a CHECK constraint. What I need here is that one of the two columns is filled in, which in this context means "different from N/A." With this in mind, writing the constraint is easy:

```
-- Add a constraint to check if either the Home_Phone_Nbr
-- or the Mobile_Nbr were properly filled in
ADD CONSTRAINT UMADB_CHP5.CHK_TBL_Persons_Contact_Nbr_Cross_Check
CHECK (Home_Phone_Nbr <> 'N/A'
       OR Mobile_Nbr <> 'N/A')
```

Remember, a CHECK constraint prevents changes if it evaluates to false. In this case, the only situation in which that happens is when both columns are "not filled in." If one of them is not equal to 'N/A', then the condition will evaluate to true and the constraint won't be "activated," thus allowing the change of values in the record to take place. Remember that this "change of values" can be either an INSERT or an UPDATE. This may sound strange, but think of the INSERT as a change from NULL to something.

Finally, rule 4 is a "regular" CHECK constraint, because there's no 'N/A' values in the Home_Address column:

```
-- Add a constraint to check if the Home_Address is valid
ADD CONSTRAINT UMADB_CHP5.CHK_TBL_Persons_Mobile_Nbr
CHECK (LENGTH(TRIM(Home_Address)) > 10)
```

Instead of just one constraint, as shown before, I'll need to add four constraints to the Persons table. This task can be performed all at once, like this:

```
ALTER TABLE UMADB_CHP5.TBL_Persons
    -- Add a constraint to check if the Home_Phone_Nbr is valid
    ADD CONSTRAINT UMADB_CHP5.CHK_TBL_Persons_Home_Phone_Nbr
```
Continued

```
CHECK (CASE
        WHEN Home_Phone_Nbr = 'N/A' THEN 'OK'
        WHEN LENGTH(TRIM(Home_Phone_Nbr)) < 10 THEN 'NOK'
        ELSE 'OK'
        END = 'OK')
-- Add a constraint to check if the Home_Phone_Nbr is valid
ADD CONSTRAINT UMADB_CHP5.CHK_TBL_Persons_Mobile_Nbr
CHECK (CASE
        WHEN Mobile_Nbr = 'N/A' THEN 'OK'
        WHEN LENGTH(TRIM(Mobile_Nbr)) < 10 THEN 'NOK'
        ELSE 'OK'
        END = 'OK')
-- Add a constraint to check if either the Home_Phone_Nbr
-- or the Mobile_Nbr were properly filled in
ADD CONSTRAINT UMADB_CHP5.CHK_TBL_Persons_Contact_Nbr_Cross_Check
CHECK (Home_Phone_Nbr <> 'N/A'
        OR Mobile_Nbr <> 'N/A')
-- Add a constraint to check if the Home_Address is valid
ADD CONSTRAINT UMADB_CHP5.CHK_TBL_Persons_Mobile_Nbr
CHECK (LENGTH(TRIM(Home_Address)) > 10)

;
```

If you want try it yourself, you'll find this statement in the chapter's downloadable source code.

Just a note about the constraints: if you try to apply these constraints in the Students table filled with the test records that were migrated back in Chapter 5, you'll get an error, because there's data in the table that doesn't comply with the constraints. Albeit a bit twisted, this is a good way to verify that your existing data is as it should be. Now let's move on to the date of birth validation.

I said earlier that this task would be tricky because I need to check whether something that represents a date, by human standards, is actually a date by computer standards. In other words, I need to check whether 20040131 is actually the date '2004-01-31' in ISO format.

I chose this format because it's a fairly common way to store dates in older applications. Some of these applications started by representing dates in YYMMDD format, which was later migrated to YYYYMMDD format because of the so-called Y2K bug. Back in Chapter 8, I created a user-defined function (UDF) that does a similar job, the IBM_Date_to_Date UDF, but now I have a date in an arbitrary numeric format. This column stores the date in YYYYMMDD format, but there might be other formats in use, such as MMDDYYYY or DDMMYYYY. This means that it's a good idea to build a more generic UDF, which will convert a number to date.

However, because we need the date separators, and those depend on the format, it might be a good idea to externalize that operation. In other words, it might be better to create a function that takes a number plus the date separators in the appropriate places. Then it's possible (if needed) to create UDFs that take numeric parameters, format them according to the appropriate date format, and call our numeric-formatted-date-string-to-date-conversion UDF. This may sound a bit confusing right now, but hopefully it will become clearer after I present the code.

Here's the numeric-formatted-date-string-to-date-conversion UDF:

```
CREATE OR REPLACE FUNCTION UMADB_CHP5.String_to_Date (
    P_DateStr VARCHAR( 10 )
)
RETURNS DATE
LANGUAGE SQL
DETERMINISTIC
RETURNS NULL ON NULL INPUT
    SET OPTION DBGVIEW = *SOURCE , DATFMT = *ISO
BEGIN
DECLARE EXIT HANDLER FOR SQLEXCEPTION RETURN '0001-01-01' ;
RETURN DATE( P_DateStr ) ;
END
;
```

This function takes a 10-character string (eight digits plus two date-separator characters) and tries to convert it to a date. If it fails, it returns the '0001-01-01' date value. This is indeed a date, but a rather unusual one. All I need to do now is call this function and check the result. If it is '0001-01-01', it means the conversion failed; otherwise the returned value will be the numeric value plus date separators transformed into an actual date field.

I'm not going to build the UDFs that take numeric values in the several possible formats; I'll just use the UDF I just discussed directly, like this:

```
(...)
DECLARE W_Date Date;
SET W_Date = UMADB_CHP5.String_to_Date
            (
                SUBSTR(CHAR(<date in YYYYMMDD format>), 1, 4)
                CONCAT '-'
                CONCAT SUBSTR(CHAR(<date in YYYYMMDD format>), 5, 2)
                CONCAT '-'
                CONCAT SUBSTR(CHAR(<date in YYYYMMDD format>), 7, 2)
            );
IF(W_Date = '0001-01-01') THEN
-- The conversion failed, handle the error accordingly
(...)
```

Note that I'm using a UDF to validate the date, and you can't use a UDF in a CHECK constraint. The other logical solution is using a trigger, so let's create one that validates the fifth rule: "The birth date must be a valid date." I want to check the birth date whenever a record is inserted or updated. In the latter case, I just need to perform the validation if the Date_of_Birth column was changed. With these requirements in mind, I wrote the following trigger:

```
CREATE OR REPLACE TRIGGER UMADB_CHP5.Trg_check_person_date_of_birth
    BEFORE UPDATE OR INSERT ON UMADB_CHP5.TBL_PERSONS
                                                        Continued
```

```
    REFERENCING NEW ROW AS UPDATED OLD ROW AS ORIGINAL
    FOR EACH ROW MODE DB2ROW
    WHEN (INSERTING
          OR (UPDATING AND (UPDATED.Date_of_birth <> ORIGINAL.Date_of_
birth)))
    BEGIN
        DECLARE W_Date Date;
        SET W_Date = UMADB_CHP5.String_to_Date
                          (
                          SUBSTR(CHAR(UPDATED.Date_Of_Birth), 1, 4)
                          CONCAT '-'
                          CONCAT SUBSTR(CHAR(UPDATED.Date_Of_Birth), 5, 2)
                          CONCAT '-'
                          CONCAT SUBSTR(CHAR(UPDATED.Date_Of_Birth), 7, 2)
                          );
        IF(W_Date = '0001-01-01') THEN
                SIGNAL SQLSTATE '75001'
                SET MESSAGE_TEXT = 'The persons birth date is not a valid
date';
            END IF;
        END;
```

This trigger's structure should be familiar by now, because I applied the same try-and-if-it-fails-signal-the-error trigger template I've been using lately. If you run this piece of code against the Persons table provided in the downloadable source code, you won't get any errors even though some of the records in the Persons table don't contain valid dates. That's because unlike a CHECK constraint, a "trigger constraint" only performs its checks when activated—in this case, by INSERT or UPDATE operations.

With the four CHECK constraints and a trigger, I managed to enforce all the rules, which were not as simple as they seemed. This mixed solution serves the purpose of reminding you that there's not one-size-fits-all solution when it comes to moving business rules to the database. Sometimes you need to improvise and use multiple "tricks" to achieve the desired results.

Enforcing the "Informal" Integrity of the Courses Table

Our database design has a little flaw, which I introduced on purpose in Chapter 5, when I created the new Courses table: the course director and teaching assistant teacher IDs are not linked to the Teachers table. They should be, because if that link is broken, we won't have any idea who is running a given course. The problem is that these columns are not part of the Courses table's keys; they are "regular" columns, but have an important dependency from another table.

This is a fairly common situation, and it's usually handled at application level, by limiting the user's choices to a subset of records of the target table (which would be the Teachers table, in this case). However, remaining faithful to the data-centric path I've chosen, I want to enforce this "informal referential integrity" between these two columns and the Teachers table. The problem is half-solved, because both columns are marked as non-nullable, but I still need to make sure that the database consistency is kept intact.

From what I've shown so far, you should know that there are two alternative paths at your disposal: enforce it via a CHECK constraint or via a trigger. The third option would be to use a referential integrity constraint, but this isn't possible because the Course_Director_Teacher_Id and the Course_TA_Teacher_Id are not part of the table's primary key. To determine whether the IDs supplied in the INSERT or UPDATE operations are valid, you can run a query to check whether they exist in the Teachers table. Something like this would do the trick:

```
SELECT Count(*)
            FROM UMADB_CHP5.TBL_Teachers
            WHERE Teacher_Id = <teacher ID from the I/O statement>;
```

If this statement returns anything other than 1, that means there's a problem, because the teacher ID should exist once and only once in the Teachers table. This is part of the final solution and also puts you in the right path, because you can't execute a query in a CHECK constraint. This means that the only viable option is to use a trigger to enforce the referential integrity.

When is the trigger activated? Whenever a change in the teacher IDs of the Courses table occurs. Before jumping to the conclusion that we're interested only in UPDATE operations, remember that an INSERT operation also changes the values of the columns (from null to whichever value was input, strange as that may seem). This leads us to the conclusion that our trigger should be activated by INSERT and UPDATE operations.

Also keep in mind that triggers are costly to execute, so they should only run when absolutely necessary. This means that we don't want our trigger to be activated by all I/O operations that update course records; instead, we're interested only in UPDATE operations that change either the course director or the course teaching assistant IDs. All that I've explained in this paragraph translates to code in the header section of our trigger:

```
CREATE OR REPLACE TRIGGER UMADB_CHP5.Trg_check_Course_teacher_Ids
    BEFORE UPDATE OR INSERT ON UMADB_CHP5.TBL_COURSES
    REFERENCING NEW ROW AS UPDATED OLD ROW AS ORIGINAL
    FOR EACH ROW MODE DB2ROW
    WHEN (INSERTING
            OR (UPDATING AND (UPDATED.Course_Director_Teacher_Id <>
ORIGINAL.Course_Director_Teacher_Id
                            OR UPDATED.Course_TA_Teacher_Id <>
ORIGINAL.Course_TA_Teacher_Id)))
```

If this looks familiar, it's because it should: I adapted it from the check teacher's salary trigger. The difference is I have two columns to check instead of just one. The rest of the code, however, doesn't resemble anything I've shown so far, so let's analyze it carefully, starting with the course director teacher ID validation:

```
    BEGIN
        -- Validating the Course Director Teacher ID referential
integrity
        IF (INSERTING
            OR (UPDATING AND (UPDATED.Course_Director_Teacher_Id <>
ORIGINAL.Course_Director_Teacher_Id))) THEN
            IF ((SELECT Count(*)
                                                    Continued
```

```
                    FROM UMADB_CHP5.TBL_Teachers
                    WHERE Teacher_Id = UPDATED.Course_Director_Teacher_Id)
 <> 1) THEN
                    SIGNAL SQLSTATE '75010'
                        SET MESSAGE_TEXT = 'The course Director teacher ID
 was not found in the teachers table';
            END IF;
         END IF;
```

You may be thinking, "that first IF is redundant." It isn't. The WHEN clause is indeed used to decide whether or not the trigger should be activated, but it doesn't make sense to check something that wasn't changed. In other words, unless an UPDATE operation actually changed the course director teacher ID, I don't have to check the column's validity. Naturally, an INSERT operation is always a change, so whenever an INSERT occurs, I have to check whether the new ID has a match in the Teachers table. If the inner IF validation fails (I explained that SELECT statement a few lines ago), then I abort the operation by signaling a user-defined error and setting the appropriate error message. Validating the course teaching assistant ID is a simple matter: just copy and paste this code and change "Director" to "TA":

```
            -- Validating the Course TA Teacher ID referential integrity
         IF (INSERTING
             OR (UPDATING AND (UPDATED.Course_TA_Teacher_Id <> ORIGINAL.
 Course_TA_Teacher_Id))) THEN
             IF ((SELECT Count(*)
                 FROM UMADB_CHP5.TBL_Teachers
                 WHERE Teacher_Id = UPDATED.Course_TA_Teacher_Id) <> 1)
 THEN
                    SIGNAL SQLSTATE '75011'
                        SET MESSAGE_TEXT = 'The course TA teacher ID was
 not found in the teachers table';
             END IF;
         END IF;
     END;
```

Note that I'm using a different SQL state code. It's a good idea to do this, because it allows programmers to prepare their applications to react appropriately to each error code. You're working at database level, but you can never lose sight of the most important clients of the database: your applications, wherever they reside.

In This Chapter, You've Learned ...

This chapter was more about applying concepts that were explained in previous chapters than about discussing new concepts. With the exception of the check constraints section, the discussion consisted of using SQL routines to create database-level business rules, thus making them independent of a specific application. The sets of business rules implemented in this chapter are fictional, but you'll probably be able to use them in real-life scenarios.

Here's what this chapter discussed:

- A quick refresher of DDL constraints, in all their different flavors: unique, referential, and check. A couple of simple examples were provided, to give you a glimpse of the real use for these constraints: the implementation of complex business rules.

- The following sets of business rules were presented and implemented using a mix of triggers and DDL constraints:

    o Implementing complex rules to prevent tampering with the teachers' salaries

    o Enforcing mandatory values on certain columns of the Persons table

    o Ensuring the "informal" integrity of the Courses table data

The next chapter will help you keep track of all the "extras" you added to your database. It will explore the system catalog and its bits and pieces, thus providing you with enough information so that you'll never lose another SQL object again.

11

Exploring the Database Catalog Information

This chapter discusses the database catalog information, providing the reader with ready-to-use queries over the database's metadata.

Wouldn't it be nice to have a place where you could find all the information about a database, or a schema within the database? It would be interesting to get to know a schema's tables and views, their constraints and triggers, and how everything is built. Sure, a "proper" database has documentation that helps, such as entity relationship diagrams (ERDs) and other documents. Unfortunately, that's not the case with most IBM i applications and the schemas that support them. If only we had a place where this information existed ....

Data About Data and the System Catalog

"Data about data" may sound redundant, but it's actually quite helpful. In order to figure out why an application is not doing what we expect, it's important to understand not just the application's logic, but also its database. Even if you haven't migrated the business rules to the database, there are certainly restrictions, triggers, and loads of other stuff that might, one way or another, influence an application's behavior. That's where the "data about data" comes in. There's a place where all the information about the database—a type of information called *metadata*—is stored. The DB2 for i database has a lot of it, as you'll see in this chapter. Let's explore this information together, starting by the way it's organized.

The database needs to know its tables, where they are, and how they're built. Whenever a statement is run, the database engine will check the validity of the statement using the database's internal metadata, a database about the database, called the *system catalog*. This set of tables keeps track of everything, from tables to user-defined functions (UDFs), including triggers, constraints, and everything in between. As you might imagine, it's a lot of data. Consider how many tables (and this definition includes both "SQL native" tables and "operating system native" physical files) and views a typical IBM i hosts. Add to that each column (or field), restriction, stored procedure, UDF ... it's an enormous amount of data, all huddled together in a few tables.

To make our lives easier, the database engine creates a subset of the catalog information every time you create a new schema. Note that I'm talking about the SQL CREATE SCHEMA statement, not the system's CRTLIB (Create Library) CL command. Whenever a CREATE SCHEMA statement is issued, the database engine will indeed create a new library. However, it will also create a set of views to filter the system catalog, restricting the information to that schema's objects. In short, there are two levels of information. The first level is the system catalog, hosted in the SYSIBM schema, which contains metadata about the entire system. It's a huge, cumbersome-to-query set of data. The second level of information is a subset, nicely filtered, which resides in each schema you create, containing only information about the SQL objects of that particular schema. Let's start by exploring the schema catalog and, whenever relevant, take a peek at the system catalog.

Where It All Starts: Tables

In a relational database, the information is stored in tables. That's where it all starts—and that's where our little tour will commence. Our UMADB_CHP5 schema contains a view called SYSTABLES. This view contains relevant information about the tables of our schema. Let's query it to obtain basic information about this schema's tables:

```
SELECT       TABLE_NAME
             , TABLE_TEXT
             , TABLE_TYPE
             , FILE_TYPE
             , SYSTEM_TABLE_NAME
             , COLUMN_COUNT
             , ROW_LENGTH
FROM    UMADB_CHP5.SYSTABLES
WHERE   SYSTEM_TABLE = 'N';
```

This will show you a list of all the SQL objects in the schema that are capable of holding data—this is a weird way of saying tables and views, which shows the object's name and text, if defined; the type of "table" (which can be either table or view); the type of file (data or source); and the system's native name for that SQL object. The SYSTABLES view also includes basic information about the structure, such as the number of columns (or fields) and the row (or record) length. Figure 11.1 illustrates the output of this statement.

TABLE_NAME	TABLE_TEXT	TABLE_TYPE	FILE_TYPE	SYSTEM_TABLE_NAME	COLUMN_COUNT	ROW_LENGTH
TBL_TEMP_STUDENT		T	D	TBL_T00001	7	230
TBL_CLASS_ENROLLMENT_PER_YEAR_LOG		T	D	TBL_C00002	7	71
TBL_TEMP_STUDENT_GRADES		T	D	TBL_T00002	4	69
TBL_CLASS_ENROLLMENT_PER_YEAR	Class Enrollment per Year Table	T	D	PFCEM	4	14
TBL_CLASS_DEFINITION	Class Definition Table	T	D	PFCLM	7	215
TBL_COURSES	Courses Table	T	D	PFCOM	9	223
TBL_CLASSES_TAUGHT_PER_YEAR	Classes Taught per Year by Teacher Table	T	D	PFCTM	2	8
TBL_CLASSES_PER_YEAR	Classes per Year Table	T	D	PFCYM	3	11
TBL_DEPARTMENTS	Departments Table	T	D	PFDPM	6	211
TBL_PERSONS	Persons Table	T	D	PFPEM	11	296
TBL_SORT_SEQ	Sorting Sequences Aux. Table	T	D	PFSRTSEQ	4	204
TBL_STUDENTS	Students Table	T	D	PFSTM	3	55
TBL_TEACHERS	Teachers Table	T	D	PFTEM	7	65
TBL_TEACHER_RANKS	Teacher Ranks Table	T	D	PFTRM	6	211
VIEW_STUDENT_INFO	Student Information View	V	D	V_STUDENT1	10	251
VIEW_TEACHER_INFO	Teacher Information View	V	D	V_TEACHER1	11	311
VIEW_COURSE_INFO	Course Information View	V	D	V_COURSE1	7	345
VIEW_STUDENT_GRADES_INFO	Student Classes and Grades per Year View	V	D	V_STUDENT2	6	189
VIEW_CLASSES_TAUGHT_PER_YEAR	Classes Taught per Year by Teacher View	V	D	V_TEACHER2	5	283
TBL_DATA_CONVERSION		T	D	PFDC	7	276
TEMP_CSV		T	D	TEMP_CSV	1	2048
TBL_COUNTERS		T	D	TBL_C00001	3	12
QSQDSRC	SQL PROCEDURES	P	S	QSQDSRC	3	160

Figure 11.1: SYSTABLE's query output

Even though the above query provides us this global view of the tables and views of our schema, it lacks detail. From this query, I can ascertain only that the TBL_DEPARTMENTS table, for instance, has six columns, but I don't know exactly what they look like. Let's go "down one level" and obtain that information from another catalog object: SYSCOLUMNS. The following statement will provide that information:

```
SELECT COLUMN_NAME
            , SYSTEM_COLUMN_NAME
            , COLUMN_TEXT
            , ORDINAL_POSITION
            , DATA_TYPE
            , LENGTH
            , NUMERIC_SCALE
FROM        UMADB_CHP5.SYSCOLUMNS
WHERE   TABLE_NAME = 'TBL_DEPARTMENTS'
ORDER BY    ORDINAL_POSITION;
```

Before showing you the output of this query, I want to mention a couple of things. First, there's more information in this table, which might be relevant on certain occasions. For instance, if you want to know whether the table has an identity column and how that column works, there are a few additional pieces of information that you might want to include in your queries over the SYSCOLUMNS table. However, these are the most commonly used columns of this table. Second, the rows in this table are ordered alphabetically by column name, which might not be very useful. That's why I included an ORDER BY clause in the SELECT statement, forcing the information about the columns to be displayed in the order in which it was written in the CREATE TABLE statement/DDS file member.

The output, shown in Figure 11.2, sheds some light on the details of the TBL_Departments table structure.

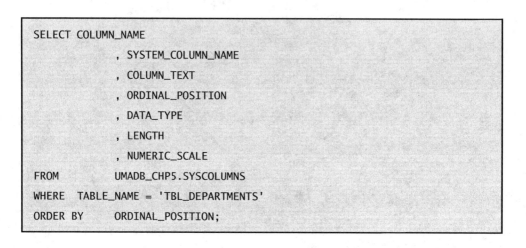

COLUMN_NAME	SYSTEM_COLUMN_NAME	COLUMN_TEXT	ORDINAL_POSIT...	DATA_TYPE	LENGTH	NUMERIC_SCALE
DEPARTMENT_ID	DPID	<null>	1	INTEGER	4	0
NAME	DPNM	<null>	2	CHAR	60	<null>
DESCRIPTION	DPDS	<null>	3	CHAR	100	<null>
DEPARTMENT_STATUS	DPSC	<null>	4	CHAR	1	<null>
CREATED_BY	DPCU	<null>	5	VARCHAR	18	<null>
CREATED_ON	DPCT	<null>	6	TIMESTMP	10	<null>

Figure 11.2: SYSCOLUMNS' query output

Unique and Primary Key Constraints

You're probably wondering where the DDL constraints of these columns are. Well, they're stored somewhere else. Actually, they're all over the place: in order to make the information readily accessible, the catalog is very "compartmentalized," and each different type of information is stored in a separate view. This means that if I want to know which are the constraints, I must query the SYSCST view. It contains, among other general pieces of information, the names and types of each constraint. To find out more about the unique and referential constraints (this topic was discussed in chapters 5 and 10), I also need to include SYSCSTCOL, which contains the primary and foreign key columns, and SQLFORKEYS, which contains information about the columns which the foreign keys point to in the other tables, in the queries. On the other hand, if I want to know the details of the check constraints, I have to look somewhere else.

I'll get to that in a moment; but first let's query SYSCST SYSCSTCOL to see which constraints are defined for the columns of the Departments table:

```
SELECT CST.CONSTRAINT_NAME
             , CST.CONSTRAINT_TYPE
             , CSTCOL.COLUMN_NAME
FROM         UMADB_CHP5.SYSCST CST
INNER JOIN UMADB_CHP5.SYSCSTCOL CSTCOL
               ON CST.CONSTRAINT_NAME = CSTCOL.CONSTRAINT_NAME
WHERE   CST.TABLE_NAME = 'TBL_DEPARTMENTS';
```

As you may recall, the Departments table doesn't depend on other tables; it has only PRIMARY KEY and UNIQUE constraints. The output of the SELECT statement I just presented, shown in Figure 11.3, reflects that:

CONSTRAINT_NAME	CONSTRAINT_TYPE	COLUMN_NAME
Q_UMADB_CHP5_PFDPM_DPID_00001	PRIMARY KEY	DEPARTMENT_ID
Q_UMADB_CHP5_PFDPM_DPNM_00001	UNIQUE	NAME

Figure 11.3: SYSCST/SYSCSTCOL query output

Foreign Key Constraints

To see how I can find information about the foreign keys, I'll need to use another table. Let's use, for instance, the Students table, which I know has a foreign key pointing to the Persons table. For a moment, let's say I don't know that this foreign key exists, and I want to find out whether there are any foreign keys in this table. You probably noticed that the SQLFORKEYS SQL object I mentioned earlier doesn't follow the same naming convention as the other views I've been using so far (SYS<*something*>). The reason for that is that SQLFORKEYS is not part of the schema's catalog; it's actually part of the system's catalog.

The following statement uses this table and the SYSCST view to list the foreign keys for a given table, as well as the "local" and "remote" columns that compose each of its foreign keys:

```
SELECT              CST.CONSTRAINT_NAME
                  , FK.FKTABLE_NAME
                  , FK.FKCOLUMN_NAME
                  , FK.PKTABLE_NAME
                  , FK.PKCOLUMN_NAME
FROM          UMADB_CHP5.SYSCST CST
INNER JOIN    SYSIBM.SQLFORKEYS FK
         ON FK.FK_NAME = CST.CONSTRAINT_NAME
WHERE         CST.TABLE_NAME = 'TBL_STUDENTS';
```

This produces the result shown in Figure 11.4. As you can see, it clearly indicates that the "local" foreign key TBL_PersonsPerson_Id refers to the "remote" Person_Id column of the TBL_Persons table.

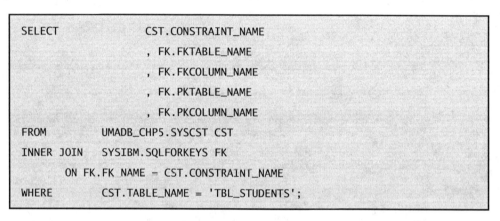

CONSTRAINT_NAME	FKTABLE_NAME	FKCOLUMN_NAME	PKTABLE_NAME	PKCOLUMN_NAME
FK_TBL_STUDENTS_TBL_PERSONSPERSON_ID	TBL_STUDENTS	TBL_PERSONSPERSON_ID	TBL_PERSONS	PERSON_ID

Figure 11.4: Foreign key details

Because of the naming convention used in the UMADB, it's almost redundant to mention the "remote" table and column, because the "local" key's name says it all. However, this is not something you'll often find in real-life databases, especially if they don't have strict naming conventions. Try adapting the query to list the foreign keys of other tables of the database and see what happens. Once you're done, continue reading, as we'll move on to another type of constraints: check constraints.

Check Constraints

In the previous chapter, I enforced a set of business rules using check constraints over the Persons table. You can find the respective source code in Chapter 10's downloadable source code, but know that the same code minus any comments is also available in the SYSCHKCST view! Here's how to get it:

```
SELECT CST.CONSTRAINT_NAME
             , CST.CONSTRAINT_TYPE
             , CSTCHK.CHECK_CLAUSE
    FROM        UMADB_CHP5.SYSCST CST
    INNER JOIN UMADB_CHP5.SYSCHKCST CSTCHK
                ON CST.CONSTRAINT_NAME = CSTCHK.CONSTRAINT_NAME
    WHERE   CST.TABLE_NAME = 'TBL_PERSONS';
```

This will show you the CHECK constraints of the Persons table, as depicted in Figure 11.5.

CONSTRAINT_NAME	CONSTRAINT_TYPE	CHECK_CLAUSE
CHK_TBL_PERSONS_NAME	CHECK	LENGTH (TRIM (NAME)) > 3
CHK_TBL_PERSONS_HOME_PHONE_NBR	CHECK	CASE WHEN HOME_PHONE_NBR = 'N/A' THEN 'OK' WHEN LENGTH (TRIM (HOME_PHONE_NBR)) < 10 THEN 'NOK' ELSE 'OK' END = 'OK'
CHK_TBL_PERSONS_MOBILE_NBR	CHECK	CASE WHEN MOBILE_NBR = 'N/A' THEN 'OK' WHEN LENGTH (TRIM (MOBILE_NBR)) < 10 THEN 'NOK' ELSE 'OK' END = 'OK'

Figure 11.5: SYSCHKCST query output

We're halfway there! So far, I've shown how you can get information about a table and most of its "moving parts." Next up are the SQL routines: stored procedures, UDFs, and triggers. Because of their direct relation with tables, let's start with the triggers.

Triggers

As you'd expect, from what I explained thus far, the information about the triggers is stored in its own views. As I showed earlier in this chapter for the tables, the triggers' metadata is also available in the schema catalog, spread over a few views. Let's start with the view SYSTRIGGER, which is somewhat similar to the SYSTABLES, in the sense that it works like a "header table" for the trigger information.

You probably recall from Chapter 9 that triggers are associated with tables or views, so it makes sense to filter the search using a table/view name. Instead of showing information about all the triggers in the schema, I'll focus on those associated with the Courses table.

Let's see what relevant information SYSTRIGGER contains about this table's triggers, by using the following query:

```
SELECT          TRIGGER_NAME
                , EVENT_OBJECT_TABLE
                , ACTION_TIMING
                , EVENTINSERT
                , EVENTUPDATE
                , EVENTDELETE
FROM     UMADB_CHP5.SYSTRIGGER
WHERE    EVENT_OBJECT_TABLE = 'TBL_COURSES';
```

Most of the columns' names are obvious, but I'll explain them anyway:

- Trigger_Name—This is the SQL (long) name given to the trigger in the CREATE TRIGGER statement.

- Event_Object_Table—This is the name of the table or view over which the trigger is built.

- Action_Timing—corresponds to the activation moment of the trigger (BEFORE, AFTER, or INSTEAD).

- Event_Insert—This column contains a 'Y' if the trigger is configured to activate when a new record is inserted.

- Event_Update—This column contains a 'Y' if the trigger is configured to activate when a record is updated.

- Event_Delete—This column contains a 'Y' if the trigger is configured to activate when a record is deleted.

As you might recall from Chapter 9, the Courses table has two triggers. I created one to maintain the "informal" integrity of the Course Director and Teaching Assistant teacher IDs and a second one to get rid of that ugly 'N/A' string in the course description column. Figure 11.6 depicts what the statement shown earlier produces.

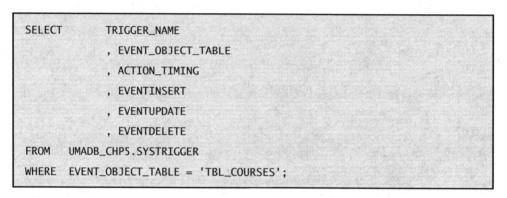

TRIGGER_NAME	EVENT_OBJECT_TABLE	ACTION_TIMING	EVENTINSERT	EVENTUPDATE	EVENTDELETE
TRG_CHECK_COURSE_TEACHER_IDS	TBL_COURSES	BEFORE	Y	Y	N
TRG_REPLACE_NA_TEXT_ON_COURSES_UPDATE	TBL_COURSES	BEFORE	N	Y	N

Figure 11.6: SYSTRIGGER's query output

The output matches our expectations, or at least part of them. If you're wondering "where's the triggers' source code?", let me tell you that it's also part of this table. I left it out because it would be too long to show in a nicely formatted figure, but it's there, stored in two separate columns: the WHEN clause is stored in the ACTION_CONDITION column, while the trigger body is stored in the ACTION_STATEMENT column.

But there's more information about triggers that you might find useful. For instance, there's a view that shows the trigger dependencies. By dependencies, I mean everything that is used by the trigger and is external to the trigger: a table, a view, a UDF, and so on.

Let's have a look at the dependencies of the trigger that replaces the 'N/A' values in the course's description. This trigger was created back in Chapter 9, and it replaces the 'N/A' with a much nicer description—something like "A *<department name>* department course, managed by *<teacher rank> <teacher name>*." To produce this description, the trigger needs to retrieve information from several tables. The following query over the SYSTRIGDEP view shows the complete list of dependencies of this trigger:

```
SELECT       TRIGGER_NAME
           , OBJECT_NAME
           , OBJECT_TYPE
FROM     UMADB_CHP5.SYSTRIGDEP
WHERE    TRIGGER_NAME = 'TRG_REPLACE_NA_TEXT_ON_COURSES_UPDATE';
```

This will show a list of dependencies, as listed in Figure 11.7. Note that I included the Object_Type column as a reminder that a trigger can depend on any type of SQL object.

TRIGGER_NAME	OBJECT_NAME	OBJECT_TYPE
TRG_REPLACE_NA_TEXT_ON_COURSES_UPDATE	TBL_DEPARTMENTS	TABLE
TRG_REPLACE_NA_TEXT_ON_COURSES_UPDATE	TBL_TEACHERS	TABLE
TRG_REPLACE_NA_TEXT_ON_COURSES_UPDATE	TBL_TEACHER_RANKS	TABLE
TRG_REPLACE_NA_TEXT_ON_COURSES_UPDATE	TBL_PERSONS	TABLE

Figure 11.7: SYSTRIGDEP query output

This trigger depends only on tables, as most triggers do, but I created another trigger, in Chapter 10, which uses a UDF: Trg_check_person_date_of_birth. This trigger's objective was to check whether a person's birthdate was a valid date. By running the same statement for this trigger, you'll see something similar to Figure 11.8.

TRIGGER_NAME	OBJECT_NAME	OBJECT_TYPE
TRG_CHECK_PERSON_DATE_OF_BIRTH	STRING_TO_DATE	FUNCTION

Figure 11.8: Another SYSTRIGDEP output example

Note the object type: it's no longer a table, because the Trg_check_person_date_of_birth trigger doesn't depend on tables to work; it depends on a UDF instead, the String_To_Date UDF. There are a couple of other trigger-related views in the schema's catalog, but (in my opinion) they don't contain relevant information in the context of this book. Feel free to explore them; their names are SYSTRIGCOL and SYSTRIGUPD. It's now time to move on to one of the trigger's "cousins": stored procedures.

Stored Procedures and UDFs

Stored procedures (SPs) share some similarities with triggers. This type of SQL routine was discussed at length in Chapter 7. However, unlike triggers, the schema's catalog doesn't contain metadata about SPs. In order to know more about SPs, I need to look elsewhere: the system catalog.

A quick search in schema SYSIBM reveals a view called SQLPROCS that might help. If you query it, you'll see that it contains most of the relevant information about a SP: schema, name, number of input/output parameters, and a few other bits of data. However, it lacks something very important: the procedure's code. To get it, we need to venture deeper into the system catalog and search in the QSYS2 schema. There you'll find the SYSROUTINE table, over which the SQLPROCS view is built. The SYSROUTINE table contains information about SPs and UDFs (after all, they both are SQL routines). This means that we can get information about SPs and UDFs with a single query. As you might recall from chapters 7 (SPs) and 8 (UDFs), these SQL routines can be either SQL native or external, have different parameter styles, and have different "levels" of SQL data access.

Here's a query that shows all of that information about the characteristics of these SQL routines:

```
SELECT      ROUTINE_TYPE
          , ROUTINE_NAME
  , SPECIFIC_NAME
                                                    Continued
```

```
                     , EXTERNAL_NAME

                     , ROUTINE_BODY

                     , EXTERNAL_LANGUAGE

                     , PARAMETER_STYLE

                     , IS_DETERMINISTIC

                     , SQL_DATA_ACCESS

     FROM            QSYS2.SYSROUTINE

     WHERE SPECIFIC_SCHEMA = 'UMADB_CHP5'

     ORDER BY        ROUTINE_TYPE DESC;
```

This produces a list of the UMADB_CHP5 schema's SPs and UDFs, shown in Figure 11.9, with the information I mentioned earlier.

ROUTINE_T...	ROUTINE_NAME	SPECIFIC_NAME	EXTERNAL_NAME	ROUTINE_BODY	EXTERNAL_LANG...	PARAMETER_STYLE	IS_DET...	SQL_DATA_AC...
PROCEDURE	REGISTER_COURSE	ADDCOURSE	UMADB_CHP5/ADDCOURSE	SQL	<null>	<null>	NO	MODIFIES
PROCEDURE	REGISTER_STUDENT_V3	ADDSTUDENT	UMADB_CHP5/ADDSTUDENT	SQL	<null>	<null>	NO	MODIFIES
PROCEDURE	DECLARE_AND_PREPARE_EXAMPLE	DECLARE_AND_PREPARE_EXAMPLE	UMADB_CHP5/DECLA00001	SQL	<null>	<null>	NO	MODIFIES
PROCEDURE	EXECUTE_IMMEDIATE_EXAMPLE_1	EXECUTE_IMMEDIATE_EXAMPLE_1	UMADB_CHP5/EXECU00001	SQL	<null>	<null>	NO	MODIFIES
PROCEDURE	EXECUTE_IMMEDIATE_EXAMPLE_2	EXECUTE_IMMEDIATE_EXAMPLE_2	UMADB_CHP5/EXECU00002	SQL	<null>	<null>	NO	MODIFIES
PROCEDURE	GET_STUDENT_DATA	GETSTUD1	UMADB_CHP5/GETSTUD1	SQL	<null>	<null>	NO	READS
PROCEDURE	GET_STUDENT_DATA	GETSTUD2	UMADB_CHP5/GETSTUD2	SQL	<null>	<null>	NO	READS
PROCEDURE	GET_TEACHER_DATA	GETTEACH1	UMADB_CHP5/GETTEACH1	SQL	<null>	<null>	NO	READS
PROCEDURE	GET_TEACHER_DATA	GETTEACH2	UMADB_CHP5/GETTEACH2	SQL	<null>	<null>	NO	READS
PROCEDURE	PREPARE_EXECUTE_EXAMPLE	PREPARE_EXECUTE_EXAMPLE	UMADB_CHP5/PREPA00001	SQL	<null>	<null>	NO	MODIFIES
PROCEDURE	PREPARE_EXECUTE_EXAMPLE_1	PREPARE_EXECUTE_EXAMPLE_1	UMADB_CHP5/PREPA00002	SQL	<null>	<null>	NO	MODIFIES
PROCEDURE	PREPARE_EXECUTE_EXAMPLE_2	PREPARE_EXECUTE_EXAMPLE_2	UMADB_CHP5/PREPA00003	SQL	<null>	<null>	NO	MODIFIES
PROCEDURE	TEST_GET_STUDENT_DATA_V1	TEST_GET_STUDENT_DATA_V1	UMADB_CHP5/TEST_00001	SQL	<null>	<null>	NO	MODIFIES
PROCEDURE	TEST_GET_STUDENT_DATA_V2	TEST_GET_STUDENT_DATA_V2	UMADB_CHP5/TEST_00002	SQL	<null>	<null>	NO	MODIFIES
FUNCTION	CALCULATE_GPA	CALCGPA1	UMADB_CHP5/CALCGPA1(CALCULATE_GPA_1)	SQL	<null>	<null>	NO	READS
FUNCTION	CONVERT_A_TO_N	CONVATON	UMADB_CHP5/CONVATON(CONVERT_A_TO_N...	SQL	<null>	<null>	NO	READS
FUNCTION	CONVERT_N_TO_A	CONVNTOA	UMADB_CHP5/CONVNTOA(CONVERT_N_TO_A...	SQL	<null>	<null>	NO	READS
FUNCTION	DEPARTMENT_CLASSES	DEPCLASS1	UMADB_CHP5/DEPCLASS1(DEPARTMENT_CL...	SQL	<null>	<null>	NO	READS
FUNCTION	GET_STUDENT_ID	GETSTUDID1	UMADB_CHP5/GETSTUDID1(GET_STUDENT_I...	SQL	<null>	<null>	NO	READS
FUNCTION	GET_STUDENT_ID	GETSTUDID2	UMADB_CHP5/GETSTUDID2(GET_STUDENT_I...	SQL	<null>	<null>	NO	READS
FUNCTION	GET_TEACHER_ID	GETTEACID1	UMADB_CHP5/GETTEACID1(GET_TEACHER_I...	SQL	<null>	<null>	NO	READS
FUNCTION	GET_TEACHER_ID	GETTEACID2	UMADB_CHP5/GETTEACID2(GET_TEACHER_I...	SQL	<null>	<null>	NO	READS
FUNCTION	IBM_DATE_TO_DATE	IBMD2DATE	UMADB_CHP5/IBMD2DATE(IBM_DATE_TO_DAT...	SQL	<null>	<null>	NO	READS
FUNCTION	IBM_DATE_TO_TIMESTAMP	IBMD2TIMES	UMADB_CHP5/IBMD2TIMES(IBM_DATE_TO_TIM...	SQL	<null>	<null>	NO	READS
FUNCTION	IS_DATE_VALID	IS_DATE_VALID	UMADB_CHP5/DA60001(IS_DATE_VALID_1)	SQL	<null>	<null>	YES	READS
FUNCTION	RETURN_VALUE	RETURN_VALUE	UMADB_CHP5/RETUR00001(RETURN_VALUE...	SQL	<null>	<null>	NO	READS
FUNCTION	RETURN_VALUE	RETUR00001	UMADB_CHP5/RETUR00002(RETURN_VALUE...	SQL	<null>	<null>	NO	READS
FUNCTION	STRING_TO_DATE	STRING_TO_DATE	UMADB_CHP5/STRIN00001(STRING_TO_DATE...	SQL	<null>	<null>	YES	READS
FUNCTION	USERREVIEW	USERREVIEW	UMADB_CHP5/USERREVIEW(USERREVIEW_1)	SQL	<null>	<null>	NO	MODIFIES
FUNCTION	USERREVIEWREPORT	USERREVIEWREPORT	UMADB_CHP5/USERR00000(USERREVIEWRE...	SQL	<null>	<null>	NO	MODIFIES
FUNCTION	USERREVIEWREPORT	USERR00001	UMADB_CHP5/USERR00002(USERREVIEWRE...	SQL	<null>	<null>	NO	MODIFIES

Figure 11.9: SP and UDF metadata from SYSROUTINE

Just as I did with the triggers, I've omitted the column that contains the routine source (it's called ROUTINE_DEFINITION), for readability's sake. In this case, things are not so simple, because these routines' code is not necessarily written in SQL. As I mentioned several times already, it's possible to define SPs and UDFs using a high-level language, such as RPG, COBOL, or C. If the routine is indeed written using SQL, then the ROUTINE_DEFINITION column will contain the body of the routine. The easiest way to find out whether the source code is available in SYSROUTINE is by checking the EXTERNAL_LANGUAGE column. If it's null, then the routine is native and ROUTINE_DEFINITION will contain the source. Otherwise, the EXTERNAL_NAME column will contain the name and location of the source member that was used to create the routine.

Now let's look at the routine's dependencies. Much like triggers, SPs and UDFs can (and usually do) depend on other SQL objects. Naturally, the system's catalog keeps track of those dependencies, in (you guessed it) a separate table: SYSROUTDEP. Instead of querying the whole table, let's focus on the Calculate_GPA UDF, created in Chapter 8. This is a fairly complex function that calculates a student's GPA. It might be a good idea to revisit Chapter 8 and reread the section that describes all that the creation of this UDF entails, to help you more easily interpret the results of the following query over the SYSROUTDEP table:

```
SELECT      SPECIFIC_NAME
          , OBJECT_NAME
          , OBJECT_TYPE
          , NUMBER_OF_PARMS
FROM    QSYS2.SYSROUTDEP
WHERE SPECIFIC_SCHEMA = 'UMADB_CHP5'
          AND SPECIFIC_NAME = 'CALCGPA1';
```

Just a couple of quick notes: because I'm using a table from the system catalog, I have to specify the schema name. I also need to indicate the specific name of the UDF. Note that is not the SQL name of the UDF, but its specific name. This is important because you can overload your UDFs (create several UDFs with the same name, but different parameters) as long as you give them different specific names. This query produces the output shown in Figure 11.10.

SPECIFIC_NAME	OBJECT_NAME	OBJECT_TYPE	NUMBER_OF_PARMS
CALCGPA1	ROUND	FUNCTION	2
CALCGPA1	SUM	FUNCTION	1
CALCGPA1	CONVERT_A_TO_N	FUNCTION	2
CALCGPA1	SUM	FUNCTION	1
CALCGPA1	TBL_CLASS_ENROLLMENT_PER_YEAR	FILE	<null>

Figure 11.10: SYSROUTDEP query output

As you can see, even the native objects used in the UDF (ROUND and SUM) are mentioned as dependencies. There's also an unusual dependency: a file(!). It's actually a table, but someone at IBM seems to have forgotten to use the proper lingo.

When it comes to SQL routines, it's also important to know what goes in and what comes out. In order words, it's important to know a routine's parameters. The PARAMETERS table, from the system's catalog, holds that information. Back in Chapter 7, I introduced SPs using a "Register Student" SP, with the specific name of ADDSTUDENT. This is relevant for the query, because (much like SYSROUTDEP) the PARAMETERS table uses the specific name to uniquely identify the SQL routine. Anyway, this SP received all the necessary information to create a student via parameters and created the respective rows in the Persons and Students table. It might be a good idea to go back to Chapter 7 and reread that particular section.

Let's see what the PARAMETERS table stores about this SP, with the following query:

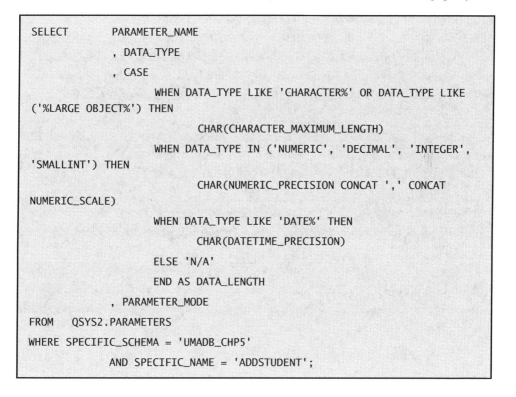

```
SELECT        PARAMETER_NAME
            , DATA_TYPE
            , CASE
                    WHEN DATA_TYPE LIKE 'CHARACTER%' OR DATA_TYPE LIKE
('%LARGE OBJECT%') THEN
                            CHAR(CHARACTER_MAXIMUM_LENGTH)
                    WHEN DATA_TYPE IN ('NUMERIC', 'DECIMAL', 'INTEGER',
'SMALLINT') THEN
                            CHAR(NUMERIC_PRECISION CONCAT ',' CONCAT
NUMERIC_SCALE)
                    WHEN DATA_TYPE LIKE 'DATE%' THEN
                            CHAR(DATETIME_PRECISION)
                    ELSE 'N/A'
                    END AS DATA_LENGTH
            , PARAMETER_MODE
FROM    QSYS2.PARAMETERS
WHERE SPECIFIC_SCHEMA = 'UMADB_CHP5'
            AND SPECIFIC_NAME = 'ADDSTUDENT';
```

Figure 11.11 shows the result of the query's execution.

PARAMETER_NAME	DATA_TYPE	DATA_LENGTH	PARAMETER_MODE
P_NAME	CHARACTER	60	IN
P_DATE_OF_BIRTH	DECIMAL	8,0	IN
P_HOME_ADDRESS	CHARACTER	60	IN
P_MOBILE_NBR	CHARACTER	15	IN
P_EMAIL_ADDRESS	CHARACTER	60	IN
P_DRIVERS_LICENSE	CHARACTER	20	IN
P_SOCIAL_SEC_NBR	CHARACTER	11	IN
P_HOME_PHONE_NBR	CHARACTER	15	IN

Figure 11.11: PARAMETERS query output

This table has some peculiarities. First, the length of the data is stored in separate columns, depending on the data type. That's why I had to use a CASE structure to present information from CHARACTER_MAXIMUM_LENGTH, NUMERIC_PRECISION, or DATETIME_ PRECISION, depending on the DATA_TYPE column value. Then there are a couple of things that I decided to omit from the code above because they're not relevant for this example, but that you might find interesting in other scenarios: the parameter's default value, which is taken directly from the code; the user-defined type's name and schema; and the character set's name and schema (applicable only to character and large object data types).

That's the last catalog component I wanted to talk about. There are a few more, but they don't contain relevant information—at least not in the scope of this book.

I tried to keep these sample queries as simple as possible, but feel free to explore the aforementioned tables and adjust the queries shown throughout this chapter to your specific needs.

In This Chapter, You've Learned ...

This was more of a demonstrative chapter, but still I hope you've managed to learn new things—or more precisely, learned where to find things. The whole point was to show where the different items discussed throughout the book, especially from Chapter 3 onward, were located in the database (system and schema) catalog. Here's a quick summary of what's where.

The metadata about tables and views, discussed in chapters 3, 4, and 5, can be found in the following tables/views:

- SYSTABLES—a schema view that has general information, such as object name and type and number of columns

- SYSCOLUMNS—a schema view that contains more detailed information about the object's structure, such as columns' names and data types

- SYSCST, SYSCSTCOL, SQLFORKEYS, and SYSCHKCST—This group contains information about the column's DDL constraints (unique, referential, and check constraints).

Even though they're directly linked with tables and views, triggers are not your typical DDL code, so they deserved special attention in Chapter 9. Their metadata is stored in the following tables/views:

- SYSTRIGGER—This schema view has general information about the triggers, such as name, activation moment, and source code.

- SYSTRIGDEP—This is also a schema view, and it contains data about the triggers' dependencies. I've shown two examples in which different dependencies are illustrated.

The last part of this chapter discussed SP and UDF metadata. I talked about these two types of SQL routines in chapters 7 and 8, respectively. It's important to mention that all three types of SQL routines (triggers, SPs, and UDFs) were used in Chapter 10 to show examples of how to move business rules into the database. Here's where the information about SPs and UDFs is stored in the catalog:

- SYSROUTINE—This system catalog table contains general information (e.g., name, type, and number of parameters, among other things) about all the SQL and external SPs and UDFs that exist in the system. This means that you need to be careful when querying it, because this table contains a lot of data.

- SYSROUTDEP—This is also a system catalog table, and it also needs to be queried with care. It contains data about the dependencies of each SP and UDF in the system, so be sure to specify a proper WHERE clause when you query it.

- PARAMETERS—As the name implies, this system catalog table stores the SQL routine's parameters: their names, data types, and lengths, among other useful information.

12

Parting Gifts

This chapter includes a few topics that are related to what was discussed in previous chapters, but were omitted from the book on purpose. This was a decision dictated by the fact that the discussion of these topics could confuse or distract the reader from focusing on what was really important in that chapter. This chapter will discuss the MERGE statement, common table expressions (CTEs), and a couple of other things in between.

As we reach the end of our time together, as you can easily grasp from the thinness of the unread portion of this book, I decided to present you with some parting gifts—things that I could have included in previous chapters but decided not to, because these topics might have confused you or diverted your attention from what was really important at the time. Some of the topics I'll explore here are relatively new, while others are old items that are often ignored, but can be useful under the right circumstances.

The Personnel Contact Information Update Scenario

The latest request that arrived at my desk, here in the University's IT department, is the perfect scenario to demonstrate the first two gifts: the MERGE statement and on-the-fly table creation. I'll start with the latter, but first let me explain what's going on.

The University's call center has been busy calling teachers and students, asking them to update their contact information. However, the call center personnel don't have enough access to update that information directly in the database, so they produced an Excel file with all the data and sent it to the IT department for processing. The first step is to analyze the file's structure, in order to create a temporary table to store its contents. Luckily for us, in this case the file structure precisely matches the Persons table structure. Immediately, you start reviewing your notes, trying to find the little script we wrote back in Chapter 5 to create the new tables. I quickly remind you that there's a "shortcut," presented a few chapters ago, which you seem to have forgotten about. Consider this your first parting gift.

Creating a Table Based on a SELECT Statement

It's a small, yet very useful thing: you can create a table on the fly, based on a SELECT statement. In this case, let's create a temporary Persons table, based on the "real" Persons table:

```
CREATE OR REPLACE TABLE UMADB_CHP5.TEMP_TBL_PERSONS
    AS (SELECT    PERSON_ID,
                  NAME,
                  DATE_OF_BIRTH,
                  HOME_ADDRESS,
                  HOME_PHONE_NBR,
                  MOBILE_NBR,
                  EMAIL_ADDRESS,
                  DRIVERS_LICENSE,
                  SOCIAL_SEC_NBR
        FROM      UMADB_CHP5.TBL_PERSONS)
    WITH NO DATA;
```

The first line of the statement looks just like any other CREATE TABLE statement. The rest of the statement also looks like any other SELECT statement. You're probably not used to seeing them together, but it works. It's a quick and dirty way to quickly create a table.

Then the sysops take the Excel file and populate this temporary table with it. In the downloadable source code for this chapter, you'll find this file with some test data. Namely, you'll find two records that already exist in TBL_PERSONS and a new one.

Your knee-jerk reaction would probably be to write a couple of statements to insert or update the records, depending on their person ID column: if the column contains a valid ID that has a match in the Persons table, then you'd update the respective row with an UPDATE statement. On the other hand, if a person ID was not supplied, or it doesn't match the existing person IDs, then an INSERT statement would be in order. What if I tell you that you can perform both operations with a single statement?

Often we're faced with the need to synchronize two tables, in such a way that the target table gets all the relevant information from the other one. For instance, imagine that you have an inventory table that receives daily updates from several stock movement tables. There are new entries to register (INSERT statements), but also item quantity fluctuations (UPDATE statements), which require separate processing. Naturally, you can also have some items disappearing from stock, and depending on how those situations are handled, these can be updates or actual deletes in the inventory table. With the MERGE statement, you can mash up those statements into a single one.

Anatomy of the MERGE Statement

Seems a bit farfetched, right? Well, once you get the hang of it, you'll see that this two-for-the-price-of-one statement is very useful. But before you're able to use it, you need to understand it, so let's take look at the anatomy of the MERGE statement:

```
MERGE INTO <Target table name>
      USING <origin table or SELECT statement>
ON <matching columns>
      WHEN MATCHED <(optional) AND <comparisons>> THEN
            <Modified UPDATE or DELETE statement>
      WHEN NOT MATCHED <(optional) AND <comparisons>> THEN
            <Modified INSERT statement>
      ELSE IGNORE
```

This seems like a lot, so let's go over it line by line, top to bottom:

- MERGE INTO *<target table name>*—indicates the name of the table or updatable view over which the I/O actions will take place.

- USING *<origin table or* SELECT statement>—indicates the exact opposite: instead of specifying where the data goes to, this line indicates where the data comes from. It can be a table name or a SELECT statement.

- ON *<matching columns>*—This line is extremely important! It explains how the records in the origin and target tables will be matched, just like you'd do in an INNER JOIN instruction.

- WHEN MATCHED <*(optional)* AND *<comparisons>>* THEN—This is where the fun begins. This and the next WHEN ... line are optional, but at least one of the two has to be specified. In its simplest form (WHEN MATCHED THEN), it indicates that the actions below it will be executed if the conditions stated in the ON *<matching columns>* line evaluate to true. Note that you can specify additional conditions to be evaluated in conjunction with the ones from the ON ... line. That's where the <*(optional)* AND *<comparisons>>* bit comes into play. This may sound a bit confusing, but I'll present an example that will help you understand what I mean.

- *<Modified* UPDATE *or* DELETE *statement>*—If a match was found, then you can perform an UPDATE or DELETE. However, note that this won't be a regular statement. It can only affect the table/view mentioned in the first line of the MERGE statement, so it doesn't make sense to include the FROM clause here. It's another of those peculiarities of the MERGE you'll have to get used to.

- WHEN NOT MATCHED <*(optional)* AND *<comparisons>>* THEN—the story for this one is similar to the WHEN MATCHED THEN, but in reverse: this specifies what should happen when the line from the origin table doesn't match the requirements—that is, when the conditions in the "ON ..." line and (if you also specify them) the ones in the <*(optional)* AND *<comparisons>>* part of this line both evaluate to false.

- *<Modified* INSERT *statement>*—If and only if a match was not found, then you can issue an INSERT statement. Keep in mind that this is also not a regular statement, because the FROM clause will be absent, as explained earlier.

- ELSE IGNORE—This is the catch-all clause, which is used as an escape when the record doesn't match any of the previous conditions. Note that you can have multiple WHEN MATCHED and/or WHEN NOT MATCHED conditions, as long as the <*(optional)* AND *<comparisons>>* part is different.

You're probably scratching your head, thinking this is confusing. It's a bit weird, I know. That was the main reason why I left it out when I revisited the DML statements, back in Chapter 2. Let's go over an example and try to clear things up.

The scenario I described earlier involves two tables: the temporary TEMP_TBL_PERSONS and the "real" TBL_PERSONS. What we want to do is update the second table with the data from the first one. With this, I've identified the origin and target tables, and I can start writing the MERGE statement:

```
MERGE INTO UMADB_CHP5.TBL_PERSONS PERSON
    USING UMADB_CHP5.TEMP_TBL_PERSONS T
```

The TBL_PERSONS table is the target table; I gave it the alias PERSON, while the TEMP_TBL_PERSONS, our origin table, has the alias T. I gave this table a short alias because we're going to use it a whole lot, and a longer alias would get in the way.

Now let's see how to match the records in both tables. I said earlier that the person ID, when the record is from an existing person in the database, is supplied in the Excel file. This is particularly handy because the Persons table primary key is the Person_Id column. With this piece of information, I can write the "ON ..." line:

```
ON PERSON.PERSON_ID = T.PERSON_ID
```

Now let's go over the rules again: if the person IDs between the temp table and the real one match, we can update the existing information with the one coming from the temp table. Let's translate that into code:

```
WHEN MATCHED THEN
    UPDATE SET  PERSON.NAME = T.NAME,
                PERSON.DATE_OF_BIRTH = T.DATE_OF_BIRTH,
                PERSON.HOME_ADDRESS = T.HOME_ADDRESS,
```
Continued

```
                   PERSON.HOME_PHONE_NBR = T.HOME_PHONE_NBR,
                   PERSON.MOBILE_NBR = T.MOBILE_NBR,
                   PERSON.EMAIL_ADDRESS = T.EMAIL_ADDRESS,
                   PERSON.DRIVERS_LICENSE = T.DRIVERS_LICENSE,
                   PERSON.SOCIAL_SEC_NBR = T.SOCIAL_SEC_NBR
```

Because I don't have additional conditions, I went for the simplest possible form of the MATCHED line: WHEN MATCHED THEN. The next few (OK, not so few) lines specify what happens when a match is found: I'll update all the Persons table columns with their namesakes from the temporary table. Note that this is not a regular UPDATE statement— it's missing the table name and WHERE clause.

The rules of the scenario described earlier also state that when a matching ID is not found, I should insert the new record in the target table. Coding this is also simple enough, but it has a catch:

```
    WHEN NOT MATCHED THEN
        INSERT (NAME,
                DATE_OF_BIRTH,
                HOME_ADDRESS,
                HOME_PHONE_NBR,
                MOBILE_NBR,
                EMAIL_ADDRESS,
                DRIVERS_LICENSE,
                SOCIAL_SEC_NBR)
        VALUES (T.NAME,
                T.DATE_OF_BIRTH,
                T.HOME_ADDRESS,
                T.HOME_PHONE_NBR,
                T.MOBILE_NBR,
                T.EMAIL_ADDRESS,
                T.DRIVERS_LICENSE,
                T.SOCIAL_SEC_NBR);
```

It's not immediately obvious, so I'll remind you of the rules: if a matching ID is not found, then I should insert the record. This means that the ID from the temporary table is useless. In other words, I don't need to (and actually can't) use it in the INSERT statement. This is not a problem, because the PERSON_ID column value is automatically generated by the database engine. Again, what you see here is a modified INSERT statement—it also lacks the FROM and WHERE clauses.

That's it! I hope this example made clear how useful and easy (after some practice) the MERGE statement can be. Here's the complete statement explained above:

```
MERGE INTO UMADB_CHP5.TBL_PERSONS PERSON
    USING UMADB_CHP5.TEMP_TBL_PERSONS T
        ON PERSON.PERSON_ID = T.PERSON_ID
    WHEN MATCHED THEN
        UPDATE SET  PERSON.NAME = T.NAME,
                    PERSON.DATE_OF_BIRTH = T.DATE_OF_BIRTH,
                    PERSON.HOME_ADDRESS = T.HOME_ADDRESS,
                    PERSON.HOME_PHONE_NBR = T.HOME_PHONE_NBR,
                    PERSON.MOBILE_NBR = T.MOBILE_NBR,
                    PERSON.EMAIL_ADDRESS = T.EMAIL_ADDRESS,
                    PERSON.DRIVERS_LICENSE = T.DRIVERS_LICENSE,
                    PERSON.SOCIAL_SEC_NBR = T.SOCIAL_SEC_NBR
    WHEN NOT MATCHED THEN
        INSERT (NAME,
                DATE_OF_BIRTH,
                HOME_ADDRESS,
                HOME_PHONE_NBR,
                MOBILE_NBR,
                EMAIL_ADDRESS,
                DRIVERS_LICENSE,
                SOCIAL_SEC_NBR)
        VALUES (T.NAME,
                T.DATE_OF_BIRTH,
                T.HOME_ADDRESS,
                                                    Continued
```

```
                    T.HOME_PHONE_NBR,

                    T.MOBILE_NBR,

                    T.EMAIL_ADDRESS,

                    T.DRIVERS_LICENSE,

                    T.SOCIAL_SEC_NBR);
```

If you want to play around with it a bit, the downloadable source code for this chapter contains all the necessary statements for creating and populating the temporary table with data that you can then use to test the MERGE statement I just explained. I should also mention that there's a bit more to the MERGE statement than what I said here. For instance, when you use multiple WHEN MATCHED instructions, the evaluation is from top to bottom and only a match per origin record is allowed. If you want to use a more complex MERGE statement, consult the *DB2 for i SQL Reference* manual and read the rules carefully. If you stick to simple statements, like the one above, you should be fine with what I explained here. And this is your second parting gift.

A Quick-and-Dirty UPDATE-only Alternative to MERGE

Let's say that the scenario I described earlier is a bit simpler, and that there are no new records, just updates. In this case, you don't actually need a MERGE statement; an UPDATE statement, albeit a bit different from what you're used to, suffices. Throughout the book I've used one of two possible syntaxes for the INSERT statement:

```
INSERT INTO <table name>
       (<Column name(s)>)  = (<Direct input value(s)>)
```

Or

```
INSERT INTO <table name>
       (<Column name(s)>) = (<SELECT statement>)
```

Yes, I did it. Check out Chapter 5's source code, and you'll find plenty of examples of the second syntax possibility. What you probably don't know is that you can do something similar to this in an UPDATE statement. It's another of those nuggets I decided to leave out because it might have confused you at the time.

Let's see how that second syntax for the UPDATE can help solve our current problem. In order to shorten the code, let's imagine that only the names and email addresses need updating. Everything else is current. I could update these two columns with the following UPDATE statement:

```
UPDATE UMADB_CHP5.TBL_PERSONS PERSONS
    SET   (NAME, EMAIL_ADDRESS) = (SELECT NAME, EMAIL_ADDRESS
                                     FROM UMADB_CHP5.TEMP_TBL_PERSONS T
                                     WHERE PERSONS.PERSON_ID = T.PERSON_ID)
    WHERE PERSONS.PERSON_ID IN (SELECT PERSON_ID
                                  FROM UMADB_CHP5.TEMP_TBL_PERSONS);
```

In case you're wondering: yes, this works. I tested it, as I did with all the code you see in this book. And yes, it's really, really weird. Let's dissect it, line by line:

- UPDATE UMADB_CHP5.TBL_PERSONS PERSONS—this is the only "normal" part of the statement, and needs no explanation.

- SET (NAME, EMAIL_ADDRESS) = (SELECT NAME, EMAIL_ADDRESS FROM UMADB_CHP5.TEMP_TBL_PERSONS T WHERE PERSONS.PERSON_ID = T.PERSON_ID—Even though it's a bit unusual, you can specify all the columns to update, enclosed in parentheses, and then all the updating values. That's what's going on here. I'm stating that I'll be updating the name and email address and then, after the equal sign, I'm saying that the updating values come from a SELECT statement. However, I'm updating only the matching records between the two tables—note the WHERE clause in the inner SELECT statement.

- WHERE PERSONS.PERSON_ID IN (SELECT PERSON_ID FROM UMADB_CHP5.TEMP_TBL_PERSONS—Finally, I'm limiting my update to the records of the Persons table that have a match in the temporary table. This may seem to duplicate the WHERE clause of the inner SELECT, but it's actually necessary. Otherwise, you'd still try to update non-matching records, and the database engine would churn out an error because the updated columns have a NOT NULL specification.

This weird syntax of the UPDATE statement is your third parting gift. Use it carefully, because it can cause serious damage if the updated columns don't have the NOT NULL specification. And remember, when you're using SELECT statements inside other statements, always test the SELECTs first!

Common Table Expressions

Earlier in this chapter I explained how to create tables on the fly. It's now time to show you how to create (a kind of) views on the fly: *common table expressions* (CTEs). CTEs are similar to derived tables or views. You can think of CTEs as temporary query definitions that can be predefined and then referenced within the same statement execution scope (kind of a prelude to a SELECT, as you'll see in a moment).

There are some half-truths regarding CTEs. Perhaps the most persistent of these half-truths is that CTEs help with overall performance. In most cases, this is not true. It may seem that way, because CTEs help simplify, for human eyes at least, complex statements, by breaking them up into more digestible and human-readable blocks. Does this help performance? Sometimes it might, but generally speaking, it doesn't.

If it doesn't, then why do we use CTEs? Well, first and foremost, because they allow you to simplify code. As you'll see in a moment, turning a nightmare of INNER JOINs into easily manageable code blocks makes it much easier to build and maintain otherwise complex statements. CTEs also help with calculated columns, allowing you to overcome some SQL limitations. But before reviewing the examples that demonstrate these features, you need to understand the anatomy of a CTE.

CTE Anatomy

Just as before, I'll start by discussing the anatomy of the CTE before showing actual examples. It's quite simple, albeit a bit weird (otherwise it wouldn't be in this chapter, right?):

```
WITH
<CTE name> (<CTE column name(s)) AS
(<CTE SELECT statement>)
<SQL instruction>
```

Let's go over this line by line, starting from the top:

- WITH—This marks the beginning of the statement and tells the database engine that you're going to define (and ideally, use) one or more CTEs.

- *<CTE name>* (*<CTE column name(s))* AS—This line has two distinct parts: the CTE name, which will identify the CTE as if it were a table/view in the *<SQL instruction>* a couple of lines down, and the CTE column name(s), which are aliases for the columns defined in the (*<CTE* SELECT *statement>*). As I mentioned before, you can have more than one CTE in a WITH statement, so each CTE name must be unique within the same statement.

- (*<CTE* SELECT *statement>*)—This is the statement that defines the CTE's characteristics. It's a regular SELECT statement, with a few restrictions. I'll address those restrictions later in this chapter. Note that the block formed by this and the previous line can be repeated as many times as you want, properly separated by commas, as long as each CTE has a unique name. I'll show examples with several CTEs within the same statement later.

- *<SQL instruction>*—Finally, this is a regular SQL instruction that uses the CTE(s) defined before it. Typically, it's a SELECT statement, but you can also use CTEs in other DML statements, such as INSERT, UPDATE, and DELETE.

A Simple CTE Example

Let's say I want to know how many teachers and/or students were born in each year. It's a simple query over the Persons table:

```
SELECT    YEAR(Date_of_Birth) AS Birth_Year,
          COUNT(*) AS Total
FROM      UMADB_CHP5.TBL_Persons
GROUP BY YEAR(Date_Of_Birth);
```

It's a bit annoying that I have to repeat the YEAR(Date_Of_Birth) scalar function in the GROUP BY clause, but this is something we're used to. It's even more annoying when you need to use a calculated column such as this one in the WHERE clause:

```
SELECT    YEAR(Date_of_Birth) AS Birth_Year,
          COUNT(*) AS Total
FROM      UMADB_CHP5.TBL_Persons
WHERE     YEAR(Date_of_Birth) > 1990
GROUP BY YEAR(Date_Of_Birth);
```

This gets even worse when the calculated column is a large or complicated formula. All the indentation in the world won't save the statement from the gruesome complexity and unfriendliness that the next guy or gal who has to understand and/or change it later will have to deal with. This is a typical situation in which a CTE is useful. Let's rewrite the original SELECT, using a CTE to simplify it:

```
WITH
Birth_Date_CTE (Birth_Year) AS
     (SELECT YEAR(Date_of_Birth) FROM UMADB_CHP5.TBL_Persons)
SELECT    Birth_Year,
          COUNT(*) as Total
FROM      BIRTH_DATE_CTE
GROUP BY BIRTH_YEAR;
```

This statement has two distinct parts: the definition of the CTE and the actual SELECT statement. In the first part, I'm creating a CTE named Birth_Date_CTE, which will have only one column, Birth_Year. The value of this column comes from the SELECT statement enclosed in parentheses, which is where I "hid" the calculated column. The second part, the actual SELECT statement, uses the previously defined CTE as if it were a table or view. However, note that I'm no longer forced to repeat the calculated column's formula, because it's now "hidden" under the Birth_Year alias. I can use it in any of the clauses that comprise the SELECT statement, as I would use a "regular" table/view column. In a way, I can say that I "moved" the complexity of the calculated column out of the SELECT statement and into the CTE.

It's important to mention that the Birth_Date_CTE doesn't exist beyond this statement. If I issue another SELECT statement after the semi-column that terminates the statement shown above, I'll get an error, saying that the Birth_Date_CTE object doesn't exist. CTEs are like temporary, created on-the-fly views. No more, no less than that.

Another CTE Example: Recreating the Student Grades Info View

Back in Chapter 5, I created the Student Grades Info view, which combined data from six different tables to present a nicely formatted "scorecard" of the students' grades, along with other relevant information, such as the course and class names. Here's what the view's SELECT statement looks like:

```
SELECT STUDENTS.STUDENT_ID
       , PERSONS.NAME AS STUDENT_NAME
       , COURSES.NAME AS COURSE_NAME
       , CLASS_DEFINITION.NAME AS CLASS_NAME
       , CLASSES_PER_YEAR.YEAR AS CLASS_YEAR
       , ENROLLMENT.GRADE

  FROM  UMADB_CHP5.TBL_CLASS_ENROLLMENT_PER_YEAR ENROLLMENT
        INNER JOIN UMADB_CHP5.TBL_STUDENTS STUDENTS
             ON STUDENTS.STUDENT_ID = ENROLLMENT.TBL_STUDENTSSTUDENT_ID
        INNER JOIN UMADB_CHP5.TBL_CLASSES_PER_YEAR CLASSES_PER_YEAR
             ON CLASSES_PER_YEAR.CLASS_PER_YEAR_ID = ENROLLMENT.TBL_
CLASSES_PER_YEARCLASS_PER_YEAR_ID
        INNER JOIN UMADB_CHP5.TBL_CLASS_DEFINITION CLASS_DEFINITION
             ON CLASS_DEFINITION.CLASS_ID = CLASSES_PER_YEAR.TBL_CLASS_
DEFINITIONCLASS_ID
        INNER JOIN UMADB_CHP5.TBL_PERSONS PERSONS
             ON PERSONS.PERSON_ID = STUDENTS.TBL_PERSONSPERSON_ID
        INNER JOIN UMADB_CHP5.TBL_COURSES COURSES
             ON CLASS_DEFINITION.TBL_COURSESCOURSE_ID = COURSES.COURSE_
ID;
```

Yes, it's long and a bit confusing, especially the INNER JOIN section. Wouldn't it be nice to simplify this statement, treating each part of it as a separate code block? With CTEs, you can! Actually, that is the most common use of CTEs. Let's see what the revamped statement looks like:

```
WITH
Course_Data (Course_Name, Course_Id) AS
    (SELECT    Name, Course_Id
     FROM      UMADB_CHP5.TBL_Courses),
Class_Data (Class_Name, Class_Year, Class_per_Year_Id, Course_Id) AS
    (SELECT    Class_Definition.Name, Classes_Per_Year.Year, Class_per_
Year_Id, Tbl_CoursesCourse_Id
     FROM      UMADB_CHP5.TBL_CLASSES_PER_YEAR Classes_Per_Year
     INNER JOIN UMADB_CHP5.TBL_CLASS_DEFINITION Class_Definition
        ON CLass_Definition.Class_Id = Classes_Per_Year.Tbl_Class_
DefinitionClass_Id),
Student_Data (Student_Id, Student_Name) AS
    (SELECT    Student.Student_Id, Person.Name
     FROM      UMADB_CHP5.TBL_Students Student
     INNER JOIN UMADB_CHP5.TBL_Persons Person
        ON Person.Person_Id = Student.TBL_PersonsPerson_Id)
SELECT  Student_Id,
        Student_Name,
        Course_Name,
        Class_Name,
        Class_Year,
        Enrollment.Grade
FROM    UMADB_CHP5.TBL_Class_Enrollment_per_Year Enrollment
INNER JOIN Class_Data   ON Enrollment.TBL_Classes_per_YearClass_per_
Year_Id = Class_Data.Class_per_Year_Id
INNER JOIN Course_Data  ON Class_Data.Course_Id = Course_Data.Course_Id
INNER JOIN Student_Data ON Enrollment.TBL_StudentsStudent_Id = Student_
Data.Student_Id;
```

Notice how I segregated the several types of information, splitting them into separate CTEs. This statement is much easier to maintain than the original SELECT statement. Also note that the INNER JOIN section of the main SELECT is now much shorter, simply linking the CTEs to the main table and/or each other when needed.

It's not always easy to find the balance between a "clean" SELECT statement and maintainable CTEs. I usually follow a few ground rules when creating CTE-infused statements:

- Each data group (usually a table, but sometimes more than one) is moved to a separate CTE. In this case, the three data groups are Course, Class, and Student. The Course_Data is the simplest of the three, as it includes only the Courses table and the absolute minimum information for the query to work (the name and ID of the course). It's usually a good idea to include the primary identifier (or a key) in order to link the CTE to the main table (or to another CTE) in the main SELECT with the minimum possible number of columns, thus simplifying the subsequent INNER JOINs.

- Each CTE gets a list of columns, even if this is not strictly necessary. In these three examples, there are some repeated column names, such as Name, but I prefer to use the CTE column names as part of the CTE definition to clarify (as much as possible) what that CTE is all about. The Student_Data CTE is an example of this principle: even though I only have two columns, I'm using the CTE column names to clearly state what this CTE has to offer.

- The CTE's SELECT statement is as minimalist as possible. Whenever possible, I strip it of everything except the mandatory SELECT and FROM clauses.

- The order by which the CTEs are defined is of paramount importance, because you can reference a CTE within another CTE, but only if the referred CTE was previously defined. Let's say I wanted to incorporate the Course_Data CTE's Course_Name column in the Class_Data CTE's SELECT statement. As they're currently defined (Course CTE first, followed by the Class CTE), this wouldn't be a problem, because Course_Data is already "known" at the time I'm defining Class_Data. However, if I switched the order in which the CTEs are defined, I'd get an error.

Here's another CTE-infused statement example. This one shows the data related to the teachers and the classes they taught. It's based on the Classes Taught per Year table, which is an association table (if you're unsure of what I'm talking about, go back to Chapter 5 and review the section "A Quick Refresher on Relational Databases"), sitting between the Teachers and Classes per Year tables. The regular version of the SELECT statement is as ugly as the Student Grades Info view's SELECT: huge, confusing, and crammed with loads of INNER JOINs. The CTE-infused version uses the methodology described above, splitting the data into groups and limiting the complexity to the bare minimum. Here's the complete statement:

```
WITH
Class_Data (Class_Name, Class_Year, Class_per_Year_Id) AS
    (SELECT Class_Definition.Name, Classes_Per_Year.Year, Class_per_
Year_Id
    FROM UMADB_CHP5.TBL_CLASSES_PER_YEAR Classes_Per_Year
    INNER JOIN UMADB_CHP5.TBL_CLASS_DEFINITION Class_Definition
        ON CLass_Definition.Class_Id = Classes_Per_Year.Tbl_Class_
DefinitionClass_Id),
Teacher_Data (Teacher_Id, Teacher_Name) AS
    (SELECT Teacher.Teacher_Id, TRIM(Teacher_Rank.Name) CONCAT ' '
CONCAT TRIM(Person.Name)
    FROM UMADB_CHP5.TBL_Teachers Teacher
    INNER JOIN UMADB_CHP5.TBL_Persons Person
        ON Teacher.TBL_PersonsPerson_Id = Person.Person_Id
    INNER JOIN UMADB_CHP5.TBL_Teacher_Ranks Teacher_Rank
        ON Teacher.TBL_Teacher_RanksTeacher_Rank_Id = Teacher_Rank.
Teacher_Rank_Id)
SELECT Teacher_Name, Class_Name, Class_Year
FROM    UMADB_CHP5.TBL_Classes_Taught_per_Year CTpY
INNER JOIN Class_Data ON Class_Data.Class_per_Year_Id = CTpY.Tbl_
Classes_per_YearClass_per_Year_Id
INNER JOIN Teacher_Data ON Teacher_Data.Teacher_Id = CTpY.Tbl_
TeachersTeacher_Id;
```

Here's how I built it:

1. First, I figured out the data groups—teacher-related data and class-related data—and created CTEs for each of them.

2. Second, I analyzed the tables and their relationships carefully, figuring out which additional columns I needed to add in each CTE to be able to link that CTE to the table in the main SELECT statement. Doing this was easy, because that table is Tbl_Classes_Taught_per_Year, which has only two columns: Class_per_Year_ID and Teacher_ID. This meant that these ID columns would have to be present in my CTEs (Class_per_Year_Id in the Class_Data CTE and Teacher_Id in the Teacher_Data CTE).

3. Third, there's data coming from a lot of tables, so it's really important to use the CTE column names "section" to bring some uniformity to the column names. If done right, this allows the next guy or gal who will look at the statement to (almost) ignore the actual SELECT statement of the CTE. For instance, the Class_Data CTE columns are Class_Name, Class_Year, and Class_per_Year_Id. This immediately tells which data is made available by this CTE, regardless of its origin.

4. Finally, I looked at the order in which the CTEs are defined. It's irrelevant in this case, because these CTEs don't interact with each other; they're directly and exclusively linked to the table Tbl_Classes_Taught_per_Year in the main SELECT statement.

If you follow these guidelines, you should be able to simplify most of the tricky, long, and confusing statements you encounter. As with almost everything described in this book, there's more to CTEs than what I explained here. For instance, you can use CTEs recursively, to navigate in a self-referencing table. I decided to omit these sorts of more complex topics from the book to provide a gentler, more manageable first (or second) contact with them. CTEs are the fourth and final parting gift I have for you. However, don't stop reading yet! There are a couple more things I'd like to tell you.

Never Stop Learning!

I don't know all the details about all the things discussed on these pages, especially because IBM is focusing its research and development efforts on SQL for i, leaving behind the native programming languages. That's why it's important to get a good grasp of the topics described throughout the book, and then, after doing some experimenting and putting these teachings to work in real-life applications, go look for the novelties or that little detail that is used in one percent of the situations. What I mean is, don't stop learning now, just because this book is ending. Actually, never stop learning! As an IT professional, it's your responsibility to keep current with the technology, and IBM usually churns out more than we can absorb. Focus on those things that yield more productive results for you and your business, but never lose sight of the bigger picture.

Let me finish this chapter (and the book) with a few topics you should learn about, which I didn't include in this book:

- Commitment control
- Online Analytical Processing (OLAP)
- Indexes and how they work
- XML-handling SQL statements
- Record-level access control and other security features
- Materialized query tables
- Other new features that IBM introduces

And you've reached the end of this book. I hope it somehow managed to teach you something useful. I learned a lot myself: I had to revisit some topics and research others in greater depth, so in a way, it was also a voyage of discovery for me. I hope that this "voyage" was a pleasant one for you. This probably won't be my last book, so keep an eye out for more! Until then, never stop learning, experimenting, and honing your skills.

Index